Revolving Gridlock

TRANSFORMING AMERICAN POLITICS

Lawrence C. Dodd, Series Editor

Dramatic changes in political institutions and behavior over the past three decades have underscored the dynamic nature of American politics, confronting political scientists with a new and pressing intellectual agenda. The pioneering work of early postwar scholars, while laying a firm empirical foundation for contemporary scholarship, failed to consider how American politics might change or recognize the forces that would make fundamental change inevitable. In reassessing the static interpretations fostered by these classic studies, political scientists are now examining the underlying dynamics that generate transformational change.

Transforming American Politics brings together texts and monographs that address four closely related aspects of change. A first concern is documenting and explaining recent changes in American politics—in institutions, processes, behavior, and policymaking. A second is reinterpreting classic studies and theories to provide a more accurate perspective on postwar politics. The series looks at historical change to identify recurring patterns of political transformation within and across the distinctive eras of American politics. Last and perhaps most important, the series presents new theories and interpretations that explain the dynamic processes at work and thus clarify the direction of contemporary politics. All of the books focus on the central theme of transformation—transformation in both the conduct of American politics and in the way we study and understand its many aspects.

Revolving Gridlock

POLITICS AND POLICY
FROM CARTER TO CLINTON

David W. Brady
Stanford University

Craig Volden
Claremont Graduate University

WestviewPress
A Division of HarperCollinsPublishers

Transforming American Politics

Copyright © 1998 by Westview Press, A Division of HarperCollins Publishers, Inc.

Published in 1998 in the United States of America by Westview Press, 5500 Central Avenue, Boulder, Colorado 80301-2877, and in the United Kingdom by Westview Press, 12 Hid's Copse Road, Cumnor Hill, Oxford OX2 9JJ

Library of Congress Cataloging-in-Publication Data
Brady, David W.
Revolving gridlock: politics and policy from Carter to Clinton / David W. Brady, Craig Volden.
  p. cm.
  Includes bibliographical references and index.
  ISBN 0-8133-2588-9 (cloth). — ISBN 0-8133-2589-7 (pbk.)
  1. United States—Politics and government—1993–   2. Coalition
governments—United States. 3. United States. Congress. House.
I. Volden, Craig. II. Title.
JK421.B73 1998
320.973'09'049—dc21   97-22279
                                                                    CIP

The paper used in this publication meets the requirements of the American National Standard for Permanence of Paper for Printed Library Materials Z39.48-1984.

10   9   8   7   6   5   4   3   2   1

Contents

Tables and Figures

Tables

Figures

Preface and Acknowledgments

The immediate origins of this book are threefold. First are the Stanford students who take Public Policy 101. Over the years the students change but their collective intelligence and their questions have pushed us to look for better explanations for why Congress passes family leave policy but not universal health care. Their intelligence and interest has been and continues to be an inspiration. Two students were particularly helpful to this project—Cameron Hamill and Brian Matsui.

Second is the extensive number of political economists at Stanford University who study legislatures. The authors were fortunate to be at Stanford when Tom Gilligan and Keith Krehbiel were working on informational models of legislatures. The intellectual challenge these models pose for the dominant distributional model of legislatures generated years of intense, informative debate and discussion of the relative merits of the two approaches. John Ferejohn, Roger Noll, and Barry Weingast ably represented the distributional side of the dispute. The discussion of legislatures spilled over into the role of the presidency in the policy process and here Terry Moe on the scholarly side and Martin Anderson on both the practical and scholarly sides were immensely helpful. Morris Fiorina of Harvard University visited Stanford's Graduate School of Business for a year and contributed to our understanding of elections and presidential success. In the same light, Nelson Polsby of the University of California at Berkeley and Joseph Cooper of Johns Hopkins University through their writings and conversations kept us from making major errors.

All of these debates about the organization of the legislature led naturally to questions about the nature of political parties and coalitions. Here again Keith Krehbiel through his research and conversations posed hard questions about what a party might be other than the aggregation of preferences. David Baron, Roger Noll, Barry Weingast, and John Ferejohn in their research and seminars provided different views and increased our understanding of the nature of coalitions and parties. Other members of the Stanford community, including Cliff Carrubba and Jon Bendor, led us to further examine aspects of our work. In addition to the group of political economists at Stanford, the work and help of Sharyn O'Halloran, David Epstein, Matt McCubbins, Ken Shepsle, Larry Dodd, Mark Hansen, Ted Brader, and the faculty and students at the Harris School of Public Policy at the University of Chicago were much appreciated. Each of us owes a long-term debt to those who have sparked our enthusiasm toward the field—to Samuel Patterson at Ohio State and to Roderick Kiewiet at Caltech.

Our thesis regarding preferences and supermajority institutions will, of course, please none of the above entirely. We will not be theoretical enough for a large number of our colleagues, and for many others we will be too theoretical and thus too simplistic in our account of the complex world of congressional policymaking. Our choice of approach benefited from the many seminars we attended and the conversations and arguments we had with our colleagues. In sum, the rich and varied group of political economy scholars at Stanford was and is first rate.

The third origin of this book is the Hoover Institution, and especially two people—one, a senior fellow, the other, a donor and friend of Hoover. Tad Taube and the Koret Foundation contributed the money to found the American Institutions and Economic Performance initiative that, along with the Smith Richardson Foundation, generated the funds necessary to finance this research. We are thus especially indebted to the Hoover Institution and the American Institutions and Economic Performance group, which includes Doug Rivers, Martin Anderson, Michael Boskin, and John Taylor, among others. We especially owe John Cogan of the Hoover Institution our gratitude. John is not only a first-rate scholar but also a practitioner. His scholarly work on the budget clarified for us the way in which organizational arrangements can shape policy outputs. And his practical knowledge of the politics of the budget (he was deputy director of the Office of Management and Budget, or OMB) is quite impressive. The number of occasions on which John gave freely of his time to explain how this or that facet of the 1983 or 1984 or 1990 budget worked (and who was for what and why) is far greater than any of us would admit.

One of the main questions we faced in this book is, what has changed Congress such that unified and divided government both lead to gridlock? The answer cannot simply be the supermajority institutions, because the filibuster and the veto have been in effect longer than gridlock issues. A large part of the answer for us is the rise of the budget as the major issue that Congress must face, and the increased difficulty of making budgetary decisions. It is in light of the role of the budget that we argue that gridlock can continue under divided and unified governments alike. The election of Bill Clinton in 1992 ended twelve years of divided government and gave rise to the notion that gridlock had ended. As Thomas Mann pointed out: "The return of one-party government after an extended period of intensely polarized divided government, especially in an era of greater party unity and at a time the Democrats were desperate to demonstrate their ability to govern . . . [and] the large freshman class and the public impatience with business as usual were also thought to provide opportunities for successful governance" (in Sundquist 1995, 10). However, as Mann, Robin Toner on health care, and Robert Reischauer on the budget have argued, there were constraints as well as possibilities.

In February 1994 the Hoover Institution's American Institutions and Economic Performance initiative was kicked off with a conference on Congress and policymaking. The opening paper was presented by Keith Krehbiel and the authors of this book. In it we argued that the failure of Clinton's legislative agenda was predictable given the distribution of congressional preferences and the filibuster. Professor Krehbiel had been working on formalizing a model of gridlock, which he published in 1996. The authors of this book pursued a slightly different path, combining the insights of Krehbiel's formal paper with the early work on preferences and supermajorities. While our analysis sometimes focuses on non-budgetary issues like family leave legislation, our main concern is the budget, which we believe to be *the* preeminent congressional issue and a further constraint on public policy.

While others have emphasized the potential constraints on Presidents as has Toner, or defended gridlock as do former members of Congress Tom Downey (D., N.Y.) and Bill Frenzel (R., Minn.), or argued for constitutional reform as does James Sundquist by urging an end to midterm elections (all in Sundquist 1995), our thesis is straightforward. If we can locate the status quo policy position along a liberal-to-conservative continuum of congressional members, we can ascertain which policy proposals will pass and which will not, as well as what concessions are necessary and whose votes will be pivotal. Emphasizing these variables surely simplifies a complex process, but such simplification avoids the optimism of Ken Duberstein and others concerning the passage of the Contract with America. The 1994 Republican takeover of the House shifted preferences to the right, but presidential vetoes, whether issued or threatened, pull policy back toward the left and into the gridlock region. The virtue of the approach taken herein is that, while straightforward, it is based on a modification of an old theory involving the median voter and adding the pivotal supermajority. Its strength is that it accounts reasonably well for policy results from 1978 to the present. We owe much to the individuals mentioned above, as well as to David G. Lawrence, L. Sandy Maisel, and Carl Pinkele, who provided insightful comments on an earlier draft of the work. Of course, we take full responsibility for all errors.

We are most indebted to our spouses and children, and thus the book is dedicated to Carolyn, Emily, Beth, and Anna on the Brady side, and to Andrea on the Volden side.

David W. Brady
Craig Volden

1

The Origins of
Revolving Gridlock

This book began as a paper on the Clinton administration's first year in office. The press had just begun to shift from positively appraising the President's job thus far to questioning how far he would get with health care, campaign finance reform, welfare, crime, and the rest of the agenda. Our view was that the quick passage of the family leave act and the motor voter act were not indicative of how successful the President ultimately would be, given the Congress elected in 1992. Subsequent events showed that unified government was not able to break policy "gridlock." The election of the first Republican Congress in forty years in 1994 and the new majority's subsequent attempt to shift policy to the right, combined with President Clinton's use of the veto to shift policy back toward the center, led us to expand the paper into a book.

In the process of expanding the work to cover the 104th Congress, our views changed regarding what caused gridlock and what could end it. In order to understand the causes of gridlock, we were forced to recognize the dominance of budget politics and policy in the Congress, and we became convinced of the importance of elections in determining where policy stands and in what direction it will evolve. Thus the book now begins with an account of the 1980–1986 period, when tax policy was dramatically modified whereas spending policies were allowed to proceed on a relatively normal trajectory. The resulting deficit, despite four major tax increases, has dominated congressional and presidential policymaking ever since. Reading new accounts of the Reagan 1981 budget battle, the Bush 1990 budget debacle, and the standoff in 1995 between the Republican Congress and President Clinton clearly leaves one with the feeling that little has changed in American politics over the past sixteen years. Given that during most of this period the government consisted of Republican Presidents and Democratic Congresses, it is easy to see why so many people believed that electing a unified government would break policy gridlock, and why many were surprised when the election of a Democratic President in 1992 did not actually do so.

As the 103rd Congress (1993–1994) ground to a close, political columnists, television commentators, Senators and Representatives, as well as the President, be-

1

moaned the lack of progress on health care, campaign finance reform, and environmental legislation. "The worst Congress in over fifty years" and "gridlock dominates" proclaimed newspaper headlines and stories. The election of a Democratic President and Democratic majorities in the House and Senate in 1992 had heralded the end of both divided government and policy gridlock. The Democratic campaign of 1992 had featured gridlock as an issue, and the early passage of family leave and the reconciliation budget was trumpeted as the end of policy gridlock. Yet by January 1994 the story began to shift, as health care and other legislation was deeply mired in the congressional labyrinth. Political scientists, columnists, Washington insiders, and other observers began to characterize the 103rd Congress as overtly partisan and controlled by "special interests"; the filibuster in the Senate was seen as largely responsible for the lack of legislative action. By early October both parties were pointing fingers, trying to interpret the inaction in ways that forwarded their own electoral purposes. Democrats, including the President, blamed Republicans for the gridlock; whereas Republicans, sensing victory in the 1994 elections, tried to make President Clinton the issue and thus the election a referendum on his performance. Congress as an institution was held in ever lower esteem, and the turnover of the 1994 elections brought in the first Republican Congress in forty years.

The newly elected Republican majority in Congress pushed through some of the reforms defined by their Contract with America—ending unfunded mandates, enacting a line-item veto, and, in the House, passing a balanced budget amendment. By April, Congress enjoyed its highest approval ratings in over twenty years, Speaker Newt Gingrich was riding high in the opinion polls, and Americans saw Republicans as the party of action, fully capable of balancing the budget. Yet within seven months all this had changed. Congress's approval rating had shrunk to about 20 percent; Speaker Gingrich's approval rating had fallen to 30 percent; President Clinton's popularity was over 50 percent for the first time in more than a year; and the government was operating on a continuing resolution (after a seven-day shutdown) while the President and the Republican Congress negotiated a new budget deal that was far to the left of the one originally passed by Congress.

What accounts for the "failure" of unified government in the 103rd Congress to break gridlock? Why, given a mandate in the 104th Congress, couldn't the Republicans have their way on policy? In the following chapters we shall attempt to define gridlock and to explain why gridlock characterized both the unified government of the 103rd Congress and the divided government of the 104th. The explanation will not focus on the role of special interests, political parties, or the media, and it does not rely heavily on presidential leadership. This is not to say that these variables don't play a role in making public policy—clearly they do. Nevertheless, our explanation for gridlock focuses on two primary factors: (1) the preferences of members of Congress regarding particular policies, and (2) supermajority institutions—the Senate filibuster and the presidential veto. We will use a simple median voter model both to define gridlock as a concept and to explain broad policy results during the 1980 to 1996 period.

The idea is really quite straightforward. When considering the U.S. Congress, instead of thinking of which party is in control, think of the members as arrayed from left to right—liberal to conservative.[1] The further left a member is positioned, the more that member favors increased government activity on health care, the environment, education, and so on. The further right one moves, the more the members favor less government activity on health care, the environment, and education; these members thus favor lower taxes. Given this ordering of preferences, what does it take to achieve a policy change?

Those who claimed that divided government caused gridlock would argue that the coupling of Republican Presidents with Democratic Congresses or vice versa was the culprit. It would then follow that having the first unified government since 1980 should have ended gridlock. But by 1994 no one was any longer making that claim. Our view is that the answer to what it takes to effectively change policy (and end gridlock) hangs on knowing the policy preferences of those members of both houses of Congress near the median (at or about the 218th member in the House and at or about the 50th member in the Senate) and on determining how close present policy (the status quo) is to these crucial members' preferences. Gridlock, for present purposes, can be said to occur when the status quo is closer to the crucial members' preferences than are the alternative policies proposed by the President or others. In short, if current health care policy is agreeable to the 218th House voter or the 50th Senate voter, then attempts at dramatic change, such as the single-payer or Clinton health care proposals, will fail—and gridlock will result.

Because in some legislation a minority of members can block a majority, the gridlock region (the range of status quo policies that is nearly impossible to change) can be sizable. Consider the filibuster as allowed by Rule XXII in the Senate. That rule, roughly, allows forty-one determined Senators to dominate floor activity so as to prohibit a bare majority from enacting its legislation. Such supermajoritarian institutions are common in state legislatures and in many foreign legislatures. The idea is that in some matters 50 percent is not enough to make fundamental changes, so rules requiring a supermajority are used. In the next chapter we will draw out this point in some detail. It is sufficient here to argue that in some issues more than a majority is required to change policy.

By narrowly focusing on preferences, supermajority institutions, and the status quo of present policies, we will leave unexplored much of the role of the parties, leadership, committee decisions, the press, and special interests in the day-to-day maneuvering that makes up the U.S. policy process. What do we hope to gain by focusing on this narrow set of explanatory variables? Our goal is to explain the broad parameters of U.S. public policy over the past two decades, and the concept of gridlock is after all not a specific matter but a general one involving deadlock in government. Moreover, the supposed culprit in gridlock—divided government—is again a rather broad concept. The narrow focus on preferences, supermajority institutions, and status quo policies is particularly informative with regard to budgetary policy, which we regard as a further cause of policy gridlock over the past two decades. Given the recent dominance of budget issues, and particularly the mounting deficit, members of Congress and the President are faced with hard choices regarding programs and funding. Increasing spending on one program often means cutting another program, not creating a new program, or raising taxes; thus in a sense funding decisions are interrelated. Programs are no longer viewed separately; rather, they are viewed in terms of trade-offs with one another—boosting one program at the expense of another, or else maintaining both at constant levels. In short, the deficit constrains all programs, forcing members to view everything within the context of the constraint.

Our argument is that, as of the late 1970s, congressional policymaking has shifted from a policy regime where new programs—entitlements and others—were added and existing programs were expanded to a policy regime where budgetary policy (focused on the deficit) encompasses and constrains all congressional policymaking. The New Deal of Franklin Roosevelt began and greatly expanded the American welfare state. Presidents after Roosevelt (with the possible exception of Eisenhower) offered new programs or packages of policies extending the welfare state. Truman's Fair Deal, Kennedy's New Frontier, Johnson's Great Society, and Nixon's New Federalism (in his first term) all testify to this phenomenon. Funding these programs took place under a budget process (aptly described by Wildavsky 1988 and Fenno 1973) where taxes rose slowly and expenditures rose roughly within the limits of increased revenues.

By the Nixon presidency, there was little room for maneuver in fiscal policy. The first two years of the Carter presidency saw the end of the old regime. By 1979 there was a tax revolt among the citizenry, the Social Security Trust Fund was nearly broke, entitlement spending from program creation and expansion in the Johnson and Nixon presidencies was rising rapidly, and the Soviet invasion of Afghanistan forced President Carter to raise military expenditures, thus canceling Congress's plan to exchange cuts in military pay for increased domestic spending. The new policy regime would be characterized by tight, real budget constraints and omnibus reconciliation budgets. Politicians who raised individual income taxes or who sought cuts in entitlements would suffer in the polls. We focus on legislator preferences and use median voter and supermajority institutional analyses to show where gridlock comes from, given the new policy regime.

A key reason to focus on preferences and supermajority institutions, rather than on special interests, parties, the media, and so on, is that in an important sense these latter variables are subsumed in the election results and the winning members' preferences. In every district and every state there are special local interests as well as national issues that play a role in the nomination and election of candidates. In Montana, wheat farmers, environmentalists, the National Rifle Association (NRA), mining and smelting interests, and labor union interests make their presence known early in the electoral process. Each interest will decide which candidates they prefer and choose a level of support. By the time of the general election, the interests and political parties will be aligned for and against the final House and Senate candidates, and the winning candidates will go to Washington with a set of established policy preferences.

Elections are in an important sense a final if temporal judgment (made every other year), based on party affiliation and personal interest, by voters determining which set of candidates will decide where public policy will be headed. In the United States, party positions on issues will vary across the country, as will the strength of interest groups. The Democratic Party in Texas, Montana, and Idaho will differ from the Democratic Party in New York and Illinois on gun control. Likewise there will be differences among local and state parties across all fifty states and 435 congressional districts on civil rights, environmentalism, tax policy, foreign policy, and any number of other issues. The congressional Democratic and Republican Parties (those members actually in Congress) will therefore be characterized by both inter- and intraparty differences. Some Democrats will be conservatives on tax policy, gun control, and environmental issues whereas some Republicans will be liberal on the same set of issues. In general, we will find that Republicans are more conservative than Democrats across a broad set of issues; however, there is enough variation in intraparty preferences to prohibit strict party control of policy. As a result, just because Democrats control the House and Senate does not guarantee that a Democratic President will get his way in Congress. Indeed, it is precisely the intraparty variance in preferences that leads to the use of a median voter model in predicting policy outcomes. Members of Congress who please their constituencies get reelected, even though they may vote against their party.

One important reason that members of the same party vary in their preferences over policy is the fact that interest groups' influence varies from district to district and region to region. Environmentalists are more numerous in the West than in the Midwest and East. The NRA is stronger in the South and the West than it is elsewhere. The National Organization for Women (NOW) has more members in the North than in the South. The National Farmers Union (NFU) has more members in the Dakotas and Minnesota than the American Farm Bureau Federation (AFBF), which is stronger, in contrast, in the lower Midwest—Illinois and Iowa. More NRA members are Republican than Democrat; AFBF members tend to be Republican; but more environmentalists, NFU, and NOW members are Democrats. Thus across districts, states, and regions interests are sorted differently and influence varies accordingly. In addition to interests and interest groups, individual voters' views matter; for example, about 70 percent of Californians are pro-choice across both parties, putting pro-life candidates at a disadvantage when running for statewide office. California Republicans like former Senator and present Governor Pete Wilson are pro-choice even though the Republican national party's official position is pro-life. One cannot simply take the Congress members' party affiliations to predict abortion policy. When Ronald Reagan was President (and pro-life) and the Senate was Republican, pro-life supporters could not pass a bill or an amendment repealing the *Roe v. Wade* Supreme Court decision. Our analysis focusing on the preferences of members of Congress should be viewed as summarizing the thousands of decisions made by voters, candidates, and interest groups, which yield an electoral result in the Congress. We simply take that end result and assume that the preferences of the members are exogenous; and we try to understand policy given these preferences that are in some large part the result of a complicated nomination and election process.

Given this assumption it should be clear that in our view the main impetus for policy change is electoral change. In general, we propose that if the same members are elected time after time, the status quo policy will prevail. If over 90 percent of incumbent members run for reelection and 95 percent of them win, then their combined preferences over major policies will not change.[2] This is especially true of budget issues, which have always been prominent and more recently have been dominant. Issues involving levels of taxation and expenditure have been featured in 1981, 1982, 1984, 1986, 1990, 1993, and 1995; and any members of Congress surviving all these changes can be said to have accurately gauged their choice and fitted it to being reelected. If one goes by party affiliation, conservative Republicans will not vote for individual income tax increases whereas liberal Democrats will not support cuts in entitlements and welfare spending. Congressional preferences since the end of the Carter presidency have shifted dramatically to the right twice—in 1980 and 1994; and once moderately left—in 1986. This does not mean that the elections in 1982 were not important—they were—only that the 1980, 1994, and 1986 elections represented more dramatic shifts.

Calling an election a "dramatic shift" sounds impressive but what does it mean? It need not indicate a new majority party throughout Congress because only 1994 yielded a new House majority. Essentially, a "dramatic shift" indicates that the new median Representative (the 218th) or Senator (the 50th) is significantly more conservative or liberal than in the previous Congress. In the case of the 104th House (1995–1996) and the 97th Senate (1981–1982), this meant that the new median member was in all likelihood a Republican rather than a moderate Democrat, as was the case in the 103rd House (1993–1994). In the case of the 97th House, although the majority was still Democratic, the median voter was now a very conservative southern Democrat rather than a moderate Democrat.

Note that for the purposes of this analysis, it does not matter whether the 50th voter in the Senate is a Democrat or a Republican. What matters is that member of Congress's policy preference and where on the spectrum that preference lies relative to the status quo and the proposed alternative policy. This is important because since at least the time of V. O. Key (1964), political scientists have pointed to differences in the parties' compositions. Key argued that each party had a presidential and a congressional branch, such that when the party controlled the presidency the presidential branch dominated, whereas without the presidency the congressional branch dominated. James M. Burns, in *The Deadlock of Democracy* (1963), argued that "the deadlock" was due to differences between the southern and northern wings of the Democratic Party, and between the northeastern (Rockefeller) and midwestern wings of the Republican Party. Southern Democrats and midwestern Republicans often voted together as a conservative coalition to block liberal policies. The point is that such "splits" or "differences" within the parties have long occurred. Moreover, when "deadlock" or "gridlock" has been broken, it is largely because an election has dramatically shifted the distribution of preferences in Congress.

Our argument here differs from previous works in the assumption that each congressional member's individual preference over a policy is the determining factor in whether that policy will find support, rather than the more general ascriptive characteristic of, for example, southern Democratic support for a Republican President. Moreover, using member preference as the fundamental building block, one can more precisely locate those groups of House and Senate members who are crucial to understanding why Congress does what it does. Granted, preferences are correlated with party affiliation—liberals are more likely to be Democrats and conservatives are more likely to be Republicans. However, what matters most are the preferences of pivotal members of Congress, such as the 218th House voter and the 50th Senate voter, when majorities are required, and not whether the policy result is the work of a so-called "conservative Democrat" or "moderate Republican." The circumstance of a unified government means very little here because a conservative Democrat would not have voted for the Clinton or Kennedy health care bills when the status quo policy was closer to that voter's preference. Hence a Democratic President elected with a Congress that was essentially the same as the Congress George Bush faced (in terms of the distribution of preferences) should *not* have been expected to enact major policy changes. Just as there was divided-government gridlock under Bush, there was unified-government gridlock under Clinton.

In essence, we maintain that the policy preferences of members of Congress at or near the median are among the crucial determinants of policy outcomes. The distribution of preferences over the members in conjunction with how many voters are needed to move the policy—one-half (a simple majority), three-fifths (to break a filibuster), or two-thirds (to override a veto)—determines policy. Thus if the preferences of key members of Congress remain similar from one administration to the next, the party of the President won't tell us much about policy results. In addition to the distribution of preferences, supermajority institutional rules, specifically the Senate filibuster and the presidential veto (or threat to veto), also affect policy in that these political instruments change who the crucial decisionmakers are—from the 50th to the 60th member of the Senate in the case of the filibuster. Given these variables of preferences and supermajority rules, all that needs to be determined are the relative positions of the present policy and the proposed policy.

This simple theory of the median voter has been circulating for some time in political science starting with Duncan Black (1958), and has been used to explain the policy decisions of school boards, city councils, and other legislative bodies for which majority rule determines decisions. A major criticism of median voter models is that, although they work in one dimension, shifting to a second dimension makes it "impossible" to determine who the median is and thus where the policy will be located. A simple example might be useful. Suppose three legislators are deciding how much to spend on defense. Legislator A prefers $100, B $40, and C prefers not to spend anything. It is obvious with a minimal amount of computation that the legislators will agree to spend $40 on defense. If we add a second dimension to the policy space, say a social budget over which A prefers to spend $10, B $40, and C $100, it can be shown that in two dimensions there is no stable solution. There will always be some other policy in these two dimensions preferred by two members over any present policy. Even the median position (B) in each dimension of spending $40 for each program could be defeated if A and C get together to increase spending for both programs. For example, if A proposes spending $50 each on defense and social programs, C will vote with A, defeating B. In turn, B could propose a point appealing to either A or C, and so on. Given that this is true in such a simple case, how could we apply such a model to anything as complex as the U.S. Congress with its thousands of programs spending well over a trillion dollars annually? This problem has largely prohibited scholars from applying the model to real legislatures.

It is our view that, even when multiple policy dimensions are present, the median members of the dimension of primary concern will be determinative of the outcome, because they will be easier to move and are thus considered pivotal. Consider a bill where member B is undecided how to vote or is mildly for or against the bill, whereas A is strongly against and C is strongly in favor. It will be easier for C (or A) to convince B to vote yes (or no) than it would be to get A (or C) to vote differently. Thus, even if B gets something in return on a different dimension—a federal building or a presidential appearance in the home district— voter B is pivotal to the issue of primary concern. In short, because B determines whether the bill will pass or not, then that legislator can largely determine the final appearance of the bill. In either case—one or two dimensions—our strategy is to focus on the pivotal voters in the relevant dimension. Where two members are needed to change policy, the median member B is pivotal. If all three are needed for a supermajority (unanimity), the member most resistant to change (closest in preference to the present policy) is pivotal.

Moving away from the three-person example it can be argued that, even though there are often relevant off-dimension policies, it is still the pivotal (and often centrist) representatives with respect to the primary policy dimension who determine policy results. For example, in trade issues there are pro–free trade representatives and pro-protectionist representatives, and in between these two positions are a smaller set of members who could vote either way. These members near the median are relatively indifferent about voting for or against a trade bill like the North American Free Trade Agreement (NAFTA). Their votes can be swayed relatively easily by appealing to them with concessions in other policy dimensions, whereas it would be prohibitively costly to sway the vote of a legislator with a strong view on NAFTA through concessions in other dimensions. In short, the votes that can be most easily swayed for purposes of gaining a majority or a supermajority are precisely those of the voters who are most indifferent about the specific issue under consideration. If the vote is on the budget, which involves programs in many dimensions and determines the rates of taxation and spending, then who determines the outcome? Those on the left who favor more spending and taxing and those on the right who favor cuts in taxes and programs will not determine the result. Rather, those members at or near the median—those favoring fewer cuts than the right and less spending than the left—will determine the final makeup of the budget. New policies can be adopted only by altering significantly who these pivotal members are or what they will support. The normal mechanism to provide such a shift in American government is an election.

In addition to the above reasons to focus on the main policy dimension despite the possibility of multiple dimensions, there is strong empirical support for the existence of a main policy dimension for a number of issues. Poole and Rosenthal (1997) address the history of roll call voting in the Congress and find that preferences along a single dimension can account for about three-fourths of the votes of members of Congress on a wide range of issues. Although member preferences may vary from issue to issue, it is preferences along the *main* policy dimension of any particular piece of legislation that will determine which policy proposals can be adopted and which will lead to continued gridlock.

In the next chapter we will present an explanation of the revolving gridlock model, using the case of minimum wage for explanatory purposes. Our intent is to bring some precision to the definition of gridlock, to show how gridlock can be explained in terms of preferences and institutions, and to determine conditions under which gridlock might end.

In Chapter 3 we will argue that the gridlock so frequently written about in the 1980s and early 1990s had its origins in the 1980 Reagan election victory. Specifically, we argue that the 1980 elections shifted the preferences of the Congress decidedly to the right and that the result was the passage of a tax policy that was significantly more conservative than the status quo policy of the time. The new tax policy eliminated "bracket creep," resulting in a constraint on spending and, with the downturn in the economy, a dramatic increase in the deficit. This legislation resulted in a new gridlock region that frustrated both the liberal tax-and-spend representatives and the tax-less, spend-less conservatives. Although modified throughout the mid-1980s, tax policy had solidified by 1986. Since then, there has been no firm coalition to support major increases or decreases in either taxation or spending. Deficit-reduction legislation such as Gramm-Rudman-Hollings in 1985 or Pay-As-You-Go (PAYGO) in 1990 linked budget and program decisions together so that increases in one area would cause decreases in another. Combined with the need for supermajorities, this constraint has been the cause of gridlock for more than a decade.

In Chapter 4 we examine legislation between 1986 and 1992, focusing on the budgetary and policy gridlock that characterized the late Reagan and Bush years. Here it becomes clear that without major changes in the preferences and positions of members of Congress, little can be done to modify policy.

In Chapter 5 we argue that this gridlock continued through the first two years of the Clinton administration. Although legislation previously vetoed by Republican Presidents was now signed by Clinton, little was actually accomplished by what was touted as a gridlock-breaking unified government. The constraints of filibusters in the Senate and the individual preferences of members of Congress guaranteed that the Democratic Party would not act as a unified force to implement the policies set forth in its party platform. Major policy actions such as NAFTA and the 1993 budget act can best be seen as a continuation of congressional policies first developed during the Bush administration rather than as a change in direction due to unified government.

In Chapter 6 we analyze the 104th Congress. We argue that the 1994 election shifted congressional preferences to the right and made Congress the agenda setter. President Clinton's major weapon in the budget policy disputes was the veto, which he used to shift policy toward the left, away from the Republican Congress's preferences. Without the ability to garner the votes of two-thirds of the Senators, the Republicans found that their Contract with America had been reduced to a wish list, left unfulfilled due to gridlock.

NOTES

1. Thinking about individuals and minority groups in government is far from a new idea. In some sense, our argumentation is consistent with that raised by Madison in *Federalist Papers* 10 and 51, that there are no natural majorities but only natural minorities, in that majorities are fleeting and exiting from them is easy.

2. The incumbency effect that allows vast numbers of members of Congress to hold their seats has been noted in political science literature for more than two decades. See, in particular, Erikson 1976, Jacobson 1981, King and Gelman 1991, Fiorina and Prinz 1992, and Alford and Brady 1993.

2

Theoretical Foundations

Presidential candidate George Bush was hitting his stride.[1] The postconvention boost in the polls had subsided and he still had a lead of five to eight points. Picking the conservative Dan Quayle had ensured support from the right, leaving Bush room to cater to the political center. With two months to go before the 1988 presidential elections, the Bush-Quayle team was looking for issues from which Bush could benefit by taking a stand as a political moderate. Abortion was out. There was no solid middle ground there. Defense was out. Testing the waters with an endorsement of "partial deployment" of the "star wars" Strategic Defense Initiative (SDI) system had found too many conservative sharks. The position was now "full deployment." Crime was out. How better to defeat Michael Dukakis than with a tough stand on crime, set against the Dukakis "policy" of granting furloughs to hardened criminals?

So the Bush-Quayle team turned its sights to current legislation before Congress. They found two bills of potential interest. The first was the family leave bill. It appeared that legislation to provide unpaid leave from the workplace to family members with newborns or ailing relatives had the support of majorities in both the House and the Senate. This issue also raised sympathy among the American people. The second issue was the minimum wage. The last increase in the minimum wage had been passed during Carter's first year in office in 1977. Due to a decade of low to moderate inflation, that wage seemed paltry to laborers and politicians alike. A wage increase also appealed to middle-class voters, whose children often worked minimum wage jobs. As such, there was broad support in Congress for a minimum wage hike, perhaps even enough support to override a Reagan or Bush veto.

The campaign team decided to support the latter legislation and oppose the former. The family leave bill would hurt small businesses and upset conservatives. Bush could stop the legislation with a veto if he were elected, enabling him to wield the power of a veto threat on other issues. The minimum wage legislation, however, had such wide support that undoubtedly something would be passed in the next Congress. If Bush opposed it, Democrats in Congress would water down the bill enough to override a veto, giving the President an early defeat. If he supported an increase, perhaps he could be involved in determining the size of the increase. It

11

could turn into a legislative victory and make him look moderate during the campaign. A winning issue.

This chapter, describing the theory upon which our book is based, is divided into five sections. First, we describe how personal preferences and congressional institutions put constraints on policy formation. Second, we address the uncertainty faced by legislators in making policy choices. Third, we look at exogenous factors affecting legislator preferences and policy positioning. Fourth, we take a closer look at the role of the President in the legislative process. Finally, we compare the revolving gridlock theory to two others that have been advanced and widely accepted as explanations of executive-legislative policy formation.

To help clarify the theory and put it in the context of the period we are studying, we will use as an example minimum wage policy throughout the 1980s. In 1977, with the Democrats in control of Congress and the presidency, President Carter called for an increase in the minimum wage and Congress exceeded his expectations. Congress passed legislation raising the minimum wage over a four-year period from $2.30 an hour to $3.35 an hour. As the 1980 election neared, President Carter asked Congress to postpone the January 1980 increase, fearing that it would add to high inflation and unemployment. The argument is that artificially high wages lead to inflated prices. Additionally, employers who could not pay the higher wages would cut back on the number of employees on their payrolls. Despite Carter's request, Congress did not delay the scheduled wage increase. When Reagan was elected in 1980 along with a more conservative Congress, the new leaders chose to leave minimum wage policy alone. There were still enough liberal Senators to filibuster any decrease in the minimum wage, but definitely too few to override the certain Reagan veto of an additional increase. Due to inflation, the 1981 minimum wage of $3.35 commanded less and less purchasing power as the 1980s progressed.

By the 1988 presidential campaign, Democrats in Congress were arguing that a minimum wage increase to $4.50 an hour would be necessary to make up for the lost purchasing power that had accumulated throughout the Reagan years. Bills that even exceeded this proposed raise were drafted in committees in both the House and the Senate. But legislators facing uncertain prospects in the upcoming elections were wary of upsetting either the labor unions or the combined forces of the national Chamber of Commerce and the National Federation of Independent Business. As such, neither chamber held a vote to pass the minimum wage hike. Conservative Senators filibustered action on the Senate Committee's bill until the Democratic leadership dropped the issue for another year. The House bill was also tabled. The issue would be faced again early in the Bush presidency.

This case study raises many interesting questions. How often are legislative changes made? What determines the legislative outcome when changes *are* made? What impact does unified or divided government have on these outcomes? The answers to these questions lead to a better understanding of what is known as policy gridlock.

Preferences and Institutions

John Chafee was being approached from all sides. When the Democratic leadership heard that George Bush was attempting to neutralize minimum wage as a campaign issue for 1988, they knew what had to be done. Majority Leader Robert Byrd called up S837, the bill supporting a $1.20 increase in the minimum wage. Byrd and Ted Kennedy, chief sponsor of the bill, were quite certain the bill would be filibustered by Republicans or vetoed by Reagan. If the bill made it to the White House and Bush did not use his influence as Vice President to gain Reagan's signature, the Democrats could claim that Bush was already breaking campaign promises. If the bill were filibustered, a weaker case could be made. As such, the cloture vote to end the conservative filibuster of S837 was a crucial one. And John Chafee, Republican Senator from Rhode Island, knew it.

Chafee was also aware that his seat was still considered "vulnerable" in the upcoming elections. In 1982, he had squeaked out a victory with 52 percent of the vote. This year his challenger in the largely Democratic state had a name that meant something to Chafee: Licht. In 1968, Frank Licht ousted Chafee from the governorship. Two decades later, his nephew Richard Licht was looking to do the same in the United States Senate. Chafee knew that the people of Rhode Island generally supported the minimum wage increase, which would have typically made his decision easy. But politics during an election year is seldom easy.

Republicans Bob Dole of Kansas and Orrin Hatch of Utah made the case in support of the filibuster. They were opposed to the minimum wage increase, claiming it was unnecessary and would hurt the economy. They were opposed to the Democratic tactic of trying to pass a bill that Reagan would veto and that would never become law. And they saw a political opportunity of their own. The last twenty-five Reagan nominees to lifetime federal judgeships were still awaiting consideration by the Senate. Perhaps there was room for a political compromise here. They would not let minimum wage go through to be vetoed until the judicial appointments had been dealt with. If the Democrats wanted to win a political point, it would be a costly one. But to pull off the compromise, they needed support and couldn't afford to lose many like Chafee to the other side.

The pressures on Chafee from home and from his party were increased by the prospects of interest group involvement. If he opposed the minimum wage hike, labor groups might throw more support to Licht. If he favored the increase, however, his support from Republican business groups might be diminished. Also, considering Licht's claims that Chafee was only responsive to his constituents during election years, Chafee couldn't be certain of getting credit for supporting a wage increase even if he did so.

On September 22, Chafee voted to end the filibuster, against the wishes of his party's leaders. Fifty-two Senators voted with him, seven shy of the sixty needed for cloture. The following day, Chafee felt more confident voting the same way on a second attempt to end the filibuster. Licht had no new issue to seize. John Chafee's decisions on this and other issues would lead him to an eight-point victory in November.

Legislators have preferences about policy decisions. These preferences are based on their partisan slant on the issues, on the degree to which they wish to be representative of their constituents' desires, on their responsiveness to organized interests, and on their personal views about politics and good government. On any particular issue, politicians will take a wide variety of positions, based on preferences ranging from very liberal to very conservative.[2] Looking at an issue, we often find the current (status quo) policy somewhere near the middle of these preferences, not as liberal as many Democrats would like it, and not as conservative as many Republicans would wish. This much is obvious, and results largely from legislative compromise.

Much more can be said about when bills will be passed and what the outcomes will be on a liberal-conservative scale. The theory on which this book focuses is introduced and analyzed formally in Krehbiel's "Institutional and Partisan Sources of Gridlock: A Theory of Divided and Unified Government" (1996). Krehbiel's *Pivotal Politics: A Theory of U.S. Lawmaking* (1997) includes a relatively nontechnical overview of the "pivotal politics theory" and subjects the theory to a wide range of empirical tests on legislative action that occurred throughout the postwar period. As a general matter, we regard his studies and ours to be complementary with respect to the tests, analyses, and interpretations. Throughout this chapter we will note differences between Krehbiel's formal analysis and our portrayal with regard to uncertainty, exogenous shocks, and bargaining between the President and Congress over final outcomes.[3]

The "revolving gridlock theory" is based on a one-dimensional spatial model.[4] We claim that, on any particular issue, legislators can be assigned positions from the most liberal to the most conservative. As a practical matter, preferences may be revealed through interest groups' ratings or other measures of legislators' positions on a variety of issues.[5] We explore these practical issues in greater detail in Chapter 3 with regard to the 1980 electoral shift, in Chapter 4 and the Appendix with regard to preferences over time, in Chapter 5 with regard to interest group ratings, and in Chapter 6 with an example of one particular representative.

In addition to the positions of individual legislators, the position of the status quo policy on each given issue likewise can be discerned. Based on the position of that status quo point with respect to the positions of the members of Congress, we can speculate with some accuracy where a bill will need to be positioned to pass successfully through the institutional structure of lawmaking. The Senate filibuster and the presidential veto provide the institutional constraints on policymaking according to the revolving gridlock theory. If a bill is to become law, it must gain a majority in both houses and must not be killed by a filibuster or a veto. We argue that these constraints caused by legislators' positions and supermajority institutions are the reason policy gridlock is prevalent in the American legislative arena today; and a change in the party of the President is not sufficient to bring about an end to this gridlock.

The first institutional feature of note is the filibuster. The Senate has always been known for its slow and deliberate consideration of issues. In particular, a Senator, once given the floor, can continue to speak for extended periods of time. When a Senator's right to hold the floor indefinitely is utilized to slow or stop the advancement of a bill, the action is commonly referred to as a filibuster. The filibuster gained particular notoriety during the passage of civil rights bills in the 1950s and 1960s. In one instance, Strom Thurmond of South Carolina, speaking out against civil rights legislation, held the floor for twenty-four hours and eighteen minutes. Obviously, filibusters could keep the Senate from acting on important legislation. As a result, the Senate has over time adopted rules limiting the use of the filibuster. Of great significance is Senate Rule XXII, allowing for a cloture vote to end debate. To invoke cloture, sixty Senators must agree that the issue has been sufficiently discussed and that the Senate should continue on with its business, often leading to a vote on the bill being filibustered. The cloture rule thus limits the power of any small group of Senators who wish to talk an issue to death. But it still allows a minority to have significant power over an issue. If forty-one Senators wish to kill a bill through a filibuster, they can do so by voting against cloture. This institutional feature thus can have a great impact on policy outcomes.[6]

Figure 2.1 helps illustrate this point. The range from F_L to F_R represents the central twenty members of the Senate, with M being the median member. The forty-one Senators to the left of and including F_L could successfully filibuster a bill. Likewise, F_R and the forty Senators to the right could successfully filibuster. The Senators are placed along this line based on their positions on the issue at hand. For example, if we are looking at minimum wage legislation, legislators could be lined up based on what dollar level they feel is appropriate for a minimum wage.[7] If the status quo (Q) on a particular issue is between F_L and F_R, we argue that no policy movement can occur. That is, if the central twenty Senators are arguing that the minimum wage should be between $4.00 and $5.00, and the current minimum wage is $4.25, that wage cannot be changed. Looking again at Figure 2.1, if the majority to the right of Q attempts to enact legislation moving policy to the right, F_L and the 40 Senators to the left will filibuster to prevent any legislative movement. This does not mean that the minority on the left can dictate policy, however. Indeed, if they attempt to move policy any further to the left, F_R and the forty Senators to the *right* will filibuster to prevent *that* movement. Thus policy Q cannot be changed by the Senate. This analysis holds true for any status quo policy in the range between F_L and F_R. Because, in this example, a majority would like to enact a more conservative policy but no change is possible, the institutional feature of the filibuster alone is enough to lead to cries of "gridlock."

This "gridlock region" within which no policy change can occur is actually even larger than described above. The reason for this is found in a second institutional feature: the presidential veto. If the President adopts a conservative position on an issue, the region of inaction is extended further to the right. The logic here is much the same as with the filibuster. If the status quo policy is fairly conservative and Congress acts to make the policy more moderate, the President can veto that legislation. Instead of needing the forty-one conservative Senators required to maintain a filibuster, the President only needs thirty-four conservatives to sustain a veto.

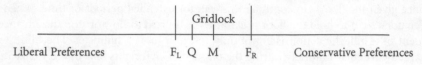

FIGURE 2.1   Policy Constraints Caused by Filibusters

Because a cloture vote requires three-fifths of the Senate and a veto override requires two-thirds, the veto provides a greater constraint on policy action. When the President is conservative and the Senators are ranked along the main policy dimension, then, this region of inaction, or gridlock, stretches from the forty-first Senator to the sixty-seventh. With a liberal President holding veto power, this region stretches more to the left, from the thirty-fourth Senator to the sixtieth. If previous policy has positioned the status quo in this region, then Congress can successfully undertake no further policy action. Movement to the left or the right will be halted by successful filibusters or vetoes, as indicated by points F_L and V in Figure 2.2.

In these diagrams, we are defining the edge of the gridlock region nearest the President to be determined by the number of legislators, based on their preferences, necessary to override a veto. However, if a President is in a position more centrist than this veto-pivotal member (denoted as "V" in the figure), the constraint will then be the President and not this member of Congress. As such, compromises will have to appeal to the President for the sake of avoiding a veto, rather than appealing to enough members of Congress to override the veto. Thus the gridlock region could stretch from the filibuster point to the veto point or to the President's ideal policy point. For extremely centrist Presidents, the veto is of little concern and the gridlock region is defined only by the filibusters, as in Figure 2.1.

After Congress passed the minimum wage increase in 1977, the new wage was securely in the region between the thirty-fourth and the sixtieth Senator. A movement to increase or decrease the wage could be stopped through either a filibuster or a veto. Indeed, even when President Carter asked his own party to delay the minimum wage increase, there was not enough support for congressional action. From 1977 to 1989, policy gridlock reigned on the minimum wage issue. Very liberal Congressmen again saw the wage slip out of line with their own preferences, and they noted that they could not change policy. They were frustrated with what they called partisan gridlock. Very conservative members, on the other hand, saw the declining value of the minimum wage as more in line with their policy preferences. They had no reason to complain about policy inaction. Eventually, however, inflation and other economic conditions caused the purchasing power of the $3.35 wage to fall so far behind that it again became out of line with the preferences of the majority of Congress. At that point, gridlock was brought to an end under a Republican President.

The assumption that the extensive use of filibusters and vetoes is favored by Senators and Presidents is questionable. Is it actually in the interest of a President

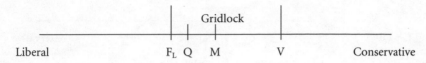

FIGURE 2.2   The Full Gridlock Region

or of a group of Senators to repeatedly veto or filibuster legislation? Would the political costs associated with being labeled an "obstructionist" not outweigh the policy benefits? George Bush's repeated vetoes perhaps even helped lead to his electoral defeat in 1992. But his defeat was not the necessary outcome of his vetoes. With an aggressive campaign, he could have used the vetoes to argue that he was fighting against the liberals in Congress. Indeed, this was precisely what he argued at the end of his campaign. As it turned out, the press had already characterized him as a do-nothing-at-home President. And, come election time, the public had bought this story.[8] And as for the conservatives filibustering early Clinton policies in the Senate, they typically represented constituents who were pleased to hear that liberal policies were being defeated. Although conservative Senators may have preferred legislative action on many issues, stopping action that would have been against their constituents' interests was considered good work. Nevertheless, it is important to be aware of how filibusters and vetoes are perceived and whether this affects how often they are used.[9]

The gridlock region described above is important with regard to policy *action* as well as policy inaction. Figure 2.3 shows the policy region for the Senate with a conservative President, stretching from the filibuster point (F) to the veto point (V). The Senator at point F plays a pivotal role in policy formation. If the status quo policy is to the right, that Senator joins the forty liberals to the left in filibustering any further movement to the right. If policy is to the left, then the pivotal Senator allows a shift to the right just so far as is in that Senator's interest. The pivotal Senator will join the forty colleagues to the left to filibuster bills that go too far. We refer to this Senator as the *filibuster pivot,* as this lawmaker plays a pivotal role in deciding which bills are satisfactory and which should be filibustered.[10] The Senator at point V holds similar powers concerning policy shifts to the left, and is referred to as the *veto pivot.* The thirty-three Senators to the right can be joined by the veto pivot to sustain a presidential veto. Likewise, the sixty-six Senators to the left can be joined to override a veto. Thus this Senator's position is pivotal in deciding whether a bill is conservative enough to pass the Senate, even with a veto threat. We call the region between the filibuster pivot and the veto pivot the *gridlock region.* Policies in this region are maintained, whereas those outside are moved inside.

Looking again at Figure 2.3, the point Q represents a status quo that is outside of the gridlock region. The Senate can thus take successful action in this policy area; but this action is again constrained by the threat of a filibuster. If the Senate

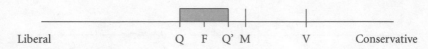

FIGURE 2.3   Possible Outcomes with a Filibuster Threat

proposes a bill that would shift policy to the right of Q', the bill would certainly be filibustered. The Senator at F and the forty Senators to the left all would be disadvantaged by a bill to the right of Q' because such a bill is further from their ideal policy than was Q. If a bill is proposed that would move policy to Q', the Senator at F is indifferent about whether to let the bill go through or to filibuster to stop it. Because of the possibility of a filibuster, the only policies that can be adopted are those in the shaded region between Q and Q'. In actuality, the predicted outcome is somewhere between F and Q'.[11] All movements from Q toward F are advantageous to the Senator at F. Only as a proposal becomes more conservative than Senator F's ideal policy does this Senator consider a filibuster to halt bill movement toward the right. The policy will end up between F and Q'; the exact position of the bill in this region is subject to agenda setting and political bargaining.[12] The conservative President and a majority of Senators prefer the point Q', but the filibustering group, often less impatient than the majority to get something passed, prefers point F. The minority might filibuster until a compromise is made, or a few Senators might find their position unpopular back home, causing the filibuster to break and the majority on the right to benefit.[13]

A diagram similar to Figure 2.3 can be drawn with regard to minimum wage legislation in 1989.[14] In Figure 2.4, the status quo policy has minimum wage at $3.35 an hour, as it was when Bush took office. The veto pivot is positioned at $4.00 an hour.[15] The region between $3.35 and $4.65 is shaded, showing policy outcomes that would be advantageous to the legislator at the veto pivot. As legislation allows the minimum wage to rise toward the $4.00 mark, the legislator preferring the $4.00 wage will vote for it over the status quo wage. That legislator would even prefer a wage at $4.50 to one at $3.35. But when the proposed minimum wage reaches $4.65, the veto pivot legislator becomes indifferent; a wage that is 65 cents too low (i.e., the status quo) and one that is 65 cents too high (i.e., the proposed new wage) are equally unpalatable. If the proposed wage is above $4.65, the legislator at the veto pivot ($4.00) and those who are more conservative will oppose the change. The bill will be vetoed by the President and that veto will be sustained.

It should be clear that the outcome of this legislative process will be a minimum wage set between $4.00 and $4.65. The vast majority, including the veto pivot, prefer a raise to at least $4.00. And the veto pivot is indifferent to a choice between the status quo wage and a $4.65 wage. Liberal and moderate members of Congress would attempt to get as close to the $4.65 wage as possible, whereas conservatives would try to keep the wage increase as small as they could. At this point there is a standoff.

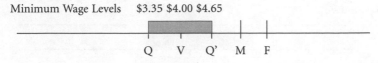

FIGURE 2.4 Possible Outcomes on Minimum Wage Policy (1989)

The initial Democratic proposal in 1989 was a minimum wage of $4.65. Bush needed to establish a counterposition. If he picked a position that increased the wage too much, his position would be frowned upon by his party and his electoral constituency. If he picked too low a wage, his coalition on the right could be broken by a compromise proposal. Some of the legislators he was counting on to sustain a veto could be won over by the majority with the argument that Bush was appearing too conservative and too much a proponent of gridlock. Bush knew that *some sort* of a wage increase would pass. The size of the increase would depend on the President's position and on the political bargaining game.

In short, the revolving gridlock theory predicts that status quo policies inside the gridlock region will be maintained, and policies outside the region will be brought inside, usually through minor policy adjustments. With very little resulting policy change, even where a majority approves change, this model starts to explain what is referred to as policy gridlock. When this gridlock occurs under unified party control of government, we call it *unified gridlock*. Unified gridlock resulted under the 103rd Congress during the first two years of the Clinton administration.

It should not be assumed that this model rests on the *observance* of filibusters and vetoes. The mere *threat* of a veto or a filibuster is often enough to kill a bill or to force it to be altered so as to override a veto or to gain sufficient votes for cloture. Successful vetoes and filibusters might actually be quite rare. Because time and effort are scarce commodities in Congress, it would be easier for the majority and the leadership to abandon a bill early on than to lose it to a filibuster or veto. However, in some circumstances politicians may wish to go down swinging.[16] Opponents can raise the issue of repeated sustained vetoes, such as those in the Bush presidency, as an example of the President and his party causing gridlock. And Democrats could claim that the repeated filibusters by Bob Dole and other conservatives in the 103rd Congress were "obstructionist." Of course, on the other side of the coin, during the 1994 elections Republicans effectively claimed that the Democrats were poor at policymaking, unable to pass major legislation even with control of Congress and the presidency.

The above discussion has concentrated mainly on the Senate. There similarly exists a gridlock region for the House. As filibusters are not allowed in the House, this region only stretches from the House median to the House veto pivot. With a conservative President, status quo policies in this region cannot be shifted to the right because a majority would not vote for such a shift, and policies cannot be moved to the left because such a shift would be vetoed and the veto sustained.

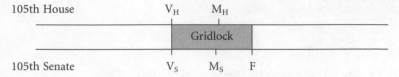

FIGURE 2.5   The Gridlock Region in the Bicameral 105th Congress

Because this region is smaller than in the Senate, it is often less of a constraint on policy.[17] However, the need for a supermajority to override a veto is a serious constraint in both the House and the Senate.

Figure 2.5 shows the bicameral situation as we perceive it today, with a fairly conservative House and Senate and a Democratic President. Here the gridlock region is defined by the constraints of the filibuster pivot in the Senate and the veto pivot in both the House and the Senate. If the House were considered more conservative than the Senate (as was the case immediately following the 1994 elections), the gridlock region in the figure would expand out to the further of the veto pivots—that of the Senate. Indeed, as we argue in Chapter 6, the constraints on policy change as outlined by the Contract with America during the 104th Congress were the presidential veto and the preferences of the veto pivot members in the Senate. The gridlock region for our bicameral system is determined on the left by the greatest restriction between the two houses on movement to the right, and is determined on the right by the greatest restriction on movement to the left. This usually means that one of the restrictions is the filibuster in the Senate, and the other is whichever veto pivot extends the gridlock region further away from the median.

The position of the President and his veto threat determines which side of the gridlock region will be stretched out to the veto pivot. With the election of Bill Clinton, the previous extension of the gridlock region to the veto pivot on the right was altered such that the filibuster pivot is now on the right and the veto pivot is on the left. Policies that were held in place by Bush vetoes were released for action by Congress. But they were still constrained by the filibuster pivot in the Senate. Unless President Clinton's proposals were made suitably conservative, the Senator at the filibuster pivot and colleagues to the right would have voted to stop the legislation with a filibuster, voting down cloture attempts until the bill died or a compromise was reached. This was the fate of many Clinton proposals in 1993, including the national service legislation and the jobs stimulus package.

Following the 1994 elections, policy proposals reflected the shift in preferences to the right, advancing more conservative policies. The limitation on these policies was the threat and use of vetoes by President Clinton. The President's successful vetoes of Republican budgets and welfare overhauls made Congress adjust their proposals more to the President's liking. Had Bob Dole been elected in 1996, the constraint on policy change to the right would have been the less-restrictive filibuster in the Senate. Many items in the Contract with America that were watered down to avoid or override Clinton vetoes could have been enacted in full.

Uncertainty

"It's Friday. Some people are confused," Bob Dole explained. The Friday in question was September 23, 1988, and the Minority Leader had just lost five more Republican votes in his attempt to keep the minimum wage filibuster going. The cloture vote had still failed, as nine Senators had not been present to vote. But Dole was concerned about the apparent weakening of his coalition. This issue was a bit complex, as they were voting on a procedural issue, not on whether to actually pass a higher minimum wage. But wasn't it a straightforward procedural vote? Maybe not.

The actual impact of an increase in the minimum wage was uncertain. Earlier in the summer, the San Francisco Federal Reserve reported that a minimum wage increase could boost inflation by a noticeable amount. Since then, several studies were released claiming that the proposed minimum wage hike could cause the loss of up to a million jobs. Such news raised questions among the Senators voting on that late September day. How soon would these effects on the economy take place? Would the voting public be able to trace the blame to those who voted for an increase in the minimum wage? Would these hardships counterbalance the benefits that constituents would perceive from increased wages for those with low incomes?

The actions of interest groups raised more questions in the minds of legislators. Even if no economic hardships materialized before the elections, would the varied interested parties influence the elections depending on my vote? If I vote for a wage increase, will my support from small businesses diminish? If I vote against an increase, will organized labor raise more support for my opponent? Even Dole was frustrated with the involvement of some of these interest groups. "How many Labor Committee bills from organized labor do we need before we go home?" he asked.

But Dole had not taken steps to make the issue clearer for his colleagues in the Senate. In fact, he muddied the waters further, by tying action on minimum wage to the approval of Reagan's nominees to federal judgeships. "I am advised by members on my side to bring this place to a halt until we get some action" on the judicial appointments, Dole said. This led to even more questions. If a Senator supported the filibuster, would he then be perceived as being involved in a type of blackmail to get conservative judgeships?

With the issue so complicated and the uncertain prospects of elections so close on the horizon, Dole should not have been surprised to see some flip-flops in voting. Over the weekend he would make sure that he would not lose the next cloture vote, leaving the Democratic leadership with the lose-lose proposition of either prolonging the stalemate or dropping the bill. By Monday it was clear that the conservative filibuster could continue indefinitely, so the Democratic leadership dropped the bill.

In forming policy, legislators face uncertainty on a number of levels. Of concern to the theory here are two types of uncertainty: uncertainty over the actual policy results of passing a bill, and uncertainty over constituent reactions to voting for or against a bill.[18] Although members of Congress are forced to live with some level of uncertainty, they take many steps to minimize that uncertainty.[19]

They listen carefully to constituents, paying attention to surveys and polls. They take advice from experts, whether committee members who have specialized in a policy area or authorities who give testimony in hearings.[20] Still, the remaining uncertainty leads to mistakes.

First, there is uncertainty over the actual policy results of passing a bill. In the above section, we assumed that the status quo policy and the alternative proposed by the bill were known and were easily placed on a one-dimensional line. Legislators then simply pick whichever policy is closer to their preferred outcome. In reality, policymaking is an uncertain activity. Budget estimates made over a five-year period are undoubtedly going to lose accuracy over time. Members of Congress cannot accurately predict which interpretations and actions government agencies and bureaus will take. Policymakers and policy analysts are unsure of just how many people will qualify for programs, find loopholes, or be indirectly affected by a policy change. Legislators try to find out as much as they can about the policy consequences of various actions, and then they must take a risk and vote.

The uncertainty of policy outcomes could have a beneficial or adverse effect on the chances of a bill's passage, depending on perceptions of the status quo. When the public seems pleased with present policies, it may be difficult to pass new legislation. Although the proposed policy could actually improve the status quo, legislators feel no pressure to take chances. Such was the case with minimum wage legislation in 1988. Pollsters predicted that incumbents would fare quite well in that year's elections. The economy was fairly strong, and it appeared that George Bush would be elected President. Congress felt that tinkering with the minimum wage while otherwise in such a strong position so close to the elections raised too much uncertainty. The San Francisco Federal Reserve reported that a minimum wage increase could boost inflation by a noticeable amount.[21] Analysts released a variety of studies claiming that a minimum wage hike could cause a loss of up to a million low-wage jobs. This potential job loss combined with the grassroots lobbying campaign by business groups led the House leadership to avoid votes on the bills proposed out of committee.[22] Although Congress did consider the issue, there was no outrage over legislative inaction, and if Congress had acted there was a great risk of making economic and political conditions worse.

In contrast to this case of uncertainty leading to inaction, at times politicians embrace an uncertain outcome. When the current policy is considered poor, the public perceives that things cannot get any worse. This paves the way for a string of new, uncertain policy proposals. Had economic conditions been different in 1988, perhaps members of Congress would have supported a minimum wage increase. For example, if there were an outcry about large numbers of working Americans living below the poverty line, legislators could address the issue through a minimum wage hike just before the election. The public would think that Congress was being responsive, and the inflation and job loss would not be felt before the election. Whereas typically members of Congress are looking to avoid uncertain options, under these conditions they may embrace a major change.

Thus uncertainty over policy outcomes can either add to or relieve policy gridlock. When legislators are uncertain about the consequences of their actions, they may either take small steps or make no changes to current policy. But when there is demand for immediate action, uncertainty could trigger a major policy change that would have been unacceptable to legislators had they been perfectly aware of the outcome. As the uncertainties are resolved over time, members of Congress can better judge what they have done. If the results are found to be in the "gridlock region," no further policy changes are made. Such was the case with minimum wage policy under President Carter. When he realized that the wage increase he had called for was hurting the economy, Carter asked Congress to delay its implementation.[23] However, so many members of Congress agreed with the wage increase that it went forward as planned. Even though the policy outcome was more dramatic than expected, the results were still in the gridlock region. If the uncertainty is resolved with the discovery that the policy enacted did not move into the gridlock region at all, or even that it overshot the region, modifications to the policy will be made. For example, when the 1981 tax cuts in concert with the economic downturn yielded large budget deficits, President Reagan supported minor tax increases over the next few years. And when the catastrophic health care measure passed by the 100th Congress was found to be catastrophic itself, it was quickly repealed.

In addition to being uncertain about where the policy outcome of a bill will lie, members of Congress face a second uncertainty: how their constituents will react to how they vote. In the above section, we argued that members of Congress are aligned from liberal to conservative. Their positions on various issues can be determined by observing how they vote over time. When they vote, members of Congress seeking reelection must be aware of how their constituencies view their votes on the issue at hand. And yet these members are uncertain as to what the reaction will be back home. Many policy votes will simply be ignored by constituents; others will be observed but play little or no role in swaying voters; and still others will become major campaign issues. Furthermore, the uncertain reaction of constituents is compounded by the uncertain policy outcomes. Even though they may have the best of intentions, legislators will be blamed for the unforeseen results of their actions (or inaction).

Because legislators are trying to maintain their popularity among constituents, they must try to resolve the uncertainties concerning voters' perceptions of the issues. In particular, members of Congress attempt to reduce uncertainty by judging the salience of an issue to the public and the leanings of the public either for or against a bill. Legislators pay attention to surveys and polls as well as to calls and letters from constituents. Over time, they settle on a position with which they are comfortable, whether they derive benefit from their party, from their constituents, from funding via Political Action Committee (PAC) support, or from a sense of doing what is right for the American people.[24] Throughout 1988 and early 1989, lawmakers were deciding on their positions regarding minimum wage increases. They were careful in 1988 not to upset the labor movement on one side of the issue or business groups on the other.[25] Either side could have helped finance challengers against incumbents who weren't carefully positioned.

As the legislators themselves are converging on their final positions on a particular issue, the bill being produced is also changing. Support for a legislative change in policy early in the formulation of a bill does not necessarily mean that anything will be done in the end. It certainly does not mean that the President or the majority party is free to push through its bill of choice. As uncertainties are resolved about where the status quo, the various new bills, and the legislators' own positions lie, we can fairly accurately predict the policy outcome. If the status quo is found to be in the gridlock region with a large number of legislators on each side of it, policy change can be stopped through filibusters and vetoes.[26] If the status quo is found to be outside the region, as was shown in Figure 2.3, it will be brought inside the region, but seldom as far as those promoting change had wished.

On many issues Congress deals with, most of the major uncertainty can be resolved before action is taken. In such cases, the revolving gridlock theory should be expected to hold without exception. Additionally, we can accurately predict *when* uncertainty will play a large role. Uncertainty influences policy when legislators face two constraints: complexity and time. When dealing with a multiyear budget and an uncertain constituent reaction, or with bills involving the one-seventh of the American economy that is health care today, legislators can make mistakes. The issues are so complex that all of the uncertainty cannot be removed. Also, when dealing with the time constraint of enacting a policy just before elections, uncertainties cannot be removed from the legislative process because all the variables cannot properly be addressed. Although members of Congress wish to campaign on the strength of a new program they have just passed, they do so at the risk of finding that they have made a mistake when they return to Congress the next year. We claim that the revolving gridlock theory will hold true generally, even where uncertainty surrounding legislative decisions makes the process more complex.

Elections and Exogenous Shocks

"I can't tell you what a very significant departure this is from what we've had over the past eight years." Democratic Senator Ted Kennedy was obviously pleased that minimum wage was again being discussed in March 1989. He had seen the wage shrink in terms of purchasing power for years, and had been a strong supporter of an increase. To raise the minimum wage to $4.60 an hour would only restore the purchasing power it enjoyed in 1981, Kennedy argued. It would not make up for the years of decline that people living on minimum wage had endured.

Now was the time to do something about the minimum wage. The newly elected President had issued a campaign promise to raise the minimum wage. And he had not brought in many conservative members of Congress on his coattails who would oppose a wage hike. As such, a large majority in both houses of Congress supported an increase.

Although President Bush had only supported an increase to $4.25 an hour, Kennedy believed that a greater increase would have enough support to override a veto. But would Bush be foolish enough to veto the increase? About 80 percent of the public favored an increase in the minimum wage. If Bush vetoed the bill passed by Congress, he would lose credit for any increase whatsoever, and would hopefully lose a veto fight as well. Kennedy therefore wanted to propose an increase that would restore much of the purchasing power of former wages, and one that would also be an embarrassment to Bush if he vetoed it. On March 23, the Senate decided on a wage of $4.55, just three thin dimes more than Bush's proposal. With the approval of the House, the ball would soon be back in the President's court.

In previous pages we defined the gridlock region and argued that policies in that region could not be changed, due to the diverse preferences of members of Congress and to the institutional structure involving the use of filibusters and vetoes. Status quo policies outside the gridlock region are brought just inside it. Because of uncertainty, policies are sometimes formulated that are outside the gridlock region. We claim that when these outlying policies are discovered, they are brought back inside the gridlock region. If all of this is true, it would seem that over time Congress would get around to dealing with every policy area, bringing each policy outcome into the gridlock region where it is then held in place. We argue that this would be the case if there were no shocks to the system. But in the constantly changing world of politics and policy, a number of exogenous factors impact upon the theory. The exogenous factors of greatest concern to us are threefold: the election of new politicians, the changing preferences of constituents, and the shifting of policy realizations over time.

Because the narrow band that we call the gridlock region is defined by the preferences of legislators in the House and Senate, a change in these members or in their preferences could alter the size and placement of the region. If such a change leads to a state in which some current policies are no longer within the region, then those policy areas are released for legislative action. The most straightforward way to change the placement of the gridlock region is to change the members who define its position. For example, if the Republicans gain a number of seats in a given election, the region is likely to shift to the right. This may result in no policy change, if there were no fairly liberal status quo policies just inside the gridlock region. Or it could result in across-the-board changes, if a large number of status quo policies are released from the gridlock region.

Thus policy gridlock depends on both the *size* and the *shifting* of the gridlock region. The size of the region is determined by the difference in preferences between the pivotal members on both edges of the region. If the preferences of the forty-first (filibuster pivot) and sixty-seventh (veto pivot) members are quite similar (as with a large number of centrists), little gridlock will occur. However, if the preferences of these members are quite different, policy changes over a vast range of policies will be unachievable. This is perhaps why commentators worry about the "lack of a political center" in today's Congress. In the Appendix, we show the distribution of preferences in Congress since 1980. Note that, given these preferences, the gridlock region has been sizable in recent years. However, not only the size of the gridlock region but also its *movement* matters. Even if the gridlock region had about the same size after the 1980 elections as before, the dramatic shift to the right released a number of policies that were formerly in the gridlock region and that could now move to better reflect the preferences of Congress and President Reagan.[27]

However, most elections do not bring about sweeping changes.[28] The vast majority of incumbents are reelected.[29] Additionally, changes at the margins often do not affect the position of the gridlock region to any great extent. If ten liberal members and ten conservative members all lose their seats and are replaced by new members on the opposite sides, the region may not be changed at all. The moderate legislators at the endpoints of the gridlock region may remain the same, whereas the legislators on the wings change dramatically. Furthermore, voters may take into account the preferences of the other members of Congress and of the President in order to strike some sort of balance or include checks on other politicians.[30] Although we are indeed interested in the link between policies and elections, our main focus is on what happens when politicians are already *in* the government, emphasizing that it takes major electoral shifts to move policy left or right.

If the gridlock region *does* move noticeably in one direction, this is often the result of the "coattails" effect frequently found in presidential elections.[31] If the party of the President changes from Democrat to Republican and a number of conservative Senators and Representatives are brought in with the new President, liberal status quo policies become vulnerable to change. The President will certainly wish to enact change in all of those policy areas before the typical loss of seats during the midterm elections.[32] This explains the phenomenon known as the "honeymoon," in which a new President is able to quickly bring about policy change on a number of issues.[33] (Often within the first few months of a presidency, most of the policies with low uncertainty are brought back into the new gridlock region.) Because policy movement is still restricted by the possibility of a filibuster in the Senate, the President often will not get all that he wants during his honeymoon. The more extreme a President's position, the more he will appear to be losing in the compromises he is forced to make. Because the policy outcomes illustrated by the above figures were not dependent on how extreme the President's position was, a President often appears more powerful by asking for what he knows can be passed rather than by asking for what he wants and then having to abandon the policy or cave in to the opposition.[34]

This is an important point in our understanding of presidential requests. It is possible that President Bush wanted the minimum wage to stay where it was. But this was an unpopular position in Congress, where a raise to at least $4.00 was inevitable. By taking a position supporting a raise to $4.25, Bush appeared to be moderate while also challenging those who wanted an increase beyond $4.25. Had he positioned his proposal any lower, he may have appeared too conservative, risking the breakdown of his coalition. Had he requested a higher wage, Bush would have been giving away more than he had to, perhaps hurting the economy as an outcome. Had he ignored the issue entirely and left Congress to pass increases that he would veto, Bush would eventually have had to give in to a small increase or risk having his veto overridden and the steam taken out of his presidency early in his first term. Bush's proposal turned a losing issue into an early victory.

After the honeymoon, the President is left to deal with those policy areas containing the greatest uncertainty, those policies that cannot easily be adjusted back into the gridlock region. This is when the legislative challenge really begins. President Reagan was able to use the uncertainty surrounding supply-side economics to his advantage. President Clinton, on the other hand, lost popularity in his first year by trying to enact his own ideal policies only to end up giving concessions to conservative Senators. In 1994, when facing the uncertainties of health care reform, members of Congress tried to distance themselves from Clinton's unpopularity.

The gridlock region can be changed not only through legislator turnover but also through a shift in the preferences of legislators. As described above, legislators' preferences are complex; they depend on party strength, on public opinion of their constituencies, on the influence of interest groups, on the amount of available information, and on the legislators' own personal preferences independent of outside forces. When any of these factors shifts dramatically, a legislator's preferences will follow.

If the President is enormously popular and has agreed to campaign for members of his party who support him, those legislators are able to vote with the President even if they lose some support from interest groups or constituents. Any such loss of support can be won back in a grand fashion if the President campaigns on behalf of the legislator. But a President without such popularity will see members of his own party distancing themselves from him. Likewise, if public opinion is shifted through advertising campaigns, such as the "Harry and Louise" ads against the Clinton health care plan, legislators may alter their voting preferences in order to please their constituents. And if interest groups join in on an issue at the last minute, or provide new information to Congress, a shift in legislator preferences is again likely.

When these shifts are dramatic, members of Congress may change their preferences to the extent that policies previously in the gridlock region are now to the left or right of it. In such cases, Congress will pass bills to bring policies back in line with the preferences of its members. Of note here is a beneficial side effect of gridlock. Because of the lack of policy movement in the gridlock region, members of Congress do not spend all of their time chasing small shifts in public opinion. If it weren't for the threat of filibusters and vetoes, legislation could be raised and passed with the slightest change in legislator preferences. These institutional constraints sometimes mean that the majority's proposals can be stopped by a minority, but they also encourage Congress to act only when significant action is needed.

The first two exogenous shocks to the revolving gridlock model—a change of legislators and a change of legislators' preferences—affected the positioning of members of Congress, and thus of the gridlock region. A third exogenous factor involves the position of the status quo policy relative to the gridlock region. As was discussed above, there is often uncertainty with regard to the actual outcome of legislation adopted by Congress. Although some laws have been unchanged on the books for decades, others are changed all the time. Congress is unable to specify a budget for more than a year or two into the future. Minimum wage, Medicare, and Social Security benefits are constantly being adjusted. With an increase in crime, a crisis overseas, a natural disaster, a dramatic increase in the cost of health care, a newly discovered disease, an economic recession or depression, or any of a number of other unforeseen events, new issues constantly arise for Congress to deal with.

When new issues arise, or old issues take on a new significance, members of Congress face a high level of uncertainty as to what should be done. Congress devotes most of its attention to dealing with these unpredictable issues when they arise, then returning to the normal business of adjusting policies that have drifted outside of the gridlock region. With the economic difficulties of the late 1970s and early 1980s, Congress dealt with the problem through an attempt at supply-side economics. When this reaction led to growing budget deficits, Congress became seriously restricted in its ability to initiate new programs and was forced to raise taxes and limit spending just to avoid a crisis.

When President Bush reacted to Iraq's invasion of Kuwait, Congress had to address the possible use of military force if the legislative branch wished to maintain a reasonable level of influence in the foreign policy arena. When hurricanes hit Florida and Hawaii and floodwaters covered the Midwest, again Congress had to act. Shocks to minimum wage policy were slower in coming. Inflation during the 1980s caused wages to lose about one quarter of their purchasing power. When the minimum wage had thus dropped to levels unacceptable to legislators, they called for a wage hike. This was not the result of a liberal shift in the preferences of members of Congress, nor in divided or unified government. Outside factors had caused the minimum wage to become skewed away from the preferences of lawmakers, who therefore changed the policy.[35]

Most of the significant action taken by Congress has occurred as a reaction to exogenous shocks to the legislative system. When new legislators are elected and there is a major shift to the left or right, new legislative action is likely. When public opinion solidifies behind an issue, such as during the Great Depression, the world wars, or the space race, the preferences of legislators are altered enough to bring about significant change. And when unforeseen policy shocks arise, legislative action is again possible. Often these shocks occur under extraordinary circumstances. The revolving gridlock theory is significant in its ability to explain the results of these occurrences as well as to address the day-to-day legislation passing through Congress. When lawmakers fail to respond to exogenous shocks, they put their seats at risk. The inability of Republicans to react to the events of the Great Depression led to enormous Democratic victories. When the Democrats failed to respond to cries for tax relief throughout the 1970s, Republicans gained control of the Senate and presidency and found enough support to enact huge tax cuts in 1981.

In the absence of major electoral and policy shocks, the government falls into periods of legislative gridlock during which either no policy is passed or only incremental changes around the edges of the gridlock region are made. It is our contention that the election of Bill Clinton with only 42 percent of the vote and few coattail victories did not represent a major shock to the American political system. As such, although the 103rd Congress and the presidency were controlled by the same political party, the government was in a period of continuous policy gridlock, with abandoned policy proposals and incremental changes. It was a unified government with unified gridlock. Just as continuous policy inaction during a public outcry for change can lead to electoral turnover, so too can there be electoral repercussions from forcing policy action. As will be shown in later chapters, the party-based pressure on some conservative Democrats to support Clinton proposals (including the 1993 budget act) led many members to vote against their constituents' preferences; this, in turn, led their constituents to vote *against them* in 1994, bringing about significant Republican gains.

These few examples of electoral reactions to policy change (or lack of change) show the dynamic nature of elections and policymaking. Exogenous shocks to policies or preferences may lead to inaction or to new policy outcomes. Such legislative action (or inaction) has electoral implications. And these elections in turn act as even further shocks to the system. It is a constant struggle for politicians to please the electorate while attempting to make compromises to break gridlock. We are describing *revolving gridlock*. Although legislators' preferences and institutional constraints always lead to a certain amount of gridlock, politicians and the electorate are always attempting new and different tactics to bring about what they perceive as good policy. Politicians are either caught in gridlock or making dramatic compromises in the attempt to overcome it. The public, when dissatisfied with congressional and presidential activities, can do little but vote them out of office.[36] Unified government was thus attempted in 1992, and Republican control of Congress in 1994. And yet, due to the reasons discussed here, this revolving of politicians did not bring an end to policy gridlock.

The Role of the President

Members of the Bush White House were pleased with their cleverness. Democratic leaders had held off sending the minimum wage bill to the White House. Congress cleared HR2 on May 17, 1989, but the Democrats wanted their new House leader-

ship in place before engaging in a confrontation with the President. On June 13, that leadership was in place, George Bush was out west on a two-day trip, and the Democrats felt that it was time. They sent the bill to the White House, and scheduled a press conference for 3 P.M. There, they would make arguments intended to give the President great discomfort if he actually vetoed the bill, which raised the minimum wage above his $4.25 target.

But Bush was ready for them. His staff had made certain that he carried his veto message with him to Wyoming. At 1:39 P.M. the President was informed aboard Air Force One that the bill had reached the White House. He immediately vetoed it, having members of his team in Washington finish the paperwork to send the bill back to Capitol Hill half an hour before the Democrats' press conference. "This may be the first faxed veto in history," White House chief of staff John Sununu joked.

The President was confident about his veto, knowing that neither the House nor the Senate had passed the bill by the two-thirds needed to override it. Additionally, he had a promise from more than thirty-four Senators that they would sustain his veto. Now if only the American people would realize that he was committed to a wage increase, but not the bloated one that had passed through the Congress . . . By undermining the efforts of the Democratic leadership to get the first punch in, Bush had taken a large step toward his objectives.

In previous sections we explain how the theory of revolving gridlock is based on the preferences of members of Congress and on congressional institutions, without much mention of the role of the President. Indeed, we feel that the President's role in policymaking is less significant than he is often given credit (or blame) for in the press and in the minds of the voters. Nevertheless, the President does play an important role in the legislative process, a role that can be brought to light through the revolving gridlock theory. He affects lawmaking in at least four areas: influencing the preferences of legislators, vetoing legislation, compromising with pivotal legislators, and raising the importance of issues he would like Congress to act upon.

The President and his party can influence the preferences of members of Congress. A popular President can help members of his party through fund-raisers, media publicity, and campaign activism. In close votes, the President and party leadership can offer side benefits to legislators in exchange for their votes, when they are indifferent to the issue at hand.[37] These benefits could come in the form of pork or of campaign financing and publicity. Additionally, a popular President can provide cover for members of Congress who are nervous about policy votes. By taking a public stand, the President provides the opportunity for legislators to say that they are voting with the President on the issue at hand rather than having to explain their position in greater detail and thus upsetting a segment of their constituency.

The most formal involvement of the President in the legislative process comes through the use of the presidential veto. As described and illustrated above, the possibility of a veto stretches the gridlock region in the direction of the

President's position. This means that policies close to the President's position often cannot be made more moderate even if a majority in Congress would prefer such a change. Furthermore, with a change in the party of the President, the direction of the gridlock region's expansion changes, often releasing policy areas that had been left alone because of veto threats by a President of the other party. In addressing these newly released policy areas, the President has a chance to gain popularity and appear active. When a newly elected President replaces a President of his own party, the gridlock region does not change (the veto pivot is still on the same side of the median). As such, not as many policies are found outside the gridlock region for the new President to act upon. This situation undoubtedly added to the impression that Bush, who replaced a President of his own party, was ineffective in the legislative arena.

When the minimum wage was raised in 1977, the constraint on this increase was the possibility of a filibuster in the Senate. Had a conservative President been in office, the constraint on policy change would have been the more-restrictive veto threat. Had Gerald Ford been reelected in 1976, the minimum wage hike would have been smaller than the $1.05 increase that President Carter secured. Likewise, had Michael Dukakis been elected in 1988, the ninety-cent increase allowed by President Bush would have been surpassed. As the theory suggests, institutional conditions and the preferences of members of Congress always constrain the size and substance of a policy change. The greater these constraints (veto threats rather than filibuster threats), the greater the cries of gridlock. In minimum wage policy, we may see a difference of a few dimes in wage increases because of the position of the President. In dealing with the defense budget and entitlements, the difference may be billions of dollars.

The third role of the President in the revolving gridlock theory relates to policy compromises made with the pivotal legislators in the model. Recall from Figure 2.4 that the policy shift from the status quo to a point inside the gridlock region could result in raising the minimum wage to any amount between $4.00 and $4.65 an hour. In this case, $4.00 was the ideal policy point for the veto pivot and $4.65 was the position that made the veto pivot indifferent to selecting between the old policy and the new. Depending on the compromise made with the veto-sustaining minority, any new minimum wage between $4.00 and $4.65 could be passed. By appearing ready to veto wage increases beyond his request of $4.25 an hour, President Bush could pull the outcome closer to $4.00, making a better deal for himself.[38] But if the President had taken the unpopular position of opposing any increase, he may not have been able to gain the votes necessary to sustain a veto. Indeed, he may have been forced to give in to a policy outcome nearer the opposing legislators' position than his own. This would have led to the appearance of caving in and thus to a drop in his popularity. Even when a President is able to influence the policy outcome, however, he seldom gains as extreme an outcome as he might want. Based on the model, Bush was faced with a policy outcome of between $4.65 and $4.00, whereas his ideal minimum wage was probably less than \$4.00 an hour. A President is always forced to accept policy results within the narrow band of the gridlock region. By taking a position of \$4.25 and vetoing any increase beyond that point, President Bush won the bargaining game with the congressional leadership. In the end, the Democratic leadership was more interested in passing the increase that Bush proposed than in risking a second loss to the President on another sustained veto.

The final significant role of the President in the theory of legislative policy-making is in bringing the public's attention to an issue.[39] Congress often has a number of issues on its plate at the same time. When a President emphasizes an issue during a campaign, a press conference, or the State of the Union Address, he is looking to bolster public awareness and encourage legislative action. Where there is a large degree of uncertainty surrounding a policy area, Congress may be hesitant to act without a push from the President. It is possible that the health care debate raised in 1994 would not have occurred without all of the publicity generated by Bill and Hillary Clinton. Whereas the revolving gridlock theory argues that legislator preferences and institutions affect *where* policy will end up, the President can help decide *which* issues will be addressed. Thus when claims were made that the Whitewater accusations would affect health care policy, the reality is that, if Whitewater had any impact, the impact was on whether health care was addressed at all rather than how liberal or conservative the health care bill was in the end. From this view, the President becomes more an agenda setter than a force influencing policy outcomes. This is not to say that once Congress starts dealing with an issue the President can back off. If he does, the bill could easily die before it ever reaches the floor. Rather, the President must keep the issue in the public eye and help to resolve uncertainty about the issue through task forces and the advice of experts and executive agencies.

Opposing Theories

To further clarify the theory we are setting forth, we have found it useful to contrast the revolving gridlock theory with two others that have been circulating in the media and academia in the 1990s. These theories have been used as assumptions in many works, but have not been fully addressed in any one work. The first is the "strong party theory," in which the control of Congress and the presidency by one party is expected to result in policy outcomes reflecting that party's ideal platform, whereas control of these two branches of government by opposing parties leads to gridlock. The second is the "compromise between branches theory," in which the Congress and the President strike a compromise between their ideal policy outcomes. According to this theory, a liberal Congress and a conservative President might agree on moderate policies, whereas a liberal President and a liberal Congress will certainly come to a (liberal) political compromise.

The assumptions of the strong party theory underlie many arguments about divided and unified government. Either explicitly or implicitly, those who write about divided government believe that control of the executive and legislative branches by different parties has policy consequences.[40] Political scientists (Fiorina 1996; Jacobson 1990; Cox and Kernell 1991) have tended to be explicit on the causes of divided government and to be less explicit about the consequences. Broadly speaking, however, the consequences can be sorted into two kinds of claims: (1) divided government makes an already unwieldy constitutional system of government unworkable; and (2) divided government obscures responsibility.

Those who focus on the claim that divided government makes the system of governance unworkable are essentially arguing that divided government yields policy gridlock. Sundquist compares divided government unfavorably with a unified model of government that assumes an active President supported by cohesive legislative majorities. Essentially, divided government gives each branch of government incentives to undermine the actions of the other branch (Sundquist 1988, 629–630). Ginsburg and Shefter (1990) make a similar argument, claiming that in divided government, governing becomes posturing and decisions satisfy no one. Although scholars who fit into the gridlock mold tend to be general rather than specific about policy consequences, some have claimed specific effects. Lloyd Cutler, for example, claims: "In modern times high deficits have occurred only with divided government. . . . The correlation between unacceptably high deficits and divided government is much too exact to be a coincidence" (Cutler 1989, 391). McCubbins (1991, 83–111) corroborates this analysis, arguing that the high deficits between 1981 and 1987 were the result of party preferences and divided control of government. Alt and Lowrey (1994) look for a connection between divided government and budget deficits in the states. McKenzie and Thornton (1996, 157) agree with the general thrust of these arguments, claiming that divided government exacerbates the problems of dealing with deficits.

Those who claim that divided government diminishes electoral accountability argue that under divided control citizens cannot tell who is to blame; thus the meaning of electoral outcomes is rendered confusing (Fiorina 1996). This line of reasoning is so enmeshed in the normative argument about responsiveness and responsibility that sorting it out depends upon one's values. Thus we deal here only with the gridlock argument.

The major case against those who believe that divided government has policy consequences is made by David Mayhew in *Divided We Govern* (1991). In this work Mayhew argues that there is no relation between divided government and significant policy results; he further argues that there is no relation between divided government and congressional investigations of the executive branch. Mayhew concludes by arguing among other things that divided government does not mean less coherence in individual laws, and that there is no evidence that those initially less well off are made worse off by divided government (Mayhew 1991, chap. 7). Mayhew's findings contradict those scholars who assume that, without a strong President and cohesive congressional majorities, policy gridlock ensues.[41] Mayhew, however, never describes the underlying model of government that would allow the passage of significant legislation even under Republican Presidents and Democratic legislatures.

Looking at the strong party theory in conjunction with the institutional constraints of the filibuster and veto in the revolving gridlock model yields a surprising result. Instead of bringing about an end to gridlock, strong parties actually *expand* the region in which gridlock occurs.[42] Imagine the Democratic and Republican Parties deciding what policy outcomes they would like. One would be rather liberal, the other rather conservative. If the status quo policy falls somewhere in between, a movement to the right would be halted by a Democratic filibuster (or a sustained veto from a Democratic President). A movement to the left would likewise be successfully filibustered by the Republicans. With each party having more than forty seats in the Senate, the strong party assumption not only expands the gridlock region, but it also predicts the *same* region regardless of the party of the President. The gridlock region for strong parties stretches from one party's ideal policy point to the other's. Thus if we observe gridlock under Bush, we should expect the same gridlock under Clinton.[43]

In 1992, the media and the Clinton campaign's rhetoric led the public to believe that Democratic control of the Congress and the presidency would end the policy gridlock of twelve years of Republican rule. There are two main problems with such an argument. The first is that this strong party model ignores the institutional constraints of the filibuster and the veto. When these constraints are included, the gridlock region actually expands out to the party ideal policies (and not just to the ideal policies of party moderates), leading to the likelihood of even more gridlock than under the weak party assumption that we have used. (Such an argument led many Democrats to the further belief that they needed sixty Democrats in the Senate to overcome Republican filibusters.) But the second problem with this theory is more dramatic: political parties in the United States are not necessarily strong.[44] Members often defect from their parties when it is in their interest to do so. Republican filibusters are broken when the policy under debate is made conservative enough to make vote switching favorable for the most liberal Republicans. Indeed, in the minimum wage example, Senator Chafee abandoned the Republican filibuster attempt in 1988. Presidents are often forced to look for votes from the other party, as Reagan did with southern Democrats, as Bush did with the 1990 budget deal, and as Clinton did with the North American Free Trade Agreement (NAFTA). When the House sustained President Bush's veto of the minimum wage increase, the President lost twenty of the most liberal Republicans, but gained twenty-eight Democrats, twenty-five of them southerners. It is our contention that the appearance of party strength comes in the alignment of preferences: conservatives are typically Republicans and liberals are typically Democrats. Only where party interests are in conflict with personal preferences would we expect to see a break with the party; such breaks, however, are commonplace. The revolving gridlock theory relies on personal preferences and constraining institutions to explain policy gridlock and the positioning of bills that do pass.[45] The strong party theory is much less explicit about the role of institutions, and has been brought into question by Mayhew and others.

Having discussed the strong party theory, we turn to a comparison of the revolving gridlock theory with the compromise between branches theory. This theory is also implicit in many works, but explicit in few; it supposes that policymaking power rests with both the President and Congress. The policy outcome will therefore be somewhere between the ideal policy of the President and the ideal policy of Congress; where in this region it will fall depends on the relative strengths of Congress and the President during the period in which policy is being formulated. If a President is strong and popular, the theory argues, he can publicize his ideal policy and gain concessions from Congress. If weak, he will be forced to the sidelines, as Congress works through the details. This theory of compromise between the branches of government is applied regardless of the party affiliations of the President and the majority in Congress, thus differentiating it from the strong party theory.

The theory's limitations are to be found in the question of where this presidential power arises in the legislative arena. A number of claims have been put forth in the literature. Some scholars claim that presidential power is the power to persuade (Neustadt 1960). According to this argument, the President can try to lead members of Congress to his point of view. When legislators are reluctant to come around to his line of thinking, the President can "go public" on the issue, hoping that constituents will persuade legislators that it is in their best interest to go along with the President (Kernell 1993). Other authors argue that presidential power originates in veto power (Rohde 1991). In essence, a President can claim that he will veto any bill that does not meet his requirements, as Clinton did with universal coverage for health care. But this argument ignores credibility concerns; if Clinton had received a health care bill covering *most* Americans, would he have vetoed it, settling for no bill over a bill that came close to what he wanted? Still others synthesize these presidential powers. Jones (1994) emphasizes a President's strategic position as it relates to public popularity, electoral mandates, and the lawmaking sequence.

The revolving gridlock theory gives the President the power to influence legislators' preferences by persuasion or by going public. It also gives the President the crucial veto power. But it does not assume that he will act in any way other than in his own interest. When a bill that has passed through Congress is closer to the President's preference than the status quo policy, he will generally sign it; when it is further, he will veto it. The result of the revolving gridlock theory presented in this chapter is not simply a compromise between Congress and the President, but a constrained policy within the Congress, with the President doing what he can to influence policy around the edges. Often, due to institutional constraints, a policy outcome is more conservative (or more liberal) than both the median member of Congress and the President would prefer; but it is the best outcome they can get, so they agree to it.

The revolving gridlock theory is a significant advancement over these prior theories, explaining executive-legislative relations in a system of relatively weak parties in a way that is unique and compelling. The theory assumes that legislators in the House and Senate will attempt to move policy toward their preferred outcomes. They are constrained in doing so by supermajority institutions. Particular members of Congress in key positions at the edges of the gridlock region enforce these constraints through support of filibusters and vetoes. Status quo policies in this region cannot be changed. Actions taken under uncertain conditions as well as exogenous shocks to the legislative system can knock policies out of the gridlock region. Congress will be able to bring these policies back inside the region only so far as is possible to keep the pivotal members from voting down cloture or sustaining a veto. Attempts to make more extreme policy shifts will be killed by filibusters and vetoes. This theory is an improvement on previous work in the field. It looks at legislators' preferences rather than simply at their partisan affiliations. It takes into account the constraining institutions ignored by the strong party theory. And it more clearly defines the nature of the compromise between members of Congress and the President.

The theory explains minimum wage policy formation quite capably. Throughout the 1980s, the minimum wage was losing purchasing power, causing the $3.35 level to fall out of line with the preferences of most members of Congress. This is an example of an *exogenous shock* (here, inflation) pushing a status quo policy outside the gridlock region. When the issue was raised in 1988, it was first used more as a political tool than as a target for policy change. The Democrats used policy proposals to call Bush's "bluff" on minimum wage policy, whereas the Republicans used the issue as an attempt to secure federal judicial positions. No bill was passed in 1988 because the situation was *uncertain* so close to the election. When would the economic downside to a wage hike come into effect? Would interest groups play a large role in the elections as a result of this issue? Would one side or the other be in a better position in the next session due to the election results? Congress abandoned the issue. In 1989 the federal government addressed the minimum wage once again, this time with less uncertainty. Bush proposed a wage of $4.25 an hour, and the Democratic leadership countered with $4.55. Either wage level was preferred by the vast majority to the current $3.35 wage. But the President was able to use the veto and his influence to win a victory for his minimum wage plan. As such, he appeared strong in his veto power and secured nearly the lowest wage politically possible. The revolving gridlock theory is clear as to why this policy outcome occurred. The constraint was the veto pivot to which Bush appealed with his veto of the higher wage. By issuing an alternative policy favorable to the veto-sustaining minority, the President was able to win his showdown with the Congress, securing the $4.25 wage in late 1989. In 1996, President Clinton took his opportunity to raise the minimum wage further. The constraint on his wage hike was the filibuster in the Senate instead of the more constraining veto pivot of conservative Presidents.

Journalists and academics have recently taken greater notice of the policy implications of the supermajority institutions of the filibuster and the veto. For example, in the conclusion of a recent article about partisanship in Congress, Cooper and Young (1997, 269) note:

> In the House a veto requires not merely 218 votes to overcome (if all members vote) but 291, and in the Senate 67 votes are required (if all members vote) not merely 51. These are very difficult levels to obtain in partisan Congresses unless majority margins are extremely high. Moreover, in the Senate, practice with respect to the filibuster has changed so that the 60 votes required in impose cloture are also required to win any major policy battle. As a result, the passage of major legislation still requires forms of behavior and negotiation that are coalitional, but in a context in which the character of party divisions provides poor incentives for such behavior. The public's disgust with paralysis may spur action when elections approach, but such a response is only the flip side of the political maneuvering to gain electoral advantage that dominates policy making and usually stymies action.

The revolving gridlock theory expands upon and clarifies this argument, noting specifics of how these supermajority institutions, along with elections, budget constraints, and members' policy preferences, lead to specific policy outcomes or gridlock in the last two decades.

In the next chapters we will take a broader policy view, attempting to explain many of the legislative outcomes of the periods of divided and unified government from Reagan's first term through the 1994 capture of Congress by the Republicans, using the revolving gridlock theory. In Chapter 3, we will take an extensive look at the budget process and how budget policies have changed since 1980. The conservative members of Congress who came in with Reagan in 1981 acted as an exogenous shock, allowing previously entrenched policies to be changed. Even still, the policies enacted were determined by those near the middle of the political spectrum. As such, Reagan needed to gain the support of conservative Democrats. He used this support to enact a huge tax break and to peg tax rates to inflation. Budgetary policy since 1981 has been limited to small changes, as no new coalitions had been formed by electoral shifts until the 1994 election. The specter of deficits as far as the eye could see left politicians no room to maneuver to break the gridlock that ensued.

As we will highlight in the next chapter, the dramatic budget deficits of the 1980s have combined with supermajoritarian institutions to further policy gridlock in four ways. First, as mentioned above, pivotal members of Congress must vote with the majority to secure policy change. These votes are typically gained either through adjusting the policy at hand toward these legislators' preferred outcomes or by guaranteeing support for these members on other bills, typically by providing them with pork in budget bills. With the budget wells running dry with the significant deficits of recent years, however, those seeking policy change found the latter option for gaining the pivotal members' support to be no longer available. As such, compromises that could be forged only through budgetary concessions now fell apart. Second, deficits led Congress to link together most budgetary decisions. Increases in one program area would need to be offset by decreases elsewhere or by increases in taxes. As can be imagined, this had a further impact in terms of policy gridlock. Once a supermajority coalition was established in support of a legislative proposal with budgetary implications, bill proponents had to convince coalition members to support tax increases or program cuts elsewhere. This was a significant enough constraint to lead to inaction on issues in which a majority or supermajority agreed that change was necessary. Third, the increasing difficulty and importance of budgetary decisions gave members of Congress even less time to deal with nonbudgetary issues. Without the necessary time to secure supermajorities or to resolve uncertainties, other issues fell into gridlock as well. Finally, the complexity of budget legislation in an era of omnibus budget bills and huge reconciliation packages led to further confusion, frustration, and gridlock.

Clearly the budget constraints on Congress combined with electoral and institutional constraints to bring about further policy gridlock. It is to these budgetary issues that we turn next.

NOTES

1. The comments, quotations, and details presented in the italicized sections throughout this chapter are drawn from various public sources.

2. While our work emphasizes the preferences of members of Congress and the President, it does not emphasize the *intensity* of these preferences. This is largely due to our focus on voting institutions within Congress that give everyone equal say. However, as Hall (1996) points out, members of Congress feel more strongly about some issues than others, leading them to different degrees of participation in committees, subcommittees, and in the brokering of deals over final legislative decisions. As we note below, the intensity of a legislator's preferences may play a role in whether others may try to influence that legislator's vote, as well as in what final bargain may be reached among the House, Senate, and the President within the limited range of possible outcomes.

3. In this work we use the term "revolving gridlock theory," but we also find Krehbiel's tag, "pivotal politics theory," accurate and appropriate.

4. Political scientists have used spatial models widely since Anthony Downs's *An Economic Theory of Democracy* (1957) and Duncan Black's *The Theory of Committees and Elections* (1958). Single-dimensional voting with a majority rule was found to lead to median voter outcomes. However, without such a limitation to a single dimension, even imposing a particular voting rule often led to indeterminate outcomes (see Arrow 1951; Black and Newing 1951; Plott 1967). The chaos result formalized by McKelvey (1976) indicated that in all but a few special cases a series of proposals could be developed to lead from any given policy status quo to any other policy in the choice space. This result troubled formal theorists more than it troubled most political scientists who, without empirical support for this "policy cycling" result, discounted the value of such spatial models. The response to this "anything can happen" view was the reassurance that there are political structures in place that keep such

ludicrous results from happening. Kenneth Shepsle's "Institutional Arrangements and Equilibrium in Multidimensional Voting Models" (1979) led to an argument about which structures or institutions are relevant in leading to various outcomes. In particular, do legislative committees with their proposal powers lead to agendas that provide them with beneficial outcomes? This article set off a debate on the power of committees, as well as on which institutions lead to the so-called "structure-induced equilibria." Major groundwork for further study of politics through spatial models was made by Romer and Rosenthal (1978) with regard to the control of legislative agendas, by Baron and Ferejohn (1989) with regard to the sequencing of proposals leading to political bargains, and by Gilligan and Krehbiel (1987, 1990) with regard to the role of information in legislative decisions. For an excellent review of these advancements through the 1980s, see Krehbiel (1988). Our view is that in the modification of spatial models in political science over the past few decades, some simple advancements and applications have been overlooked. In particular, even restricting the model to a single dimension, much can be gained by looking at the institutional structures that require supermajorities to pass legislation. See Krehbiel (1997, chaps. 7, 8) for an excellent analysis of how the single-dimensional pivotal politics theory works in the face of empirical findings regarding agenda setting, partisanship, uncertainty, and presidential influence.

5. Poole and Rosenthal (1991a, 1997) provide an excellent compilation of voting in Congress and thus legislator preferences.

6. Binder and Smith (1996) provide the most comprehensive analysis of filibusters to date. For a further summary of the use of filibusters throughout the history of the Senate, see the 1987 *Congressional Quarterly Weekly Report*, 2115–2120. For more information on the rise of the filibuster and other changes leading to a more individualistic and competitive Senate, see Davidson 1985 and Sinclair 1989.

7. Krehbiel and Rivers (1988) use such an alignment in their analysis of committee positions and proposals with regard to minimum wage.

8. For a similar argument of how the press portrayed the economy in 1992 and how it led to Bush's defeat, see Hetherington 1996.

9. Some theories would suggest that members of both houses err on the side of willingness to use blocking tactics in order to avoid blame, on the assumption that avoiding blame is more important than taking credit. See, for example, Weaver 1986 and Arnold 1990. We raise some of these concerns below in our discussion of uncertainty.

10. What is important to us here is the near indifference of this pivotal legislator to the proposed policy change. This indifference may make this pivotal individual the target of persuasion to either cement the deal or sabotage it. Although we do not explore the matter of legislator preference intensity here, in a similar fashion, legislators who have a low intensity of preferences (for whom the issue at hand is not very salient) might also be easily persuaded to vote for or against the legislation. For more on legislator preference intensity and the resultant participation decisions, see Hall (1996).

11. Note that policies in the region between Q and F are outside the gridlock region, and thus will not be adopted by the Senate.

12. This result is different from that derived by Krehbiel (1996). Krehbiel limits the interaction to a single veto and override attempt. In actuality, legislation that is vetoed may be attempted again in a revised form. We do not derive results from a formal game of this nature here, but simply note that the ensuing action is a form of bargaining in which the resultant outcome is in the range between the main actors' ideal points and is dependent on their bargaining strengths. Additionally, if the President or congressional committee

makes a proposal in this range under a closed rule, it will be accepted by the pivotal members who prefer the proposal to the status quo; while under an open rule, the median member and concurring majority will push policy toward the median (although the policy is still constrained by Q'). As such, our finding is not inconsistent with the seminal agenda-setting work of Romer and Rosenthal (1978).

13. The *intensity* of preferences may play a role in influencing the patience of the actors who participate in the bargaining (Hall 1996) and what final outcome is reached.

14. The minimum wage increases from left to right on the diagram. Therefore the figure does not fit the traditional left-to-right spectrum, in which conservatives are positioned on the right and liberals on the left. Here, the position of Bush and the conservatives is on the left, favoring a lower minimum wage. We hope that this arrangement is less confusing than the inverse, with dollar amounts decreasing from left to right.

15. This assumption is justifiable in hindsight, based on voting behavior, but may have been a bit trickier to judge at the time. Nevertheless, Democratic leaders had proposed a $4.65 minimum wage, claiming that they could collect enough votes to override a veto. This would be the case with a veto pivot at $4.00, where that legislator would be indifferent to whether the minimum wage were 65 cents higher or 65 cents lower. Volden (1997) explores the positions of legislators (and the possibility of their voting strategically) with regard to the 1989 minimum wage vote, corroborating the values set forth in this chapter as quite accurate in representing legislator preferences.

16. Gilmour (1995) notes conditions under which Congress might provoke vetoes or otherwise promote stalemate through strategic actions.

17. On legislation that cannot be filibustered in the Senate, the gridlock region in the Senate becomes like that in the House, stretching from the median to the veto pivot. Such legislation includes budget reconciliation as well as trade bills set on the "fast track." This smaller gridlock region acts as less of a constraint to policy change, thus allowing for more policy action and limiting the power of a minority to stop legislation. While the lack of a filibuster threat on such legislation affects the size and shape of the gridlock region, it does not affect the overall theory with regard to this region. Status quo policies in the gridlock region cannot be changed. Those outside of the region will be brought in, with limitations similar to those seen in Figure 2.3. The theory surrounding this smaller gridlock region will be clarified further in the next chapter, which attempts to explain the major budget changes that have passed Congress since 1980.

18. Note that Krehbiel's work (1996) does not contain uncertainty. Nor do we introduce uncertainty in a formal modeling sense here. Our point is that uncertainty and the complexity of forming legislation may lead to further policy gridlock under certain conditions. This thesis is explored in greater detail in later chapters.

19. Where this uncertainty cannot be suitably resolved, legislators might try blame-avoidance tactics. See Weaver 1986 and 1988, and Arnold 1990.

20. For an analysis of the information provided by committees and the surrounding incentives to gaining expertise, see Krehbiel 1991.

21. Reported in the *New York Times,* July 6, 1988.

22. For more on the pressures surrounding this decision, see the 1988 *Congressional Quarterly Almanac,* 255.

23. Reported in the *New York Times,* December 8, 1978.

24. These decisions are part of the strategic choice process followed by politicians with regard to elections. See Jacobson and Kernell 1982; Jacobson 1983 and 1989; and Rosenstone and Hansen 1993.

25. As reported in the *New York Times*, September 19, 1988, members of Congress were being very careful about their positions on minimum wage.

26. Stopping policy change does not necessarily mean that no bill will be passed. For political reasons, legislators could pass a "hollow" bill, one that does not change policy to any great degree.

27. Thus, in focusing only on expansions and contractions in the gridlock region, Krehbiel (1997) is missing part of the story, that of electoral shifts.

28. See Brady 1988.

29. See Erikson 1976; Fiorina 1991b; Jacobson 1991; Ansolabehere, Brady, and Fiorina 1992; and Alford and Brady 1993.

30. Our view is not inconsistent with that held by Alesina and Rosenthal (1989, 1995) who argue that voters at the margins will choose liberal Democrats to counter conservative Republicans. Fiorina (1991a, 1996) presents the case that voters may want to elect politicians who will provide a "check" on other politicians. As a baseline against which voters might decide to temper policy outcomes, voters often perceive particular politicians as espousing particular issues or viewpoints. Jacobson (1990) and Petrocik (1991) present a form of "issue ownership" argument. Jacobson argues for the public perception that Democrats might better address local problems and Republicans national issues (although with Clinton as President, the opposite might now hold true). Petrocik argues that each of the parties owns a set of issues, with Republicans seen as preserving low taxes and pursuing prosperity and Democrats seen as espousing kindness through social spending.

31. The "coattails" effect refers to the election of other members of the President's party to their respective offices due to a surge of presidential supporters going to the polls. See Ferejohn and Calvert 1984.

32. See Erikson 1988.

33. See Brody 1991 for views on the role of the "honeymoon" in assessing a President.

34. Rivers and Rose (1985) discuss how the size of a President's program affects its likelihood of success.

35. Weaver (1988) attempts to explain conditions under which Congress indexes programs to inflation, leading to "automatic government" without the need to continually deal with the exogenous shocks of inflation.

36. Hibbing and Theiss-Morse (1995) explore this public dissatisfaction with Congress, finding that the actions and activities of politicians disgust the public equally regardless of the political party. Politicians of both parties are seen as being identical in the types of actions they take, regardless of the distinctions they attempt to make on particular policy issues. This is consistent with our belief that politicians act on their own preferences, using the institutions of government to their best advantage. Often this is to the best advantage of their constituents as well, and, when this is perceived by the public, the politicians are reelected.

37. The effectiveness of using presidential popularity to aid members of Congress is brought into question by Collier and Sullivan (1995).

38. Volden (1997) argues that this bargaining process is complex, often leading to members of Congress voting against their immediate preferences in what is referred to as a "sophisticated vote."

39. Important theoretical and empirical work on this issue has been advanced by Samuel Kernell (1993).

40. See Fiorina 1996 for an excellent summary of the literature pertaining to divided government.

41. James Pfiffner (in Thurber 1991) argues that unified governance with strong parties is necessary for directional coherence of legislation.

42. For further details and a formal proof of this finding, see Krehbiel 1996.

43. Some views of the strong party assumption consider only a strong Democratic party. This would still lead to an expansion of the gridlock region when compared to our weak party assumption of individual preferences mattering more than the party preferences, but the expansion would be only to the left.

44. It is not our intention here to become enmeshed in the debate about how strong or weak political parties are. It is clear to us that, as Cox and McCubbins (1993) suggest, parties can use various powers, acting as "legislative cartels," to gain mutually beneficial compromises. We also recognize, as Krehbiel (1993) does, that parties are limited in their abilities and that a strict test of party strength is a difficult endeavor. Our view of political parties in the United States today is that party leaders and the President can influence the preferences of members of Congress, but cannot dictate how they will vote. Party members also have other interests, mainly reelection. We believe that parties are weaker than they once were (for a view on parties at a time when they were stronger, see Brady and Epstein 1997). We also see a strong link between preferences and party, with conservatives tending to be Republicans and liberals tending to be Democrats. (In Krehbiel's view this is exactly what parties are—aggregated preferences.) In some ways our view is not unlike that found in the political science literature of the 1960s and 1970s. Following E. E. Schattschneider's responsible party thesis (1942, APSA 1950), David Truman's work (1959) reversed the strong party notion by focusing on congressional parties as blocs of voters with party leaders near the party's center. We speak of preferences where Truman, as well as Burns (1963), focused on blocs or wings, but their view of parties as aggregates of different views is not unlike our own.

45. In this way, our work complements that of John Gilmour (1995), who argues that the need to satisfy constituents (preferences) often leads to pursuit and avoidance of ideas and proposals, with politicians provoking vetoes (supermajority institutions) and taking positions that cause greater difficulty in the negotiations necessary to reach compromise (gridlock).

3

The Rise of Reagan
and Budgetary Politics

Making public policy in the United States is obviously a complex business. The opinions of voters and interest groups, institutions like the separation of powers and federalism, and changing economic and world events shape the making of public policy. In this book we simplify this elaborate, complicated process by proposing that one can identify the basic location of public policy if one knows the preferences of members of Congress, the location of the status quo policy, supermajority institutional conditions, and the position of the newly proposed policy (often the President's proposal). The ultimate goal is to explain why a unified government such as Bill Clinton's didn't end "gridlock" as many commentators thought it would. We define "gridlock" as a situation in which the status quo cannot be changed by any new policy proposal. If the status quo policy point is near the preferences of moderate members of Congress, then we predict that, regardless of unified or divided government, policy will not shift dramatically. Presidents who propose policies to the left or right of the "gridlock region" will see their policies either fail or modify to accommodate the preferences of moderate Representatives and Senators. In our view the major factors that account for policy shifts are electoral. In other words, if an election results in a shift of member preferences to the right or left, then policy may shift right or left accordingly.

Elections are complex events in which voters choose between candidates who normally differ in personal characteristics, party identification, and policy preferences. Voters' choices are affected by domestic and global events, and in turn electoral results change policy. Thus in the early 1960s, when African Americans campaigned for equal justice and Lyndon Johnson buried Barry Goldwater in the 1964 election, policy on civil rights began to change. Likewise during the late 1970s, when income, property, and state taxes increased dramatically, voters signaled a desire to reduce taxation; in the early 1980s, major changes in tax policy resulted. Each of these changes in policy brings about both a new policy status quo and a new set of problems. The civil rights movement raised the issue of compensatory justice and gave rise to affirmative action policies; affirmative ac-

43

tion has led to a new set of problems.[1] Likewise tax cuts in the 1980s generated economic effects that led to new problems and solutions for the 1990s.

In an important sense, current policy (the status quo) is normally within the gridlock region and, as the civil rights and tax examples indicate, those regions can shift left or right or remain stable depending upon the preferences of members of Congress. To understand why President Clinton, with strong majorities in both the House and the Senate, failed to shift policy, we need to understand the gridlock region and how it evolved in the years prior to 1992. This is essentially a story of increases in entitlement spending, a shift in the tax burden, and largely defense-related external events that have occurred since the end of World War II. Because these factors are important to our argument, we will present a brief overview of budget politics prior to the Reagan, Bush, and Clinton years. It is important to note that in the post–World War II years, government policy came to be dominated by budget issues, including both taxation and spending. We will outline the changes in federal spending during the postwar period and then turn to tax policy over the same period. These postwar policies led to a budget situation by the late 1970s that would be difficult for *any* President and Congress to solve. Reagan's resolution of these problems established a new status quo point and led to the formation of a new gridlock region.

As was noted in the previous chapter, gridlock is typically broken only by significant external shocks; these shocks are primarily in the form of changes in the legislative composition due to elections. In this chapter we describe the events that led to the 1980 elections, the results of those elections, and how the results temporarily ended gridlock on tax and budgetary issues. The inability or unwillingness of Congress throughout the 1970s to redress the grievances of a large part of the public who felt overtaxed led to the rise of pundits, political entrepreneurs, and candidates who advocated tax cuts and supply-side economics. The election of Ronald Reagan, along with sizable numbers of conservatives in the House and Senate, allowed for the possibility of a major policy shift toward lower taxes and lower spending. The income tax cuts achieved in 1981 were actually in excess of the decreases in spending passed by Congress. A reduced tax base plus the increased expenditures generated by the 1981–1982 recession led to significant budget deficits. When Reagan's popular support diminished and when congressional Democrats picked up twenty-six House seats in 1982, tax policy was adjusted somewhat back to the left in 1982 and 1984. But the overriding policy of lower tax rates was solidified by the 1986 tax act, which made future tax adjustments extremely difficult. Budget policy from 1981 on became more conflictual, with decisions to increase spending for one program often linked to cuts elsewhere.

It may seem ironic that the Reagan revolution helped bring about further gridlock. Indeed in Chapter 2 we argued that significant electoral change brings an end to gridlock. But, as will become evident, preferences, policy outcomes, and elections are all interrelated. The 1980 elections led to changes among the pivotal members of Congress and their preferences; these changes in preferences allowed for policy modifications; and the new policy of cutting taxes and indexing them to inflation led to yet another region of gridlock and changed conditions such that budget agreements were even harder to reach.

In this chapter we will flesh out the theoretical arguments of the previous chapter in the context of budgetary policy. The chapter is divided into four sections. In the first section, we will discuss the conditions that led to the need for policy change regardless of who was elected in 1980. In the second section, we will describe how the election of conservatives in 1980 led to a coalition on the right and how that coalition came together with regard to the policies adopted in 1981. In the third section, we will argue that reactions to this conservative shift in income tax policy were manifested in minor shifts back to the left in 1982, 1984, and 1986, with the last of these setting tax policy in place for years to come. It is through this set of events that budgetary politics has become more important and more divisive than ever before. In the fourth section, we will make explicit the ties between the new budgetary politics and the revolving gridlock theory.

Precursors to Change

The taxing and spending decisions of today are not made in a vacuum. They are influenced by past policies, by preferences, and by institutions. Some of the most important restrictions on budgetary changes today have their origins in these conditions as faced by Congress and the President in the early 1980s and in their decisions to, among other things, cut income taxes and peg them to inflation. Just as decisions today do not occur in a political vacuum, so too is it necessary to place the decisions made in 1981 and afterward in their proper context.

Budget Expenditures

To understand the constraints that the budget places on congressional politics and policymaking, it is necessary to examine how large categories of the federal budget have changed over time.[2] Table 3.1 highlights these changes for the period from 1948 to 1988.

In 1948 national defense accounted for 3.7 percent of the country's gross national product (GNP), human resources accounted for 4 percent of GNP, and net interest on the debt was 1.8 percent of GNP. A decade later, defense accounted for 10.4 percent of GNP and 56.8 percent of the budget, whereas human resources accounted for 5 percent of GNP and 27 percent of the budget, and net interest had fallen to 1.2 percent of GNP. By 1968 defense had fallen whereas human resources climbed and net interest remained steady. By 1978 national defense had been cut to 4.8 percent of GNP, human resources soared to 11.2 percent, and net interest was 1.6 percent. After eight years of the Reagan presidency, national defense had risen to 6.1 percent of GNP, human resources were still at 11.2 percent, whereas the net interest had climbed to 3.2 percent. Thus, contrary to what many commentators have claimed, at the end of the Reagan period national defense was about half of what it

TABLE 3.1   Budget Expenditures, 1948–1988 (as percentage of GNP)

Major Categories	1948	1958	1968	1978	1988
National defense	3.7%	10.4%	9.0%	4.8%	6.1%
Human resources	4.0	5.0	6.5	11.2	11.2
Net interest on debt	1.8	1.2	1.3	1.6	3.2
Combined	9.5	16.6	16.8	17.6	20.5

SOURCE: Cogan 1997.

had been in 1958 in terms of percentage of GNP, whereas human resources and net interest were two and three times higher than they had been in 1958.

The rise in expenditures for human resources from 1948 through 1988 was largely the result of entitlement programs enacted in the 1965–1968 and 1969–1975 periods. The 1948 figure for human resources (4 percent of GNP) largely represented programs enacted during Franklin Roosevelt's New Deal. The last New Deal entitlements were enacted in 1935 (unemployment compensation, Aid to Families with Dependent Children, and Social Security). The only entitlement program enacted from 1935 through 1964 was the Social Security Disability Insurance Act of 1956. Thus in 1961, John Kennedy's first year as President, only 5.8 percent of GNP was spent on human resources (30.5 percent of the federal budget).

Beginning with Johnson's Great Society and proceeding through the Nixon years, a spate of entitlement programs was passed. Table 3.2 gives a list of these programs. We divide the programs into two eras mainly for political reasons. The Great Society programs were passed largely by a Democratic majority, whereas the 1969–1975 programs were passed by a bipartisan majority both in Congress and across institutions—specifically, a Republican President and a Democratic Congress. In terms of cost, the two major programs are Medicare and Medicaid. These programs grow as the population ages and the number of eligible recipients increases. In 1970, for example, five years after Medicare was originated, the federal government spent $10.7 billion on the program (all figures in terms of real 1995 dollars). By 1981, Ronald Reagan's first year as President, Medicare expenditures had grown to $65.7 billion and they were estimated to rise to $140.6 billion by 1990. The increase from 1970 to 1980 was by a factor of greater than five. It is easy to see how the growth of these entitlements increased the proportion of the budget and the GNP devoted to human resources, which accounted for 9.9 percent of the budget and 2.6 percent of GNP in 1946, but 53 percent of the budget and 11.7 percent of GNP in 1980.

Tax Policy

Changes in tax policy during this period did not parallel budget changes in that the percentage of taxes paid as a share of GNP remained stable. However, within

TABLE 3.2   Major New Entitlements (1964–1975)

Program	Year	Public Law
Food Stamps[a]	1964	PL 88-525
Medicare	1965	PL 89-97
Medicaid	1965	PL 89-97
Guaranteed Student Loans	1965	PL 89-329
Child Nutrition Programs[b]	1966	PL 89-642
Social Services Block Grant[c]	1967	
Black Lung Benefits	1969	PL 91-173
General Revenue Sharing	1972	PL 92-512
Supplemental Security Income[d]	1972	PL 92-603
Pension Benefits Guarantee	1974	PL 93-406
Child Support Enforcement	1975	PL 93-647
Earned Income Tax Credit	1975	PL 94-164

[a]From 1961 to 1964, the program operated under an Executive Order issued by President Kennedy.

[b]The main nutrition program, the National School Lunch program, was created in 1946. The 1966 law authorized an open-ended appropriation and transformed the program into a mandatory program.

[c]In 1956, state social services expenditures for welfare recipients became eligible for federal matching funds. In 1967, states were required to establish a single organizational unit for administering social services, and the federal social services program was formally separated from the cash assistance welfare program. In 1975, the Social Services Block Grant program was formally established by the enactment of Title XX.

[d]The SSI program replaced the Federal Grants to States for old-age assistance and for the permanently disabled.

SOURCE: Cogan 1997.

that figure there were significant changes. In the 1930s individual income taxes were about 1 percent of GNP and corporate taxes averaged about 1.5 percent of GNP. The need to finance World War II drove income taxes up to over 8 percent of GNP and corporate taxes to over 7 percent, and, in spite of the resumption of a peacetime budget in 1945, income taxes never fell back below 5.9 percent of GNP. After the Korean War income taxes were fairly stable—a low of 7.1 percent of GNP in 1964 and a high of 9.6 in 1981. This overall stability in the rate of income taxes masks important changes.

In the 1950s and 1960s, state and local taxes grew. More important for our purposes was the change in the composition of tax receipts. Social Security taxes have risen by roughly 3 percentage points per decade. The combined employee-employer contribution was 6 percent in 1960, 12.3 percent in 1980, and was projected to be over 15 percent within the next decade. These increases caused Social Security tax rates to rise to over 5 percent of GNP by 1979 (Steuerle 1992, chap. 3).

Given the increase in state, local, and Social Security taxes, and the fact that overall taxes remained stable, some taxes must have been reduced. Excise taxes went down as a percentage of GNP largely due to two factors: the tax act of 1965, which cut excise taxes, and inflation, which caused them to erode. Corporate income taxes also fell during this time period; corporate profits as a percentage of GNP fell and taxes fell correspondingly, and rates for deductible interest rose.

The changes in the *mix* of taxation rather than the *level* is what is important for understanding the "tax revolt" of the late 1970s. During the years following World War II, "excluded income" grew. For example, employer contributions to health, pension, and profit-sharing plans are excluded from an employee's taxable income. From 1947 to 1979, these excluded employer contributions grew from 0.7 percent to over 4 percent of personal income. Other nontaxable exclusions include Social Security income and home mortgage payments. Altogether, total exclusions grew from roughly 10 percent of personal income in 1942 to about 20 percent by the late 1970s. Itemized deductions on tax forms also increased during this period, from about 4 percent to over 9 percent of gross income. By far, however, the most dramatic change was not the increase in exclusions but rather the decline of the personal exemption. Between 1945 and 1979, the personal exemption fell from almost 25 percent of gross income to less than 10 percent.

These factors, the increase of excluded income and the slippage of the standard exemption, brought about great changes in *who* was taxed. In 1948, in all taxpayer filing categories, 46.8 percent of all income was exempt from taxation. In 1981, prior to the Reagan cuts, taxpayers with four dependents were only able to exclude 13.3 percent of their income. Increases such as these, plus Social Security tax increases, meant that by the mid-1970s the working poor and middle-class families were paying higher rates.

The rise of inflation in the late 1960s and 1970s raised incomes into new marginal tax rates (the rate paid on the last dollar earned) and shifted the tax burden. C. Eugene Steuerle (1992) has calculated the effect of these changes on marginal and average tax rates for the middle class (at the median income), the poor (at one-half the median), and the well-to-do (at twice the median). Between 1960 and 1980 the average tax rate for those with twice the median income rose from about 12 percent to over 18 percent, while their marginal rate went from 21 percent to over 40 percent. Average taxes for median income earners rose from about 7 percent to just over 10 percent, while their marginal rate dropped from 20 percent to about 18 percent. For those with incomes at one-half the median, average taxes rose from around 1 percent in 1960 to over 5 percent by 1980, while their marginal rate went from 0 in 1959 to about 18 percent by 1980.

Before the 1980 elections, human resources expenditures were clearly increasing as a percentage of both the budget and the GNP. The rise in entitlement programs, namely Social Security, Medicare, and Medicaid, was the driving force behind these increases, which could only increase further with the aging population. The increase in expenditures was not accompanied by a corresponding increase in federal taxes; rather, there was a shift in the pattern of who paid taxes. The median taxpayer's income tax rate rose only slightly, whereas taxes for those at the lower end (one-half the median) and the upper end (twice the median) increased. Those at the lower end now paid Social Security and Medicare taxes, while the wealthy saw both their average rates and their marginal rates increase. In addition, state (income) and local (property) taxes more than doubled during these two decades. The tax burden on middle- and upper-middle-class voters had increased to cover the larger entitlement and social expenditures.

These changes in the distribution of taxes, together with the shifts in the budget, moved the United States toward a new era of policymaking—one that was inevitable no matter who had been elected to the presidency or the Congress. As Steuerle put it, "In this new era, reforming old expenditure or tax rules or meeting new priorities required that trade-offs be made explicitly among many existing programs. Tax reform, for instance, provided for lower rates and tax relief for the poor by reducing expenditures hidden in the tax code" (1992, 3).

The high rate of inflation during the 1976–1980 period exacerbated the problem. The percentage increase in the consumer price index (CPI) from year to year during this period was never below 6 percent; it reached 11.3 percent in 1979 and 13.5 percent in 1980. This pushed taxpayers into higher brackets, thus increasing both average taxes paid and the number of people at higher marginal rates. The effect on the government's budget was to ensure a steadily increasing stream of revenue. In fact, as Don Fullerton has so ably shown, *every pre-1981 budget projection showed a surplus in the budget within three years.* "As a result, legislators always seemed to find themselves with surplus revenue that could be used for some combination of increased spending or decreased taxes" (Fullerton 1994, 170). Under these conditions, legislators of either liberal or conservative bent could please constituents. Conservatives could claim that the revenue measures that they enacted lowered taxes (Merrill, Collender, and Cook 1990). Liberals could continue to spend in their programs because analysts had shown that within three years there would be a budget surplus.

Although inflation aided politicians who could promise tax reductions and increase spending simultaneously, the reality of increased taxes at both the federal and state levels hit home. Higher average taxes and marginal rates upset voters, while at the state level inflation caused housing prices to soar, thus raising property taxes at reassessment time.

Simply examining federal expenditures and taxes as percentages of GNP would not by itself accurately portray the extraordinary politics of the 1980s. Economic conditions had changed such that any politician elected in 1980 would have had difficulty dealing with the situation, given the conditions. The increase (and inevitable future increases) in social expenditures and the tax revolt in the states clearly indicated budget difficulty. Inflation helped budget revenues, but the reality of tax increases caused a voter revolt signaling to all politicians that taxes had to be cut. The Democrats under Carter already knew in the 1970s that taxes had to be reduced, thereby putting pressure on expenditures. The Carter administration proposed cutting defense expenditures and shifting the savings to social expenditures. The Soviet invasion of Afghanistan, however, ended this strategy, and Carter proposed major increases in defense in his last two budgets. In addition to this revenue dilemma, the Social Security Trust Fund was in trouble, and it became clear that fixing it would entail increased taxes.

Thus the government faced a situation in which expenditures would necessarily increase given entitlements and the need for a growing defense budget, and revenue would surely decrease given the mood of the electorate. Steuerle (1992, 3) put the dilemma as follows: "The agony of moving to the new era came not from demands that were extraordinary by historical standards, but from the simple requirement that meeting new demands required politicians to identify losers." In the realm of ideas, supply-side economists came to the fore. Taxpayers, first in California and then later across the country, signaled their growing anger over increased taxes and the "stagflation" that characterized the economy during the Carter presidency. This anger led to extraordinary election results in 1980. The 1980 national elections shifted the presidency and the Congress to the right. The Republicans controlled the Senate for the first time in twenty-six years, and in the House they picked up forty-six seats in the 1978 and 1980 elections.

The newly elected members of Congress faced a new policy world. Inflation was over 13 percent; interest rates were over 18 percent; and the unemployment rate remained high as well. Moreover, most budget expenditures were for cash transfer and income transfer programs that are statutory, and Social Security was expected to be running a deficit within five years. Taxpayers had signaled that they wanted tax relief. The choice would no longer be easy. Congress could not both reduce certain taxes *and* continue to fund programs as though the revenue flow were guaranteed to increase. The politics of taxing and budgeting would have to change.

The Politics of Taxing and Spending

We have seen how expenditures and taxes shifted during the 1946–1979 period. Now we turn to the *politics* of taxing and spending during this period. The classical period of budget politics, according to Wildavsky (1988), occurred from 1946 to 1973. There is some debate about when the classical period ended—1967, 1969, or later—but this is not of primary importance.

During the classical period the appropriations process was dominated by the President and the Appropriations Committees in the House and Senate. Fenno's work (1973) shows that the Appropriations Committees were successful (by winning on the floor) when they reached a consensus in the committee and reported out a "committee bill" that all members—liberal and conservative, Republican and Democrat, northern and southern—could support. Fenno's analysis further shows that during the classical period the Appropriations Committees were able, with few exceptions, to achieve a consensus. The consensus was achieved in large part because the members agreed on a few basic principles. Wildavsky (1988) identifies these principles as follows: (1) deficits are bad; (2) spending helps those in need but must be paid for; and (3) taxes are necessary but they must be silent taxes.

Members of the Appropriations Committees faced a dilemma—how do we retain power yet maintain the support of our colleagues who want programs funded? Power originated from the ability to cut presidential and agency requests; yet cutting spending too much would cause members in the House and Senate to limit the Committee's power.[3] This dilemma was resolved by cutting particular agency budgets in any given year but allowing expenditures generally to rise over time. In sum, the committees adopted and Congress approved an incremental solution. There would be balanced budgets from year to year and, if there were room to increase programs, those increases would be marginal so as not to increase taxes or borrowing. And if conditions were tough, Congress would make the President act first.

The tax committees were able to keep revenues roughly equal to expenditures by virtue first and foremost of the growth of the U.S. economy. Hidden taxes did, however, increase. Individual deductions were eroded, the level of tax payments increased due to bracket creep (caused by inflation-driven higher incomes), and increases in Social Security taxes on individuals were enacted. Thus liberals were able to fund their programs. Conservatives also served their interests by lowering overall rates (although because of loopholes few ever paid the full rates) and by passing necessary adjustments in depreciation and business taxes.[4]

This system of spending and taxing worked well as long as the economy was expanding and revenues were increasing. The system began to break down as expenditures on nondiscretionary social programs and the Vietnam War increased. President Johnson's policy of "guns and butter" without tax increases was financed by increased borrowing and by allowing the replacement of borrowing authority monies to be reallocated off-budget (Cogan, Muris, and Schick 1994). In 1965 President Johnson added a surtax on income to increase revenues, and in the following election House Democrats lost seats. The reaction to the surcharge was a harbinger of the tax revolt of the 1970s.

In 1969 President Nixon was faced with a serious budgetary problem. Increases in social expenditures, increases in defense spending, and the opposition to the surtax left Nixon with little room to maneuver. The Appropriations Committees found that more and more of the budget was committed to uncontrollable expenditures and, as Schick shows (1981), members of Congress continued to vote for new entitlements and for expanding old ones by increasing eligibility and indexing them to inflation. These pressures on expenditures and the reluctance to tax directly led to the breakup of the relatively consensual politics of the classical period. In the era of steady growth (roughly 1946–1966), expenditure decisions were decentralized to Appropriations subcommittees and to authorizing committees, while the tax committees could adjust revenues when necessary. As expenditures for entitlements increased and taxes increased due to inflation and the loss of deductions, budgetary decisions became more difficult.

President Nixon's reelection in 1972 and his subsequent decision to impound funds appropriated by the Congress further exacerbated the breakup of the classical consensus. The President's impoundments in effect told the Congress, "I don't care what you appropriate, I will decide what will be spent" (Schick 1981, 135). The conflict between the Republican President and the Democratic House over who controlled expenditures was dramatically altered by Watergate. As the status of the presidency fell, Congress became bolder and, after the 1974 election, changed the budgeting procedure by passing the Budget and Impoundment Control Act of 1974. Details regarding the exact changes brought about by this act can be readily found elsewhere (Sundquist 1981; Shuman 1984; Davidson 1992); for our purpose it is sufficient to state that the new procedure added a new level of activity to an already cumbersome process. Appropriations had been conditioned by authorizations under the classical system. Under the new system both authorizations and appropriations were to be based on budget resolutions. In short, Congress created overarching Budget Committees, which were to coordinate budget policy. In order to achieve this end, Congress created the Congressional Budget Office (CBO) and changed the appropriations procedures. Because it is not our purpose to describe the budget process in full, suffice it to say that however one feels about the new 1974 budget process, the fundamental underlying problems did not go away. Expenditures for entitlements stayed up and effective tax rates were still increasing.

The choices were tougher and the consensual decisionmaking of the classical period was breaking down under the strain. The number of amendments per appropriations bill (a measure of consensus between the committee and the floor) increased fivefold from 1963 to the mid-1970s. By the late 1970s the increase in amendments was twentyfold over 1963. Stanley Bach of the Congressional Research Service put it this way: "Increases in the number of amendments proposed in recent years, and increases in the percentage of winning amendments, suggests that the [Appropriations] Committee has had increasing difficulty in accommodating to the preferences of the House and in anticipating and settling potential controversies in advance" (Wildavsky 1988, 196). The politics was harder in large part because the economic policies of the past were constraining members' ability to tax and spend. The dilemma would get more difficult.

The 1970s were characterized by inflation; during the Carter presidency, inflation was particularly high. Inflation had a positive effect on the budget because as inflation rises, wages and prices rise, pushing taxpayers into higher brackets and thus increasing the amount of revenue collected by the government. This increase in taxes collected during the 1970s kept the deficit low relative to the GNP. In fact, every budget projection by the CBO from 1975 through 1980 showed a surplus three years down the road. This allowed Congress to somewhat reduce marginal tax rates, increase the personal deduction for tax filers, and speed up depreciation rates for business investments, while simultaneously continuing to fund entitlement programs. The rise of inflation, however, had a down side from a politician's viewpoint. Taxpayers knew that, despite their higher salaries, they had less real income; and taxpayers on fixed incomes were hurt by increased taxes on private property. During this period the dominant Keynesian economic model was questioned, and supply-side theorists came to the fore. Proposals to cut taxes were generated by academic think tanks, by citizens groups, and by elected representatives. Beginning with Proposition 13 in California, voters clearly signaled that they were very unhappy with increased taxes. Thus while inflation helped keep the deficit low, it also helped trigger a tax revolt across the country.

Going into the 1980 elections, the following set of conditions were present, and would squarely face whoever won the election.

1. Entitlements as a percentage of the budget were high and rising, and they were statutory, not discretionary.
2. Taxes on the average had been rising, especially for high- and low-end taxpayers, and effective marginal rates had also risen. Voters across the country had clearly signaled their desires—lower taxes.
3. Defense spending, which had been decreasing as a percentage of the federal budget, was now rising again. The Soviet invasion of Afghanistan together with the Iranian hostage crisis had led President Carter to ask for large increases for the military, and opinion polls showed that Americans favored a stronger military.
4. Members of Congress knew that the Social Security Trust Fund was to be in deficit within the next few years, and that they would have to deal with it.

In short, public policy regarding taxing and spending needed to be addressed regardless of who won the election. Members of Congress faced brutal choices. Taxes had to be reduced because voters wanted them reduced. Expenditures for social programs were statutory and growing, and the plan to shift money from defense to entitlements was no longer viable. Budgetary matters were about to move from being *part* of governing to being *most* of governing. That is, the politics of taxing and spending would take up most of Congress's time. Finally, the combination of brutal choices and the increased importance of budgetary politics hardened members' attitudes. Conservatives favored cutting taxes and programs; liberals favored raising taxes for the wealthy and corporations in order to fund needed programs. Moderates were fewer in number and were pressured by the harsh economic necessities. Comparing the classical period of budgeting to the late 1970s (and 1980s) shows that legislators of both periods believe that deficits are bad. However, legislators and others were also raising serious questions about the benefits of government spending, and the taxes to fund this spending were no longer silent taxes.

Coalitions for Tax and Budget Reform

Prior to 1981, Congress and the President, liberals and conservatives, could have their cake and eat it too. That is, conservatives got tax cuts passed when pressure mounted, and liberals could vote for the decreases (or not contest them) because they were assured that their programs would continue to be funded. Conservatives could not block increased expenditures because they were in the minority, but were able to appease their constituents with tax cuts and other victories. The 1980 election changed all this. The Congress elected with Ronald Reagan marked a distinct shift in preferences to the right. The Senate was Republican; and the 192 Republicans, together with conservative southern Democrats, made a working majority in the House.

The policy result of this preference shift was that "1981 represents a watershed year in the making of tax policy, from an era of constantly projected surpluses to one of constantly projected deficits. . . . The making of tax policy would never be the same" (Fullerton 1994, 171).[5] The two key pieces of legislation were the Economic Recovery Tax Act (ERTA) of 1981, initiating tax reduction and indexing, and the Omnibus Budget Reconciliation Act (OBRA)of 1981. These acts were passed as a result of the newly elected conservative majority. Republicans hung together and with the support of very conservative Democrats changed tax policy dramatically. The recession of 1981–1983 together with the tax cuts caused dramatic increases in the deficit. Policy after 1981, especially the tax acts of 1982, 1984, and 1986, all increased taxes in an attempt to deal with the deficit. In 1982 and 1984, the very conservatives who had supported Reagan in 1981 defected. That is, after 1981 there was a new status quo point and from 1982 through 1986 centrists in both parties built strong bipartisan coalitions to shift policy leftward. The end result was a new gridlock region in which the left could not seriously increase taxes and the right could not decrease expenditures, leaving programs and taxes basically intact. The Bush 1990 budget deal and Clinton's 1993 budget reconciliation are testimony to that gridlock region. In short, the battles between liberals and conservatives became bitter, or hardball.

None of this is to say that there were no budget battles during the Johnson and Nixon-Ford eras. Rather, our claim is that policy shifted partly as a result of exogenous conditions (the economy) and the concomitant shifts in preference that were reflected in the Congress. Votes were more divisive after 1981—there were winners and losers—and liberals and conservatives became more strident because there was more at stake.

We now turn to an analysis of what President Reagan pushed through Congress in 1981 and how he got Congress to go along. The recession of the early 1980s increased the deficit and forced the President and Congress to pass two major tax increases in 1982 and 1984 and to then revise the tax code in 1986. In our terms, this means that the initial effect of the 1980 election results was to shift tax policy to the right of the status quo. Subsequent economic events forced policy adjustments to the left. Each of these shifts—first to the right and then to the left—was achieved by appealing to different coalitions. In addition to explaining the politics involved in these actions, we will also document the rise of new reconciliation procedures to "facilitate" passage of the budget, and address the increasing dominance of the budget in American politics.

The Rising Importance of Budgetary Politics

There are a number of ways to demonstrate that budgetary politics constitutes an ever increasing share of total congressional politics. One can highlight the attention paid to the budget by the media. As the budget becomes a larger part of politics, stories about the budget in the broadcast and print media ought to rise dramatically. Additionally, one can show how over time the nondiscretionary portion of the budget has grown. The larger this "mandatory" percentage of the budget becomes, the less control the President and Congress have over appropriations, leading ultimately to little or no room for new programs. In this section we will show that media attention to the budget has grown enormously since 1980, and that mandatory expenditures take up an ever increasing share of the budget.

In 1968, 14.4 percent of the U.S. GNP was available for discretionary spending, while mandatory budget expenditures (including interest) accounted for 5.3 percent of GNP. When Jimmy Carter became President in 1977, the figures were 10.8 percent discretionary and 9.5 percent mandatory. When Ronald Reagan took office in 1981, discretionary expenditures were 10.5 percent and mandatory expenditures were 9.9 percent. These figures had reversed by the time of Bill Clinton's presidency, with 10.7 percent of GNP reserved for mandatory expenditures and 8.7 percent available for discretionary programs. Mandatory spending now comprises over one-half of the budget of the U.S. government. As shown above, the big-ticket items other than Social Security are Medicare, Medicaid, and interest on the debt.

Mandatory spending growth squeezes the discretionary portion of the budget. The squeeze gets even tighter if one notes that well over one-half of all discretionary spending goes for national defense, leaving less than 20 percent of the total budget for other programs. With over 80 percent of the budget reserved for mandatory and defense spending, those favoring new government programs have less and less of the budget to work with. Environmentalist, agricultural, and business interests must work harder to keep expenditures for the Environmental Protection Agency and the Departments of Agriculture and Commerce at what they deem reasonable levels. Liberal members of Congress have a difficult time pushing new programs, given the budget squeeze and the opposition to serious tax increases. Conservatives, on the other hand, have not been able to make major cuts in the mandatory portion of the budget; thus they are forced to try to cut from the discretionary portion of the budget's non-defense-related expenditures. In short, liberals and conservatives are fighting over an increasingly smaller and smaller part of the budget. Military spending can't go below a given amount; as a result, agricultural, environmental, and other domestic programs are all that are left to fight over. The budget has become more important because conservatives can't cut big entitlements and, where they can cut, there are smaller savings. Liberals cannot raise taxes to fund new programs and have to work hard to keep domestic discretionary programs funded at adequate levels.

Given the above circumstances, it is not hard to understand why budget politics has come to dominate Congress and media coverage of Congress. This is reflected in the *New York Times*'s coverage of Congress and the budget from 1970 through 1995. During the 1970s the *Times* ran an average of 2,300 stories per year on Congress; about 200 of these stories also focused on the budget. In 1980 the number of stories on Congress rose to 4,705, and from 1981 through 1995 never fell below 5,407 (there were over 7,000 stories each year from 1981 through 1987). The number of stories on Congress *and* the budget rose to 927 in 1979 and thereafter averaged about 1,800 a year.

Figure 3.1 shows the increase in *New York Times* stories on the budget as a percentage of stories on Congress. The increase clearly shows the new importance of the budget in congressional politics.

Another indicator of the "new" importance of the budget is the change in the rules, procedures, and institutional arrangements that govern budgetary politics. As budget decisions became more stark, Congress was forced to move away from the incremental decisions and arrangements that had governed budget politics during the classical period. As we shall see, the adoption of the budget resolution and the increased use of the reconciliation budget testify to both the increased importance of the budget and to the complexity of the decision process.

New Procedures

Budgetary politics became a larger part of American politics because the choices faced by Congress became more difficult, thereby forcing Congress to change the rules and procedures by which it considered budget choices. The major change was the Budget and Impoundment Control Act of 1974. Prior to this act, Congress worked within a decentralized authorization and appropriation process wherein substantial committees such as Agriculture and Armed Services dealt with issues and authorized expenditures for programs. These authorizations then went to the Appropriations Committee and its subcommittees where monies were appropriated for authorized expenditures. The resulting thirteen appropriations bills were never combined until the end of the process. In short, Congress had no mechanism for determining the effect of the budget on the economy.

In the reforms of 1974, Congress established a comprehensive budget process, but in order to keep most members involved they overlaid the existing procedures with the new budget resolution procedures. Congress attempted to keep the decentralized revenue and spending process intact and at the same time to add an

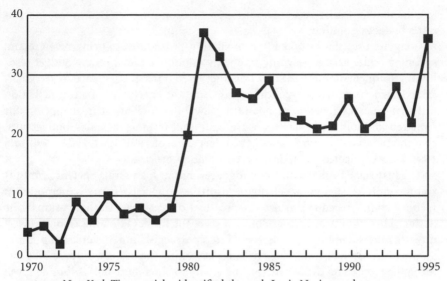

SOURCE: *New York Times* articles identified through Lexis-Nexis searches.

FIGURE 3.1   Percentage of *New York Times* Articles on Congress Also Dealing with the Budget

integrated system. In Allen Schick's words (1995), "This combination has made for complicated, ever changing relationships between Congress's budget process and its other budget related activities."

In passing a budget resolution, Congress specifies budgets for five years with binding aggregate budget figures. The main aggregates in the resolution are: total increases or decreases in revenue; total new budget authorities (money that can be spent) and outlays (money actually spent); total loan obligations and guarantee commitments; the deficit (or surplus); and total public debt. The resolution specifies these five levels over twenty functional categories including national defense, energy, health, and Medicare. Allocations to the functional categories must add up to the corresponding budget aggregates.

Under the rules, the Budget Committees of the House and Senate must present a budget resolution to Congress by April 15 of each year (May 15, prior to the Gramm-Rudman-Hollings deficit reduction act of 1985). After adoption of the resolution, the regular authorization and appropriation process works it way through Congress within the constraints imposed by the resolution. In practice, the resolutions do not meet the deadline, and at least twice have been over a hundred days late. There are many reasons why the resolutions are late but the primary reason is political. Given the tough choices and the differences in philosophy between Republicans and Democrats, agreement has been hard to come by. Conservatives do not want to vote for tax increases. Liberals do not want to vote for program cuts and can't get tax increases. Because setting priorities is not easy to achieve, the regular authorization-appropriation process often proceeds without a budget resolution.

Congress uses the so-called "reconciliation procedure" to bring revenue and spending under existing law into line with amounts set forth in the budget resolution. Reconciliation involves two distinct operations: the issuance of reconciliation instructions that set spending limits, and the enactment of a reconciliation bill that changes revenue or spending laws. Reconciliation is an option for Congress and it is used when there are significant revenue increases, budget cuts, or a combination of both. The major budget shifts of 1981, 1982, 1984, 1990, and 1993 were all enacted through the reconciliation process.

The first stage begins with the budget resolution instructing specific committees to report legislation that changes existing laws. Social Security is exempt from reconciliation procedures as are (in practice) discretionary authorizations. The designated committees then attempt to meet the limits set by the resolutions. If more than one committee is instructed to report legislation, the bills are put into an omnibus reconciliation bill. The rules governing the passage of these bills differ in the House and the Senate but the ability to amend the bills is limited given their complexity. Add to these basic reforms the Gramm-Rudman-Hollings rules of 1985 and the Pay-As-You-Go (PAYGO) rules adopted in 1990, and it is clear that budget bills and procedures have become more complex. Congress's attempt to solve hard budget problems by layering over a decentralized process with a resolution-reconciliation integrative process has not solved the deficit problem. These changes have, however, increased greatly the amount of time that members of Congress must spend on budget matters.

The reconciliation process *did,* however, bring about one change that has made politics easier. Given the complexity of the omnibus budget packages and the reconciliation process, Senators agreed that no filibusters would be allowed during reconciliation. With regard to the revolving gridlock theory, this means that, if a budget is passed under the reconciliation rules, the gridlock region is defined by the veto pivot and the *median* member in both the House and the Senate. Thus the President and Congress face a choice of using either the budget reconciliation with its complex processes but a simple majority rule, or the nonreconciliation rules under which filibusters are allowed.

Arrival of the 97th Congress

The revolving gridlock theory presented in Chapter 2 depends on determining the preferences of members of Congress. In this section, we attempt to show how preference shifts resulting from elections can be meticulously documented, leading in the end to conclusions about which individuals became the pivotal members of Congress in 1981.

The newly elected 97th Congress came to Washington in 1981 with a new President and an old agenda—rising entitlements, high taxes, Soviet involvement in Afghanistan, and a rapidly decreasing Social Security Trust Fund. The new Congress differed significantly from the 96th Congress. The Senate was Republican for the first time in twenty-six years; liberal Senators including George McGovern (D., S.Dak.), Birch Bayh (D., Ind.), Gaylord Nelson (D., Wis.), and Frank Church (D., Idaho) had been defeated in 1980. They were replaced by conservative Senators like Dan Quayle (R., Ind.), Robert Kasten (R., Wis.), Steven Symms (R., Idaho), Charles Grassley (R., Iowa), and James Abdnor (R., S.Dak.). The eleven defeated or retired Democratic Senators had a mean Americans for Democratic Action (ADA) score of 55.5 and a median ADA of 50 in 1980.[6] In the first session of the 97th Congress, the Republican Senators who replaced them had a mean ADA score of 6.8 and a median of 5. In short, the election had resulted in a significant shift of the preferences of the U.S. Senate to the right. Equally important were the facts that the Republicans were now the majority party, and the preferences of the committee chairs had also shifted to the right.

In the 96th Congress, the Chairs of the Finance, Appropriations, and Budget Committees were Russell Long (D., La.), Warren Magnuson (D., Wash.), and Edmund Muskie (D., Maine). Long, a conservative southern Democrat, had an ADA score of 28 in the last session of the 96th Congress. His replacement, Senator Bob Dole (R., Kans.), had an ADA score of 22 in the same session. Magnuson's ADA score in 1980 was 72 whereas his replacement, Senator Mark Hatfield (R., Ore.), had an ADA score of 50. Senator Muskie's 1979 ADA score was 53 whereas his replacement in the 97th Senate, Senator Peter Domenici (R., N.Mex.), had a 1979 ADA score of 5. In each case there was a move to the right, with the shift in the Budget Committee being the most noticeable. Given that the Republicans chose to use the reconciliation procedure, the shift was important because the Budget Committee would set the spending limits during the first budget resolution.

Although the shifts in the Appropriations and Finance Committees appear to be less decisive, there were major shifts in subcommittee chairs. Senator Thomas Eagleton (D., Mo.) chaired the Agriculture subcommittee of Appropriations in 1980 and his ADA score was 78, whereas his replacement in the 97th Congress, Senator Thad Cochran (R., Miss.), had a 1980 ADA score of 22. In 1980 the chair of the Interior subcommittee of Appropriations was Senator Robert Byrd (D., W.Va.), whose 1980 ADA score was 56; his replacement in the 97th Senate, Senator James McClure (R., Idaho), had an ADA score of 17.

The shift from a Democratic to a Republican majority in the 1980 elections had major effects on other committee chairs as well. The leadership of the Judiciary Committee went from Senator Ted Kennedy (D., Mass.) to Senator Strom Thurmond (R., S.C.). The Committee on Banking, Housing, and Urban Affairs went from Senator William Proxmire (D., Wis.) to Senator Jake Garn (R., Utah). In the 1980 session of the 96th Congress, Garn had an ADA score of 17 whereas Proxmire scored 56. The Energy and Natural Resources, Agriculture, and Labor and Human Resources Committees all had similar shifts from 1980 to 1981. Agriculture went from Herman Talmadge's (D., Ga.) ADA of 33 to Jesse Helms's

(R., N.C.) ADA of 11. On the Energy and Natural Resources Committee, the ADA scores of the chairs shifted from Henry Jackson's (D., Wash.) 72 to James McClure's 17. Labor and Human Resources's new chair was Orrin Hatch (R., Utah), who had an ADA score of 17 in 1980; in contrast his predecessor, Harrison Williams (D., N.J.), had a 1980 ADA of 72.

Although these shifts are illustrative, more compelling evidence can be obtained by comparing Senate means and medians by election over time. We calculated the mean, median, and standard deviation for ADA scores over all sessions of the Senate from 1969 through 1990.[7] Table 3.3 shows these figures arranged by Presidents. During the Nixon-Ford and Carter years the median Republican ADA score was about 17 while in the 1981 session of the 97th Congress the median had dropped to 10. In addition to the drop in the median, the spread of preferences had tightened. Republican ADA scores ranged from 0 to 55 (Weicker, Conn., and Hatfield, Ore., scored 55), which was the narrowest spread during the 1969–1990 period. Analyzing mean scores and variance shows the same tightening phenomenon at work. The mean Republican ADA score in 1981 was 16.8 with a standard deviation of about 16. Both the mean and the standard deviation show about a 40 percent drop from any Senate scores over the 1969–1980 period. The reduced range and variance of scores around the median and the mean indicate that not only did the center of the party shift to the right but also that the number of liberal and moderate Republican votes was greatly reduced in the first session of the 97th Senate.

Even with this shift to the right in the Republican Party, the Democrats had opportunities to at least delay legislation, and in some instances to successfully filibuster if they could hang together. The election resulted in a shift to the left among Democratic Senators—the median Democratic Senator in the Nixon-Ford and Carter years scored an average ADA of between 56 and 66 while in the first session of the 97th the median had risen to 70. The spread around the Democratic median, however, was the full 100 points, from a conservative 0 to a liberal 100. The variance around the mean increased, meaning that although the median Democrat was a liberal with an ADA score of 70 there were a large number of Democrats far to the right of the median. Three Democratic Senators had ADA scores of 15 or less—Stennis (Miss.), Long, and H. Byrd (Va.)—while another three, Johnston (La.), Bentsen (Tex.), and Zorinsky (Nebr.), had ADA scores of 20 or 25.

The floor median ADA score in the 97th Senate dropped to 35, about a 10-point drop from the Nixon-Ford and Carter years. There were twelve Senators near the floor median, with ADA scores between 30 and 40. Of the twelve, eight were Republicans and four (Heflin, Nunn, Boren, and Cannon) were Democrats. This is in contrast to the 96th Congress where, as we have seen, the Republican median was higher and the Democratic median lower. In the 96th Senate, five Republicans were at or about the Democratic median—Hatfield, Weicker, Mathias (Md.), Durenberger (Minn.), and Javits (N.Y.). At or about the floor median in the 96th

TABLE 3.3 ADA Score Summary (Senate)

	Nixon 1969–1972 Averages	Nixon/Ford 1973–1976 Averages	Carter 1977–1980 Averages	Reagan 1981	Reagan 1982	Reagan 1983	Reagan 1984	Reagan 1985–1988 Averages
Republicans								
Median	18	17	17	10	15	15	15	11
Mean	27.4	28.7	26.2	16.8	25.1	22.1	25.8	20.4
Standard deviation	27.6	29.0	22.5	16.0	23.6	19.5	24.9	23.7
Democrats								
Median	63	66	56	70	70	75	75	78
Mean	56.9	59.0	54.2	65.1	67.7	68.3	74.0	71.6
Standard deviation	31.5	28.8	23.4	26.7	24.5	21.7	23.3	21.9
Entire Senate								
Median	42	52	44	35	45	40	50	48
Mean	43.9	46.7	43.1	39.5	44.7	43.3	47.5	46.2
Standard deviation	33.2	32.4	26.8	32.5	32.0	30.9	34.1	34.2

Senate were fifteen Senators, nine Democrats and six Republicans (Cohen, Maine; Durkin, N.H.; Heinz, Pa.; Kassebaum, Kans.; Packwood, Ore.; and Pressler, S.Dak.). Clearly the 97th Senate was more conservative and under Republican control. The median voter was twice as likely to be a Republican than a Democrat, and if a Democrat then a conservative one. The Republicans were a tightly clustered conservative group, whereas the Democrats ranged from very conservative to extremely liberal.

The 1980 elections brought the Republicans to the majority in the Senate and shifted preferences to the right, resulting in a majority for more conservative policies. In addition to the Republican majority, there were a sufficient number of conservative Democrats to ensure that the filibuster could not be used often or effectively. In short, the Democrats in the 97th Senate were badly split, with conservative Democrats reading the election as a mandate for a policy shift to the right. A second factor increasing the prospect for a conservative policy shift was that President Reagan would be setting the agenda. This meant that even liberal to moderate Republicans like Cohen, Heinz, Mathias, and Weicker were reading the election results as a Reagan-right mandate. One way to show this effect is to look at those Senators who were in both the 96th and 97th Senates and to compare the shift in the direction of their ADA scores. Technically, the scores are not comparable because they are calculated over different votes. However, if we simply ask whether Senators in both Senates have become more or less conservative, the results will be indicative. The expectation is that the Republicans will become more conservative across the board whereas the Democrats will split, with northern Democrats becoming more liberal and southerners (on the average) becoming more conservative. Because ADA scores only indicate the percentage of times a member voted liberally, we broke the results down as follows: major change, measured as at least two votes in the 97th Senate (10 ADA points) more conservative or more liberal than in the previous Senate; slight change, measured as one vote (5 ADA points) more conservative or liberal; and no change from the 96th to the 97th Senates. Of the thirty-five Republicans in both Senates, only two (Pressler and Hatfield) changed in a liberal direction (one major and one slight). Eighteen Republicans changed by more than two votes to more conservative positions; nine shifted to the right by one vote; and six did not change from the 96th to the 97th Senate. In sum, the analysis is consistent with the notion that the Republicans present in both Senates read the results of the 1980 election as a mandate for a conservative shift, and their voting patterns followed suit. Even considering that the votes were over different issues, these results show that Republicans strongly supported conservative positions on a range of issues after the 1980 election.

There were forty-five Democratic Senators in both the 96th and 97th Senates. The hypothesis is that the Democrats, unlike the Republicans, will split and go both directions—liberal and conservative. Fourteen of the forty-five (31 percent) did not change direction; of the remaining thirty-one Senators, twenty became more liberal while eleven shifted to the right. Sixteen Democrats voted significantly more liberally (at least two votes) while seven, mainly southerners, became significantly more conservative. The eight Democrats exhibiting slight changes in directions split evenly: four more liberal and four more conservative. In sum, Democrats read the 1980 election in different ways, splitting about two to one in favor of adopting more liberal positions, whereas Republicans overwhelmingly read the election as a signal to shift to the right.

The 1980 House election yielded somewhat different results. The Republican party gained a net of 33 seats, taking them to 192 total seats in the 97th Congress. Although this was their highest total in over a decade, the Republicans still needed to hold all their members and convince twenty-six Democrats to vote with them in order to achieve the 218 votes needed for a majority. The House elections shifted the preferences of members to the right, because the Democrats who lost or retired were on the average more liberal than the Republicans who replaced them. The shift to the right was not as significant as in the Senate for a number of reasons. First, the Democrats were still the majority party and as a result the conservative shift did not *appear* as dramatic. Second, the chairs of the major committees were either returned or replaced by similarly minded Democrats. These factors dictated that House Democrats still controlled the machinery and timing of the institution, and that old-line Democrats like Rostenkowski (Ill.), Dingell (Mich.), Wright (Tex.), and O'Neill (Mass.) would control the Democrats' response to the Republicans' budget policies. Representative James Jones (Okla.) would chair the Budget Committee, while Rostenkowski would chair the Ways and Means Committee (in charge of tax policy); it was clear that their preferred policy would be to the left of Reagan. Without a majority and with Democrats in control of the House's machinery, the Republicans' major battles would be in the House. The gain in seats gave conservatives a chance at winning but it would be harder than in the Senate.

While these details get at the heart of the political scenario as Congress entered its 97th session, the extensive findings can be boiled down to a simple preference shift. Figure 3.2 illustrates the 1980 election results in the format introduced in the previous chapter.

The 96th Congress, under President Carter, faced gridlock from the veto pivot in the House to the filibuster pivot in the Senate. The House was more liberal than the Senate. The President was a Democrat, and thus the gridlock region extended to the left. The possibility of filibusters in the Senate constrained policy movement to the left, whereas the President's veto and the difficulty of overriding such a veto in the liberal Democratic House stopped policy movements to the right.

The 1980 elections shifted the median in both the House and the Senate to the right, with Republican gains in both chambers. The most dramatic shift in the gridlock interval, however, came as a result of the Presidential election. No longer would the threat of a Presidential veto extend the gridlock region to the left; now the region would extend toward the conservative preferences of Ronald Reagan. The gridlock region for the 97th Congress was defined by the filibuster pivot in

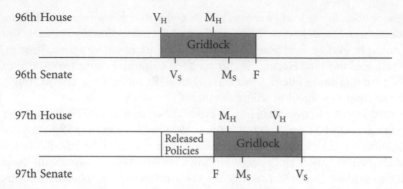

FIGURE 3.2   The 1980 Elections

the Senate and the veto pivot, also in the Senate. This meant that the gridlock region shifted dramatically to the right, releasing policies that had formerly been held in place by the preferences of a Democratic Congress and a Democratic President with veto powers. Republicans could seize on these released policies, shifting them to the right, back into the gridlock region.

The constraint on policy change would generally be the filibustering of Democrats in the Senate. However, with regard to budget issues, the President could opt to use the reconciliation rules that would prevent budget resolutions from having to gain supermajorities in the Senate to overcome filibusters. As such, with regard to budget issues, the President was constrained not by the filibuster in the Senate but by the need to construct a majority in the Democratic House. Pivotal members on nonbudgetary issues would be conservative Democrats in the Senate, and on budget issues they would be conservative Democrats in the House. As such, the new President looked to southern Democrats to round out his new coalition.

Turning Election Results into Policy Outcomes

Given the dilemma facing the country in 1981—high entitlement expenditures, a much-needed increase in defense spending, voter anger about taxes, the drying up of the Social Security Trust Fund, and a stagflated economy—it was clear that a tax cut, increases in defense spending, and cuts in some programs would be forthcoming. The debate would be over *how much* to cut taxes, *how much* to increase defense, and *which* programs should be cut back. President Reagan had the first move; between his inauguration and State of the Union Address, the President and his director of the Office of Management and Budget (OMB), David Stockman, worked the Hill to prepare members for the magnitude of the cuts. Stockman's "Black Book" revealed that the President would ask for $50 billion in spending cuts. Among the targeted programs were the National

Endowment for the Arts, Social Security benefits for students, food stamps, comprehensive employment training, research on synthetic fuels, and urban development. In tandem with these program cuts, the President also proposed the adoption of the Kemp-Roth tax cut—a 10 percent cut in income taxes in each of three years—and a $50 billion increase in defense spending.

In his February 18, 1981, State of the Union Address, President Reagan warned of a "day of reckoning" if Congress did not act immediately to cut taxes and expenditures. Reagan promised to maintain the safety net for the truly needy. He proposed the 10-10-10 tax cut effective July 1, 1981, and cuts in eighty-three programs ranging from food stamps to mass transit grants to dairy price supports. The assumption underlying these proposals was clearly supply-side economics.

Stockman and the President chose to use the reconciliation process to push the policy shifts through Congress. Roughly, the process calls for the House and Senate Budget Committees to first pass resolutions placing limits on expenditures within functional categories and instructing committees to reconcile their decisions with the aggregate totals in the budget resolution. After passage of the resolution, the regular appropriating and taxing process would go to work. The decisions made by the committees would result in two bills: an appropriations bill addressing all the cuts and the increase in defense, and a tax bill. The consolidation of all these issues under the reconciliation rules enabled the President to appeal to the American public just before the voting, rather than having to deal with thirteen regular appropriations bills spaced out over time.

Democratic opposition to the tax cuts and spending cuts was immediate. They did not question that these cuts would be made; they questioned the magnitude. Their strategy was to appear responsible before the electorate while waiting to sort out the potential effects of Reagan's proposals. Representative Rostenkowski put it best: "We are still debating exactly what it was that voters expressed at the ballot box last fall" (1981 *Congressional Quarterly Weekly Report,* 377). Reagan and Stockman understood from the start that they would need conservative Democratic support, so their House lobbying activity focused on southern Democrats. House Speaker Thomas P. (Tip) O'Neill and the Democratic leadership also focused on southern Democrats. Representative Hefner's proposal to increase defense spending by $6.6 billion more than Reagan's proposal was meant to entice southern Democrats to vote for the Democrats' budget.

Republicans in the Senate pressed ahead on the resolution and in March the Senate Budget Committee voted unanimously to approve a reconciliation resolution cutting $36.4 billion from Carter's 1981 budget plan. Republicans "exhibited unprecedented solidarity" whereas Democrats "squabbled openly around the conference table" (1981 *Congressional Quarterly Weekly Report,* 499). Ten separate Senate committees were given reconciliation orders. On April 2, 1981, the Senate passed a budget resolution that cut $36.9 billion in expenditures, and assumed revenues based on Reagan's 10-10-10 tax cuts. The House Democrats meanwhile were developing their own counterproposal, which featured a smaller, one-time tax cut and expenditure cuts that were $19.4 billion smaller than those proposed by the Senate resolution. Even though the Democratic proposal was less severe than Reagan's request, it represented "a major rightward shift by the majority party in the House" (1981 *Congressional Quarterly Weekly Report,* 622). Representatives Phil Gramm (D., Tex.) and Delbert Latta (R., Ohio) proposed a substitute for the Democratic plan that was much closer to the Reagan budget; the Gramm-Latta proposal was defeated 13-17 by the Budget Committee. The Budget Committee, however, did not represent the floor. On May 7, 1981, the House of Representatives voted for the Gramm-Latta substitute. Sixty-three Democrats joined Republicans to support what was essentially the basic Reagan proposal. The vote "provided cold, hard proof that the fragmentation among the Democrats . . . is extremely serious" (1981 *Congressional Quarterly Weekly Report,* 783). Given this decisive victory in the Democrat-controlled House, the House-Senate conference agreed and both bodies passed the budget resolution. The resolution was a victory for Reagan's policies because it included $36 billion in budget cuts, assumed a $53.9 billion reduction in taxes (a 5-10-10 cut), and instructed committees to reconcile their numbers with the resolution.

But the battle was not yet over. The committees, particularly in the House, would not all meet their instructions and there would be a series of votes on the final omnibus reconciliation bill. In addition, the House and Senate tax committees had to draft bills to actually reduce taxes since the budget resolution is not binding in law. "The first true test of how serious Congress is about cutting federal spending in the budget will be how the committees respond to their reconciliation instructions" (1981 *Congressional Quarterly Weekly Report,* 839). The Democratic strategy in the House was to hope that the President's popularity fell or that economic conditions deteriorated such that deep cuts in the budget would become untenable. Interest groups pushing to reverse budget cuts turned to the committees.

In late June, House Republicans were faced with major problems, as seven of fifteen committees were short on their reconciliation proposals. The Republican-controlled Senate had already presented a reconciliation package that even exceeded the first resolution by trimming $39.6 billion (the goal was $35.1 billion). Several House committees, however, failed to meet the targets in agriculture (Agriculture), impact aid for school districts (Education and Labor), park acquisition (Interior), funding for the arts (Appropriations, Interior subcommittee), Medicaid (Energy and Commerce), and subsidized housing (Banking, Finance, and Urban Affairs), among other program areas. Republicans had to choose between accepting the committees' results or pushing for an alternative that cut expenditures to a level consistent with the first resolution. The alternative plan was referred to as Gramm-Latta II, and the vote would be tough because now it was actually a vote to cut whereas the first vote had no legal status.

The crucial budget reconciliation votes would occur on the rule under which the bill would be reported and on the actual Gramm-Latta substitution. Roughly, the Democrats wanted a rule that would force Republicans to vote separately for every cut greater than what the committees had proposed. Republicans wanted one vote—up or down—on the whole package. The Republicans, with the support of very conservative southern Democrats, prevailed on the rule, and on June 26 the House accepted the Gramm-Latta substitute by a 217-211 vote. The Gramm-Latta bill cut $38.2 billion in 1982 and was compatible with the Senate bill. The majority favoring Gramm-Latta was composed of a unified Republican party together with conservative Democrats. Figure 3.3 shows the array of Democratic support for President Reagan's policies by ADA score in the first session of the House. The results show that the more difficult the vote, the further right the Democrats supporting the action were. Cutting taxes is much easier to vote for than cutting programs and, as can be seen, Democrats supporting both the tax cut and the first Gramm-Latta substitute (which was not binding) were more conservative than those who only supported the tax cut. The twenty-nine Democrats supporting Reagan all the way on tax cuts and the tough Gramm-Latta II proposal were very conservative.

The first budget resolution had accepted the broad outline of the Reagan tax policy, and it seemed clear that the Republican Senate would not present much of an obstacle. In the House of Representatives there were two major concerns to be addressed in order to pass the tax bill: (1) should the cuts be multiyear or one-time; and (2) who should benefit from tax relief? Senator Dole's Finance Committee proposed a 25 percent cut with 5 percent the first year followed by two 10 percent cuts in each of the next two years. House Democrats insisted that the beneficiaries be those with annual incomes of $20,000 to $50,000. The tax bill also included a drop in marginal tax rates and additional retirement and business-related breaks. The debate, however, would center around the multiyear proposal and the question of who would benefit.

The Republican Senate proposed a three-year, 25 percent tax reduction package that did not target "middle income earners" in any specific way. The Senate also approved indexation beginning in 1985, which meant that bracket creep would be eliminated. The House Democrats countered with a two-year, 15 percent cut in individual taxes skewed to provide most of the relief to those earning less than $50,000 annually. Their alternative allowed a third-year cut if certain conditions were met. Given that Republican unanimity for the three-year Reagan-Dole proposal guaranteed only 192 votes, the bill was still 26 votes shy of passage. Under these circumstances, the President began to court the members of the conservative Democratic Forum. The forum consisted of forty-seven Democrats of whom forty-four were from southern and border states.[8] Kent Hance (Tex.) and Charles Stenholm (Tex.) were among the House leaders of the Democratic Forum. In short, in order to pass, the tax bill would have to appeal to the median voter, who was surely in this group of forty-seven conservative Democrats. On the liberal side, Rostenkowski and Jones were leading the battle for those favoring a one-time cut aimed at earners with incomes below $50,000. The liberals too knew

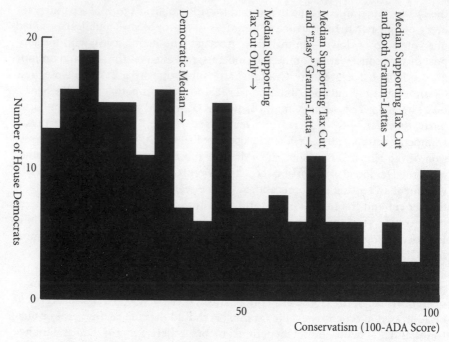

FIGURE 3.3   House Democratic Support for Reagan (1981)

that to win they had to woo conservative southern Democrats. The shift to a two-year, 15 percent tax cut was indicative of this strategy.

Liberal Democrats were more than a little annoyed by the Republicans' wooing of conservative Democrats. Representative Moffett (Conn.) sought punishment for Democrats voting too often with Republicans. Representative Long, the chair of the Democratic caucus, openly spoke of disciplining maverick Democrats. The Democratic leadership, however, refused to agree to any sanctions largely because they knew they would need the help of conservative Democrats in the future for other purposes. The fate of the Reagan tax bill would be decided by members of the Democratic Forum. Representative Hance told Rostenkowski that he would carry the President's bill—a three-year, 25 percent individual tax cut (5–10–10) with significant tax cuts for corporations—to the floor. One important side issue was indexation of the individual income tax. This would involve indexing taxes, like entitlements, to inflation so that inflation could not force wage earners into higher brackets. The Senate included indexation in its tax bill. On each of the crucial indexation votes in the Senate, a block of conservative Democrats voted with the Republicans.

With the Senate firmly in place and the House outcome in some doubt, President Reagan on July 27, 1981, again appealed to the public, arguing that the tax cuts were as crucial as the budget cuts he had won a month earlier. In the

House, "both the President's and the Democrats' bills have been laden in recent weeks with myriad benefits and sweeteners for different groups of taxpayers, as each side has sought to put together a coalition of support" (*New York Times*, July 27, 1981). Needless to say, the arguments for these sweeteners were complicated and arcane. The point is that the benefits were offered to southern and border state Democrats who were on the fence between the Reagan bill and the Democratic bill. The President's speech cut through the distracting complications by focusing on the need for a major tax cut. Reagan also made a plea for indexing, arguing that without it taxes would rise automatically over the long run.

On July 29, 1981, the House of Representatives voted 238-195 to adopt a bill close to Reagan's original proposal, sponsored by Conable (R., N.Y.) and Hance in place of the Democratic bill drafted by the House Ways and Means Committee. Forty-eight Democrats voted with Reagan whereas only one Republican (Jeffords, Vt.) opposed. Thirty-seven of the defecting Democrats came from the South; Texas accounted for eight defectors and Georgia seven. In conference, Senator Kennedy kept the Senate in session for two days trying to send the bill back to committee to remove the breaks for big oil. In the end, the basic Reagan package survived: a three-year (5-10-10) individual income tax reduction with income taxes indexed after 1985; a major increase in the depreciation allowance for corporations; and a major reduction in the top corporate tax bracket (from 70 to 50 percent). In sum, the President's basic tax package had carried the day.

Our thesis has been that the 1980 elections shifted the preferences of the U.S. Congress to the right and that the major policy shifts of the Reagan revolution were achieved in the Senate by virtue of the Republicans' majority status (with conservative Democratic support) and in the House by garnering votes from the conservative Democratic Forum. Figure 3.2 shows the shift in the gridlock region, leading to the establishment of conservative Democrats as the pivotal voters. Figure 3.3 shows the array of preferences in the House and indicates the preferences of key Democratic defectors. The broad array of Democratic preferences from very conservative to very liberal highlights the difficulty of organizing unified Democratic action. Representative Hefner validated this phenomenon when he said: "Even when the Democrats are together, we're still fragmented. We're a party made up of liberals, moderates and conservatives. We don't have the luxury of the Republicans, who know exactly who their constituency is" (1981 *Congressional Quarterly Weekly Report*, 786). The Reagan victory was achieved by the unified Republicans plus conservative Democrats; Senator Breaux (D., La.) said that his vote couldn't be bought but "it can be rented" (1981 *Congressional Quarterly Weekly Report*, 1169).

As was hypothesized in the previous chapter, the shift in preferences and pivotal members after the 1980 elections released spending and taxing decisions from a state of legislative gridlock. The movement was to the right, for lower taxes and lower spending. This shift was moderated by pivotal members—southern Democrats in this case. The votes of the pivotal members were secured by moderating policy somewhat (from 10-10-10 tax cuts to 5-10-10) and by including sweeteners in the tax and budget bills.

Adjustments and Solidification of Policy

The U.S. economy fell into a severe recession in late 1981 and the effect on the budget was ominous. Revenue was down because taxes were lower and fewer people were employed. Expenditures for programs such as unemployment insurance and food stamps were up. The decrease in revenues plus the increase in expenditures generated a major increase in the budget deficit. Early in 1982 it was clear that the budget would have to be modified. There are only two real ways to reverse deficits: raise taxes or cut expenditures. Cutting expenditures is a conservative response whereas raising taxes is a liberal response. Which way the President and the Republican Senate would move depended upon where they could find the votes.

After 1981: Reagan's Abrupt Shift

In 1982 taxes were raised far more than expenditures were cut because a majority in favor of cutting expenditures could not be established, leaving the tax increase as the primary weapon of deficit reduction. In short, the second session of the 97th Congress was not as hospitable to conservative ideas as was the first session. With a sour economy and a lower level of support than in 1981, Reagan could not appeal to the public as before to pressure members of Congress to support his conservative agenda. Because tax policy was now shifting to the left (favoring increased taxes), we expect to find the majority for the new policy to differ from the majority formed for the 1981 tax cuts and reconciliation budget. We expect conservative Republicans to be the major opponents of the 1982 tax increases.

Interest rates and inflation dropped during 1982, but at a price. Unemployment reached 10.8 percent by late 1982 and industrial production continued to decline. The budget deficit was projected to be about $180 billion in 1983 with an annual deficit of over $300 billion by 1988. Representative Latta summed up the problem simply in January 1982: "The honeymoon is over."

Democrats in the House were reluctant to take up the tax issue, given the upcoming 1982 elections. Members were leery of voting for tax increases and then having the President campaign against them as tax-and-spend Democrats. Thus in an unusual fashion Representative Rostenkowski, Chairman of the Ways and Means Committee, chose to wait until the Republican Senate and the President had acted. In the Senate, President Reagan's call to plug tax loopholes and require a minimum corporate tax was treated as insufficient.

The Senate Finance Committee proposed (on an 11-9 straight party vote) a $98 billion tax increase: $21 billion in the first year, $34 billion in the second, and $43 billion in the third. The bill raised taxes on corporations, cut back some business benefits given in the previous year's bill, and established a minimum tax on high-income individuals. The committee attached its bill to H.R. 4961, a minor tax bill passed by the House in 1981, thereby meeting the constitutional requirement that tax bills must originate in the House. Committee Democrats advocated repealing the 1983 individual tax cut (10 percent). The Senate voted on July 23, 1982, to accept the Finance Committee's report by a 50-47 vote. Several amendments to cut the 1981 tax reductions were defeated on the floor largely because Senator Dole assured his colleagues that repealing the 1981 tax reductions would guarantee a presidential veto.

In the House, the Ways and Means Committee was having trouble agreeing on what to include in their own revenue agreement, so on July 28 they agreed to go directly to conference on the Senate bill. Later that same day the full House agreed to go along with the Ways and Means Committee's plan to go directly to conference. The advantage of this strategy was that members anxious about their re-election bids would not be voting on a Democratic plan but rather on a Republican plan, and the Republican Senate and President could be held responsible for the tax increase.

The battle in conference took eight full days and was painful. Increasing taxes and cutting spending in an election year are not popular activities among members of Congress. Battles over restoring the 1981 cuts in welfare and limiting Medicare reimbursements and Medicaid co-payments highlight the policy differences between Democrats and Republicans and between House and Senate. In the final analysis, $17.5 billion in spending cuts over three years were accepted. On the tax side, the chief battle was over the proposed $38 billion increase in corporate taxes. The Democrats prevailed by dropping the indexation of taxes on capital gains, defeating Republican liberalization of capital gains taxes, and increasing the minimum tax on wealthy individuals.

Final passage of the 1982 Tax Equity and Fiscal Responsibility Act (TEFRA) depended upon President Reagan's willingness to lobby on its behalf. Although in principle Reagan did not like increasing taxes, he had prevented any increase in personal taxes; the indexed 5-10-10 tax cuts would stay intact; and some of his original loophole-closing proposals made it to the final package. Without Reagan's backing, Democrats would not deliver the votes needed for passage, while with Reagan's public sponsorship they could cleanly run for reelection saying that they had supported the President's bill. In order to assure Democrats that he was committed to the bill, the President promised to send personal letters to all who supported it, thus giving the Democrats electoral cover. The question then became whether Reagan could convince enough Republicans to support the bill. To this end the President went to the Hill and pressured Republicans to support the 1982 tax increases. On the crucial votes, from the Rousellot (R., Calif.) motion that the law was unconstitutional to final passage, only 75 to 88 Republicans voted with about 150 to 170 Democrats to pass the bill. A majority of Republicans voted against the President and the compromise. In the Senate the bill also passed, but 11 Republicans voted against it and 9 Democrats sided with the majority to fashion a 52-47 victory.

To sum up, the downturn in the economy along with the 1981 tax cuts had created a large deficit that had to be brought under control; the director of OMB, his deputy, and other Reagan strategists clearly indicated that no further "real" expenditure cuts were possible. The administration decided that raising business taxes and closing loopholes were preferable to losing part of the tax cut. Thus, in order to cut the deficit, the compromise proposal adjusted tax policy to the left, away from the 1981 tax act. Since Senators' and House members' preferences were fairly stable, the majority for the leftward shift differed from the majority that had passed the key items of the 1981 Reagan revolution a year earlier.

Specifically, the hypothesis is that the Republicans who defected from the President will be the most conservative. Likewise, Democrats who voted for the President's tax and reconciliation bills in 1981 and against the 1982 deficit reduction act will be the pivotal moderate to conservative Democrats. On the Republican side, stalwart conservatives like Barry Goldwater (Ariz.) and Jesse Helms voted against the tax hike. The median 1981 ADA score of Republican defectors was 5 while the mean was a scarcely higher 10.4. Conservatives like Senators Zorinsky and Boren (Okla.) were among the Democratic defectors who had, for example, supported the President on indexing taxes and denying amendments to increase spending in 1981. The median ADA for Democratic defectors was 45. In contrast, the median for the eleven Democrats voting for the tax increase was 90; these liberals included Senators McGovern, Kennedy, and Cranston (Calif.). The story in the House was the same. Eighty-eight Republicans voted for the tough Gramm-Latta bill and the tax cut in 1981 and then deserted the President on the 1982 tax increase; twelve Democrats followed the same voting pattern. The median ADA score of these Republicans and Democratic defectors was about 7 while the mean was 10. In short, in both the House and Senate, the 1982 coalition to increase taxes was "middle-to-left" or "middle-out" (with some liberal Democrats refusing to join the coalition in order to either force moderate Republicans to vote for tax increases or gain further concessions in exchange for their votes), whereas the 1981 "cut-taxes-and-spending" crusade had been a middle-to-right coalition of Republicans and very conservative Democrats.[9]

The 1980 elections had allowed for a significant shift to the right in tax policy. The coalition for this shift was conservative, made up of both Republicans and southern Democrats. When the economy declined in 1982, budget deficits indicated that the tax cuts had gone too far, leaving policy to the right of the median in both the House and the Senate. However, preferences and constraining institutions prevented a full shift back to the left. When the President supported shifts back to the left, Congress was able to move policy back toward the median members. When the President opposed the shifts, there would be gridlock. Reagan promised to veto legislation that attacked his 5-10-10 indexed individual income tax cuts, and there certainly were not enough votes to override this supermajority constraint. As a concession and a response to the budget deficits, Reagan agreed to tax increases elsewhere. A coalition in support of such a policy would have to come from the left, with conservative Republicans deserting. In order to avoid the blame for the tax hikes, House Democrats forced the President and the Republican Senate to initiate the proposals. This new coalition responding to the ballooning deficit would cooperate in another tax increase in 1984, but then find no further common ground after the 1986 tax act.

The Refinements of 1983–1986

The 97th Congress had come to Washington with a new President facing a tax revolt, a Social Security system nearing bankruptcy, a need to increase defense spending, and ever growing entitlement expenditures. In the first session the new conservative majority passed a 25 percent (5-10-10) tax cut that would be indexed after 1985, an increase in defense expenditures, and a reconciliation budget that cut $35.2 billion from the Carter budget. The majority favoring these policies in the House were the unified Republicans joined by about thirty conservative, mainly southern, Democrats. In the Senate, where Republicans were the new majority, southern Democrats again voted with Republicans to pass conservative legislation. The 1980 elections had shifted preferences, and the response was a shift in policy to the right. These changes and the downturn in the economy produced the largest deficit since World War II. Given the state of the economy and the upcoming election, moderate Republicans and Democrats sought a tax increase to lower the deficit. Conservative attempts to further cut expenditures were voted down and in 1982 Congress passed and President Reagan signed a deficit reduction bill that increased taxes on corporations. Liberal attempts to postpone the last two years of income tax cuts were defeated. The deficit reduction package ultimately backed by Reagan was passed with the support of a new centrist coalition of moderate Democrats and moderate Republicans. Conservative Republicans and Democrats who had voted with Reagan in 1981 defected and voted against the 1982 deficit reduction package.

Public policy from 1983 to 1986 was, in effect, an adjustment of tax and budget policy, a shift slightly to the left. In 1983 Congress passed an adjustment to Social Security that raised taxes. In 1984 Congress again passed a tax increase, the Deficit Reduction Act (DEFRA), and in 1986 Congress passed a major tax act. For the remainder of this chapter we will briefly show that: (1) the 1982 elections shifted Congress to the left; (2) attempts by liberals to raise taxes failed as did attempts by conservatives to cut expenditures (other than defense); and (3) the 1986 tax act was a continuation of the policies begun in 1981. Congressional politics had become budgetary politics, and budgetary policy could no longer be shifted in any dramatic fashion because neither the liberals nor the conservatives had the votes to do so.

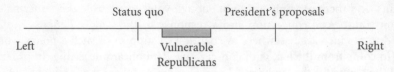

FIGURE 3.4   Vulnerability in Republican Districts

The 1982 elections to the U.S. Senate produced little change. Newly elected Senators Trible (Va.) and Hecht (Nev.) replaced Democrats, while the Democrat Bingaman (N.Mex.) replaced a Republican, yielding a one-seat Senate gain for the Republicans. The 98th Senate would be much like the 97th Senate. In the House elections there was a shift to the left as the Republicans lost twenty-six seats to the Democrats, primarily in the southern and border states, in the Midwest, and in the Northeast. Moreover, the Republicans who lost had been supporters of the President's policies. To compare these results with the congressional changes faced by Reagan's immediate predecessors after two years in office, President Carter lost eleven Democrats in 1978 and President Nixon lost twelve Republican seats in 1970.

One way to think about the 1982 elections is that President Reagan's policies were very conservative and put at risk those Republicans who came from moderate districts. A President puts at risk those congressional members furthest from his own policy proposals. Republicans from moderate districts like Jim Leech (Iowa) had constituencies that were likely to oppose some of Reagan's policies. These representatives face a dilemma. If they vote for the President's policies they will face an electoral opponent who will paint them as too conservative for the district. If, on the other hand, these representatives vote against the President, they will fall out of favor with the White House. Figure 3.4 shows the district preferences of these vulnerable members.

Due to pressure from their party in Congress or from the White House, Republicans feel that they sometimes must vote with their party even in cases where they should rightly vote against the party because of the preferences of their constituents. In doing so, they are putting their seats at risk.

Brady and Cogan (1997) support this theory over a variety of elections from 1954 to 1996. For example, they find electoral vulnerability and losses in 1982 for moderates who supported Reagan's early policies, and in 1994 for moderate and conservative Democrats who supported Clinton's early proposals (analyzed in Chapters 5 and 6). In order to determine if district characteristics and voting support played a role in the 1982 election, Brady and Cogan analyzed the election results for Republican incumbents in the House. The results support the claim that Republicans who came from the least conservative districts and who voted with the President were the most likely to be defeated in 1982. In short, the Republicans from moderate districts who voted with Reagan paid a price, whereas the so-called "Gypsy Moth" Republicans (who voted against Reagan after the 1981 Christmas break) were reelected. Once again, the point is clear: members of

Congress who please their constituencies are most likely to get reelected; and sometimes voting for the district means voting against the party.

The new House in 1982, with 269 Democrats and 166 Republicans, was more liberal than the 97th House. Attempts to further roll back spending for social programs and governmental services were doomed to fail. President Reagan's economic performance ratings fell to 30 percent; the "voting scores for the 57 newly elected House Democrats [were] the most liberal since the class of '46" (Palazzolo 1992, 148). As George Miller observed, "Last fall's election really put the leadership on the cat bird's seat" (Palazzolo 1992, 149). Moreover, from the 98th through the 100th Congresses, the Democratic leadership made sure that the Budget Committee was stocked with liberal Democrats. (In 1983 no Democrat with an ADA of less than 50 was appointed.)

The 1983 budget was Reagan's first full budget, and it included large cuts: the Department of Energy was to be dismantled, many programs such as Amtrak were to be zeroed out, Urban Development Action Grants (UDAG) were zero funded, and the Environmental Protection Agency (EPA) was cut. We interviewed top-ranking Reagan OMB personnel regarding the spending envelope. One knowledgeable participant claimed: "[It is] not fair to say that we had reached the outer edge of the spending envelope. But any more that could be done was marginal because: (1) the recession was deep; (2) it was coming on to the 1984 elections and the mandate had worn off; and (3) the interest groups that lost in 1981 had regrouped."

Another Reagan appointee said that in 1983 and 1984 the stumbling blocks were Waxman (D., Calif.) in the House on Medicare and Medicaid; Weicker in the Senate on Health and Human Services (HHS) and harbor matters; Cohen on rural housing; and Stafford (R., N.H.) on educational programs. Senators Dole, Packwood, and Baker (R., Tenn.) set the parameters for debate. In short, conservatives no longer had a majority and policy shifted slightly back to the left. Expenditures would not be cut, defense would receive less than Reagan wanted but more than the House wanted, taxes on corporations would be raised, and tax loopholes would be plugged; the 5-10-10 indexed individual income taxes, however, would not be touched. The political coalitions necessary to pass the slight shift were middle-out coalitions. Across a whole set of votes from the 1983 budget resolution through the 1984 DEFRA tax hikes, the twenty-one Republican Senators who supported the compromises had a median ADA score of 50 and a mean of 50.8. The cast was familiar: Weicker, Cohen, Percy (Ill.), Mathias, Danforth (Mo.), Andrews (N.Dak.), Kassebaum, Chafee (R.I.), Gorton (Wash.), Stafford, Hatfield, and Packwood, to name a few. The Republicans not voting for compromises had a mean ADA of 12.4 and a median of 7.5; they included Helms and East (N.C.), Wallop (Wyo.), and Kasten (Wis.). Democratic supporters of the compromises were familiar moderates such as Chiles (Fla.), Dixon (Ill.), Bradley (N.J.), Moynihan (N.Y.), Sasser (Tenn.), and Bentsen. On the House side, the story was the same. The conservative Democratic caucus split over the compromises whereas moderate-to-liberal Democrats and moderate Republicans voted for compromise. The Republicans who voted against Reagan in 1982 voted against him again in 1984. In sum, after 1981 the readjustment to increase taxes was passed by middle-out or middle-to-left coalitions *in stark contrast to* the middle-to-right coalition that had passed the major 1981 conservative legislation.

The 1986 Tax Act

Many have interpreted the 1986 Tax Reform Act as a reversal of previous practice. Birnbaum and Murray (1987) and Beam, Conlan, and Wrightson (1990) argue that the 1986 act was true reform. Our interpretation agrees with Fullerton, namely that "It [the 1986 Tax Reform Act] was indeed important legislation. But the direction of tax policy-making had really changed by 1981" (Fullerton 1994, 190). The politics of the 1986 act had already been established by the switch to the right in the 1980 election, Reagan's conservative legislation of 1981, and the two adjustments again raising taxes in 1982 and 1984. The Tax Reform Act of 1986 was the result of four developments that pushed the tax code together; Fullerton lists these developments as follows. First, supply-siders continued to affect tax policy. Calls for a flat tax or a modified flat tax were gaining ground. Second, the tax system had become too complicated both in terms of its legal complexity and the amount of time it took the "average" taxpayer to fill out the forms. Third, public confidence in the tax system was low, in large part due to reports that large corporations and wealthy individuals paid no taxes. Fourth, marginal effective tax rates were shown to have high disparities between different types of assets or financing (see Fullerton 1994, 192ff.). Note that the issues of progressivity and considerations of revenue are missing from this list.

The goals of the tax legislation that culminated in the 1986 act were lower marginal tax rates, less complexity, similar tax burdens for those with similar income, and a more efficient allocation of resources. Senator Bradley was probably the first to formulate this overview and to push it in the Bradley-Gephardt fair tax proposal of 1982. The Bradley-Gephardt plan was not taken too seriously in 1982; however, the Reagan 1984 reelection campaign staffers were worried that Walter Mondale would endorse the plan and gain an advantage in the 1984 election. The President thus announced that the Department of the Treasury would conduct a study on taxes, but that it would not be due until after the election. The Treasury report, like the Bradley-Gephardt proposal, endorsed a modified flat rate (of 15, 25, and 35 percent) on individuals and a shift of $150 billion from individual taxes to corporations (a rise to a 33 percent rate). In short, the relevant proposals were revenue neutral, distributionally neutral, and designed to level the playing field.

The Treasury proposal was opposed by business and other interests because they saw it as restricting capital investment. Senator Packwood, the chair of the Finance Committee, said that he liked the tax code as it was, and the American public was indifferent to the reform given its complexity. Secretary Baker modified the Treasury proposal by reducing indexation and integration, strengthening the acceleration of depreciation allowances, and restoring tax breaks for oil and gas and other benefits. Baker kept the 15, 25, and 35 percent brackets, although in order to make the proposal revenue neutral he added a windfall recapture tax.

On the House Ways and Means Committee, Chair Dan Rostenkowski restored (under pressure) additional benefits that caused the top rates to go to 38 percent and shifted $140 billion over five years from individual to corporate taxes. House Republicans led by conservatives and aided by southern Democrats killed H.R. 3838 on a procedural vote. Again, as in 1982 and 1984, President Reagan went to the Hill encouraging Republicans to keep reform alive, and promised to veto the bill if changes were not made in the Senate. The Senate Finance Committee increased excise taxes, reduced corporate taxes below the levels proposed in the House, and killed the rise to 38 percent in the top personal rate. The result was a projected revenue shortfall, and Packwood stopped the mark-up, thus momentarily halting tax reform. The Finance Committee then proposed a top rate of 27 percent, but ensured higher real revenues by fully taxing capital gains and disallowing some "passive losses." The House-Senate conference raised the top personal rate to 28 percent (actually 33 percent for the highest income brackets for whom a 5 percent surcharge could be applicable).

The summary results of the tax changes from 1981 to 1986 are as follows: (1) marginal tax rates were reduced; (2) politicians now paid serious attention to estimates of revenue impact, in which revenue considerations dominate all discussions of tax reform; and (3) the five-year budget has been established as the primary budget-planning vehicle. These changes all began with the 1981 Economic Recovery Tax Act, modified by the 1982 and 1984 tax bills. "The new era of tax policy was in effect as of August 1981, but its first products were not evident until TEFRA in 1982 and DEFRA in 1984. These bills closed loopholes, slowed depreciation, and started to level the playing field. By 1986, in these respects, the Tax Reform Act of 1986 was simply more of the same" (Fullerton 1994, 206).

The politics of budget formulation also shifted during this period. Any President facing the U.S. economy in 1980 would have had to address tax reform, Social Security reform, defense increases, and spiraling entitlement expenditures. The major shift in policy was the 1981 ERTA bill, which was passed by the newly elected conservative majorities in the House and the Senate. The revenue shortfalls generated by the recession caused the President to favor eliminating loopholes, shifting taxes to corporations, and leveling the playing field. In order to achieve these ends and keep the reduced average and marginal tax rates, the politics shifted to the center and those who were crucial in passing the 1981 reform were most opposed to the 1982, 1984, and 1986 reforms. The election of 1982 was particularly important for the expenditure side of the equation because the twenty-six Republicans who lost in the House had been supporters of the 1981 budget changes. From 1982 through 1986 it was clear that the votes to seriously decrease expenditures were no longer there, and there were also not enough votes to increase individual taxes. Thus it seems clear that by 1986, budget policy either had been perfected or was mired in gridlock. Despite the fact that future budget deals would need only bare majorities, between the House and the Senate no majority agreement could be reached, either for tax increases or for spending cuts. Deficits became institutionalized and the national debt grew.[10]

Budgets and the Revolving Gridlock Theory

Some would argue that budget politics are far too complex to be captured in a model as simple as the one proposed in the previous chapter. Rather than being one-dimensional, budget decisions appear to be particularistic, with each member of Congress trying to bring goodies back to the home district. The reconciliation rules call for majorities, not the supermajorities prominent in the revolving gridlock model. The coalitions that come together often take odd forms, with extreme liberals and extreme conservatives voting together against specific packages. Taxing and spending decisions are extremely complex. In many ways, we would agree with this assessment. But we raise the topic of budgetary politics here and give it prominent consideration because we think it is complementary to the revolving gridlock theory.[11] In the previous chapter, we argued that preferences and institutions, uncertainty and elections, all play a role in determining policy outcomes. We find the same to be the case in budget policy.

In its simplest sense, raising taxes and social expenditures constitutes a policy shift to the left, whereas cutting taxes and spending (other than defense) is a move to the right. In the classical budget period, with the possibility of budget surpluses three to five years down the road, majorities were easy to form. Conservatives supported tax cuts, targeting particular cuts to gain the pivotal members needed to secure majorities or supermajorities. Likewise, liberals supported new programs and expanded spending, securing particular benefits for key members who were needed to vote for their bills. Budget deals could include proposals pleasing both sides—and thus enjoyed nearly universal support and consensus.

Beginning in the 1970s, Congress and the President had to make much tougher budget decisions, as the public began to resist further taxes, entitlements were rising uncontrollably, military spending required new commitments, and Social Security was nearing a crisis. High inflation allowed politicians to mask the need for dramatic action for a short time, but by the 1980 elections it was clear that something had to be done by whoever was elected. The question was whether the pain would be shared, as the benefits had been shared during periods of surplus, or whether a coalition would form to move policy strictly to the left or the right. The 1980 elections answered this question: Ronald Reagan's election coupled with the Republican gains in Congress signaled a shift to the right. In 1981, tax cuts were not accompanied by general spending increases, but by moderate spending *cuts* (with the exception of defense spending). Liberal to moderate Democrats voted against the tax and budget bills. As the revolving gridlock theory predicts, the pivotal members in this shift were the conservative Democrats near the median in the House.

But the results of the policy change were uncertain. The tax cuts, along with the increases in defense spending and the recession, led budget analysts to predict sizable deficits within the year. Two solutions were possible: the initial Reagan coalition could hold together and propose deep spending cuts, or policy could be moved somewhat back to the left with tax increases. Given the options of either tax increases or spending cuts, there are no longer budget winners, only budget losers. The shifts to the right in 1981 had gone too far, and the only reasonable solutions were the tax increases of 1982 and 1984 and the final consolidation of 1986. The Reagan solution was to raise corporate taxes and plug loopholes, but not to touch income tax or the indexing provision.

In the era of budget deficits and public pressure to address the deficits, coalitions take odd forms. There is no majority favoring tax increases in both houses of Congress. Likewise, there is no majority favoring spending cuts, especially cuts in major entitlements. As such, when Congress and the President need to deal with the deficit, they attempt to reach compromises that involve a combination of tax increases and spending cuts. This combined strategy of moving both to the left in raising taxes and to the right in cutting spending pleases no one—at best it spreads the pain of cutting the deficit. When politicians can pass the blame off to members of the other political party, they will do so. Democrats in 1982 forced Reagan and the Senate Republicans to propose and support the painful tax increases, even avoiding the constitutional requirement that budget bills must originate in the House. This made for the odd "middle-out" coalitions, with extreme Democrats and Republicans defecting. As we will address in the next two chapters, Democrats were again able to pass the blame for the pain of the 1990 budget deal onto Republicans, this time to President Bush, who had made his famous "no new taxes" pledge. But the unified Democratic government that passed the 1993 budget act had no one else to blame. Politicians bringing home nothing but bad news are unlikely to be reelected. As such, the Republicans lost House seats in 1982, the Senate in 1986, and the presidency in 1992. But Democrats faced the same tough decisions as Republicans, and passed equally painful legislation.

No matter which politicians are in office, they face the need to deal with difficult issues and to secure majorities (and even supermajorities) of members with diverse preferences. The complexity of budget decisions leaves politicians little time to form coalitions on other issues, and few resources to create sweeteners—tax cuts and spending increases. Without such resources to secure pivotal members for policy change, gridlock continues.

NOTES

1. For a discussion of how events transform voters' preferences, which in turn transform the political agenda both generally and as it regards racial policy in the United States, see Carmines and Stimson 1989.

2. While we focus here on broad categories of taxing and spending, the actual decisions that lead to these overall figures are of greatest importance. The "microbudgeting" approach studies these decisions in detail. Among the best work in microbudgeting is that of Cogan, Muris, and Schick (1994). See especially Cogan's chapter on the dispersion of spending authority.

3. Some of the best work on the politics of the appropriations process with regard to political parties, the influence of the President, and the delegation of appropriations authority has been conducted by Kiewiet and McCubbins (1988, 1991).

4. For an excellent analysis of the politics of finance in the House Ways and Means Committee, see Manley 1970.

5. McKenzie and Thornton (1996) discuss how the need to cope with the budget deficit has influenced economic policymaking in the United States.

6. The ADA score is the member's ranking constructed from a set of roll call votes chosen by the Americans for Democratic Action to represent issues important to liberals. Thus if there were twenty such roll calls and a member voted with the ADA all twenty times, that member's score would be 100. Conversely a conservative member who never voted with the ADA would receive a score of 0.

7. Because ADA scores are based on twenty different votes each year, comparing them over time could lead to some biases and inconsistencies. Groseclose, Levitt, and Snyder (1996) attempt to deal with these inconsistencies by setting up an "inflation index" to construct "real" ADA scores. We display these adjusted scores over time in the Appendix. However, even in their raw form, the ADA scores and their variances do show patterns of who voted in what fashion in any given Congress. For our purposes, we mean to use these scores only to demonstrate that in 1981 the Republicans held together as a conservative group and Democrats splintered, with southern Democrats joining the Republican coalition.

8. With the attempted passage of the Fair Labor Standards Act of 1938, the northern and southern wings of the Democratic Party differed on issues other than race. At various points the conservative (mainly southern) Democrats were part of the Conservative Coalition, the Reagan Democrats, and so on. The press has referred to them at different times as the conservative Democratic Forum, the Conservative Democratic Caucus, or Blue Dog Democrats. The point, however, is not the name but the fact that there have for some time been conservative Representatives within the Democratic Party.

9. This type of "middle-out" coalition appears from time to time. In such a coalition, despite the fact that they might approve of a policy change, extreme members may refuse to vote for the package in order to gain greater concessions or to get members of the other party into political trouble for voting on a difficult issue. When these extreme members hold secure seats, this type of voting is likely to be more prevalent. As a result, amendments moving bills either left or right must be carefully crafted to ensure that there are not too many defections from the extremes on either side. This phenomenon does not adapt to the revolving gridlock theory very well, as we assume that these extreme members will vote for all changes that support their preferred policy positions.

10. The U.S. tax code had been riddled with special loopholes and specific taxes built up over four decades such that the special circumstances of 1986 allowed the bundling of and then the elimination of tax loopholes, thus simplifying the tax code. One might expect that over time Congress and the President might seek to reinstate loopholes and special taxes, and indeed they have done that via increased tax rates and surcharges on individual income, tax

reductions for families with children in college, and passive real estate losses. However, it is our belief that such loopholes and taxes are harder to come by under deficit conditions than they were in the postwar boom economy. Furthermore, the establishment of PAYGO and Budget Caps in 1990 show that the Congress recognized its need to restrain itself regarding special taxes and loopholes. Nevertheless, some still are legislated.

11. If nothing else, it provides the exception that proves the rule.

4

Reagan's Last Years and the Bush Interregnum

The passage of the 1986 tax act was the culmination of the 1981 Reagan tax revolution. The dramatic lowering and indexing of individual income taxes over the 1981–1986 period had dropped average taxes and dramatically decreased marginal tax rates. The original decrease was a direct result of the 1980 elections, which shifted the preferences of both the House and Senate to the right, and it was conservatives who passed the 1981 tax policy. The recession of 1982–1983 resulted in high deficits, and as a result Congress twice passed major tax increases. President Reagan beat back Democratic attempts to shift taxes to individuals (through dropping the last two years of the 1981 act's tax cuts) by threatening vetoes that would have been sustained. The 1982 and 1984 tax increases were restricted to corporations and to closing loopholes, and both were passed without the support of the conservatives who had passed the 1981 tax cut. Individual income tax cuts were built into the 1986 tax act and were now untouchable.

The issue of expenditures did not go as well for the President. The 1982 election had shifted the House somewhat back to the left, and it was clear that there was no majority for dramatic cutbacks in expenditures. Twice the Office of Management and Budget (OMB) put forward tough budget resolutions and twice they were dead on arrival. The best that can be said on the expenditure side is that the *rate of growth* in expenditures was slowed (Cogan, Muris, and Schick 1994). In effect, after 1986 it was clear that taxes could not be raised without dire consequences for the politicians proposing the raises, and expenditures could not be cut—in other words, the deficit was here to stay. No five-year budget projection since 1981 has shown a budget surplus, whereas every five-year budget projection prior to 1981 showed a surplus starting two or three years out.

In this chapter we will focus on the period from 1986 to 1992. It is during these years that we begin to see how the dominance of the budget combines with preferences and constraining institutions to lead to policy gridlock. After highlighting the preeminence of budgetary issues and the failure of the Bush election to produce a change in the gridlock region, we will turn to an analysis of the 1990 budget act. This budget deal was a strong indication that consensual politics was dead with regard to budgetary issues. We conclude this chapter by noting how other scholars have viewed the 1990 budget deal and how many of them predicted that an end to divided government would end the gridlock associated with the Bush presidency.

The Domination of the Budget

The budget's domination of American politics since 1981 is indicated by the increased coverage given to this issue in the media. More significantly, there were important side effects. New policy proposals were harder to come by and major policy changes were off-budget—their costs were borne by business, consumers, and state governments rather than by the federal government through taxes. With regard to domestic policy, President Bush's Americans with Disabilities Act and the 1993 amendments to the Clean Air Act were both off-budget. If, as we claim, American politics had become budget politics by the end of the 1980s, we should expect to see that the number of major policies passed by Congress decreases over this period, and that the ratio of off-budget policies to budget policies increases. That is, as the budget constrains contemporary programs, new policies requiring money will be harder to come by and members will turn to off-budget policies because these don't directly affect the budget numbers.

Defining "major policy" is not an easy thing to do because people disagree about which policies are important; however, David Mayhew (1991) has defined "major policy" by objectively ascertaining the amount of press coverage given to issues before the Congress. His purpose in defining major policies was to determine whether divided government affected policy results. Although our purpose differs, we can use his careful selection of public policies from 1946 through 1996 (Mayhew 1997) to corroborate our point about the declining importance of general policies and the increased importance of budget policies.

Beginning with John Kennedy in the 87th Congress (1961–1962) and ending with Richard Nixon's 92nd Congress (1971–1972), on the average about eleven major policies per Congress were passed that had direct budget implications. Most of these policies involved domestic discretionary or entitlement expenditures; fewer than 5 percent were tax decreases. In contrast, these same Congresses each passed an average of about six major pieces of legislation that were non-budgetary. Thus an average of about seventeen significant policies were passed per Congress, and the ratio of budget to off-budget policies was about 2 to 1.

During the Nixon-Ford and Carter years (1973–1980) the number of major budget-related issues fell to just below six whereas the number of major off-budget pieces of legislation rose to more than eight per Congress. In Reagan's first Congress, the budget dominated policymaking: of nine significant pieces of legislation, seven were on-budget whereas only two were off-budget. The 98th and 99th Congresses (1983–1986), in which Republicans controlled the Senate, passed on the average four on-budget policies and four off-budget policies. In the

Democrat-controlled 100th Congress (1987–1988), the Democrats passed some social legislation such as water quality improvements, aid for the homeless, and catastrophic health insurance that had on-budget implications but in general the amounts passed were quite small because the budget was under Gramm-Rudman-Hollings restrictions. In sum, from an average of seventeen significant pieces of legislation per Congress during the 1961–1973 time period, with a 2-to-1 budget-to-nonbudget ratio, the number of significant bills passed in Reagan's last three Congresses fell to about nine per Congress, with a 1-to-1 ratio between budget and nonbudget items. The amount of significant legislation stayed at about these levels during the Bush presidency. In Bush's first two years (the 101st Congress, 1989–1990) there were five on-budget items and four off-budget items including the Clean Air amendments and the Americans with Disabilities Act. The 102nd Congress was clearly gridlocked, with only seven pieces of legislation deemed significant (by Mayhew's criteria) and with off-budget proposals out-numbering on-budget proposals. This on-budget to off-budget ratio continued into the Clinton administration, although the Republican-controlled 104th Congress enacted a number of additional off-budget reforms such as the Congressional Accountability Act. Table 4.1 reiterates these numbers from 1960 through 1996.

It is clear that, as budget difficulties grew, the amount of significant legislation passed by each Congress diminished and, with reconciliation, the number of on-budget items declined relative to off-budget items. Moreover, although the data shown do not list the amounts of budget authority, it is clear that the budget implications of the Johnson-Nixon era were larger than those of the Reagan-Bush era on the expenditure side. The Kennedy-Johnson-Nixon years resulted in: the Economic Opportunity Act, the Food Stamp Act, the Urban Mass Transportation Act, the Elementary and Secondary Education Act, and rent supplements under the Housing and Urban Development Act; increases in Social Security of 13 percent (89th Congress), 15 percent (91st Congress), 10 percent (91st Congress), and 20 percent plus indexation (92nd Congress); and major expansions in unemployment compensation and food stamps. In Reagan's last three Congresses there was a $4.6 billion antirecession jobs bill, an agricultural subsidy bill that increased subsidies by about $10 billion, and a $1.7 billion antinarcotic bill. The Bush administration bailed out savings and loans under Federal Deposit Insurance Corporation (FDIC) obligations and passed a small block grant to increase affordable housing.

The Gridlock of George Bush

In an important sense divided government became an issue when George Bush was elected President (Fiorina 1996). Prior to Bush's victory, the Eisenhower, Nixon, and Reagan presidencies could be dismissed as circumstantial. That is, Ike won because he was a war hero, Nixon because the Democrats were badly divided

TABLE 4.1   Legislation with Budget Consequences and Off-Budget Legislation

	Congress	President	Budget-Related	Off-Budget
1961–1962	87th	Kennedy	11	4
1963–1964	88th	JFK/LBJ	9	4
1965–1966	89th	Johnson	15	6
1967–1968	90th	Johnson	6	11
1969–1970	91st	Nixon	14	7
1971–1972	92nd	Nixon	11	5
1973–1974	93rd	Nixon	8	14
1975–1976	94th	Ford	5	9
1977–1978	95th	Carter	5	7
1979–1980	96th	Carter	5	5
1981–1982	97th	Reagan	7	2
1983–1984	98th	Reagan	3	4
1985–1986	99th	Reagan	5	4
1987–1988	100th	Reagan	7	5
1989–1990	101st	Bush	5	4
1991–1992	102nd	Bush	3	4
1993–1994	103rd	Clinton	5	6
1995–1996	104th	Clinton	4	11

SOURCE: Mayhew 1991, 1997.

in 1968, and Reagan because of economic stagflation. With Bush's victory over Dukakis, scholars, journalists, and others began talking about divided government as a permanent feature of American politics. Most political scientists focused on why voters elected divided governments.[1] Some focused on the consequences of divided government; and it was these scholars who coined the term "gridlock."[2] Forgetting the variants, the gridlock theme was essentially the same—divided government produces policy stagnation. Thus the analysis of Reagan's last two years and George Bush's four years points to a quintessential period of gridlock—a Democratic Congress and a Republican President with few legislative achievements between them.

The 100th Congress returned the Democrats to majority status in the Senate and brought James Wright (W.Va.) to the speakership of the House. Given control of the Senate and bright prospects for winning the presidency, the Democrats, especially Wright, wanted to establish a policy position that distinguished them from Reagan. The Democrats passed an $18 billion sewage treatment bill and an $88 billion transportation bill over Reagan's veto. They also passed the small ($443 million) Homeless Shelter Act and a $30 billion housing bill. In addition, Speaker Wright pressed for a larger role in U.S.–Central American policy. Despite the Democrats' victory in the 1986 elections and Speaker Wright's aggressive use of his office, not many objective observers would give the 100th Congress high marks for significant legislation. President Reagan's actual and threatened vetoes and the Gramm-Rudman-Hollings sequestration threats helped define the "gridlock region," which left little room for major changes in budget resolutions and appropriations bills. There were no individual or corporate tax increases and no major cuts or increases in expenditures.

George Bush's presidency did not give rise to many significant domestic policy shifts. The Gulf War, the collapse of communism, and the defeat of the Sandinistas in Nicaragua were the major events of the Bush presidency. On the domestic front, the major legislation was off-budget. Interviews with Bush OMB officials generated comments like, "We knew that if he was going to do anything for the environment and education and keep the Reaganites we would have to figure out how to do it without adding to the budget," or "They [the Reaganites] never trusted us so we had to be especially careful on how we created a kinder, gentler America." The Clean Air amendments and the Americans with Disabilities Act were both carefully crafted to be off-budget, as was the minimum wage increase.

Theoretically it is not surprising that George Bush had few initial legislative victories. Policy gridlock is overcome by major shifts in the gridlock region through elections. With a switch in the party of the President, the boundaries of the gridlock region change, with the filibuster pivot replacing the veto pivot and vice versa. The less-restrictive supermajority constraint of the filibuster often dictates that some policy areas (where legislation was vetoed by previous Presidents) are released for movement toward the President's position. Because Bush replaced another Republican President, he did not have this advantage and was therefore handicapped from the beginning by a lack of issues that he could successfully act upon. At best, policy change could come through Bush refusing to veto legislation that Reagan had vetoed, but this would result in policy shifts to the left, away from the majority of his party. In addition to the President's position remaining almost the same from Reagan to Bush, the makeup of Congress was unchanged by the 1988 elections, so no new policy initiatives could be expected from a change in congressional preferences. Along with the deficits that discouraged tax cuts and new expenditures, there was little room for President Bush to maneuver on the domestic agenda. Figure 4.1 shows the identical gridlock regions for the 100th and 101st Congresses; as usual, V represents the House and Senate veto pivots, F the Senate filibuster pivot, and M the medians.

Although George Bush won the 1988 presidential election by a relatively comfortable margin of 54 to 46 percent over Michael Dukakis, the congressional election results differed very little from those of the 100th Congress, in which the Democrats retook the Senate and increased their House majority. In the 100th House the Democrats held 258 seats to 177 for the Republicans whereas in the 101st House the Democrats actually increased their number to 260, reducing the Republicans to 175. There were 230 Democratic incumbents up for reelection in 1988 and 218 of them won, meaning that all of the leaders of the Democratic 100th House would be back. Moreover, in districts where both Bush and Republican House candidates won, the President ran behind the congressional

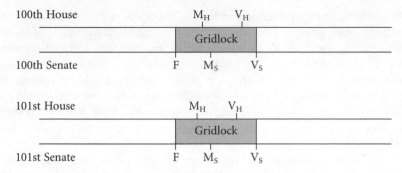

FIGURE 4.1 The 1988 Elections

candidate 85 percent of the time. In short, the 1988 congressional elections re-turned to Washington the Congress elected in 1986 plus some new Democrats. Thus, unlike all Republican Presidents of the twentieth century save William Howard Taft, George Bush's victory had actually generated a loss for his party. In the Senate the numbers stayed the same from the 100th to the 101st Senate—55 Democrats to 45 Republicans. The President faced a Congress dominated by Democrats who had felt *no* effect from his personal victory over Dukakis.

In our view, the major policy battle during the Bush presidency was the 1991 budget deal (which was voted on in 1990 prior to the midterm election). Bush's now-famous "no new taxes" pledge in his acceptance speech at the Republican Convention; his breaking the promise; and the subsequent defeat, impasse, and pas-sage of the budget are a classic example of our view of how "gridlock" operates. We now look at this turning point in Bush's domestic presidency with the intention of showing how the consensual bipartisan coalition strategy, which had been success-ful in the classical budgeting period, failed in this new era of budgetary dissensus.

The 1990 Budget Crisis

Since the 1981 tax act, the idea that individual income taxes were as high as they should be was the majority position. Politicians who attempted to raise these taxes had (like Walter Mondale) been defeated; the median position in the Congress was to leave income taxes alone. The 1982, 1984, and 1986 tax acts had not violated this principle. Corporations paid higher taxes and loopholes were closed, but average and marginal tax rates were lower in 1987 than they had been in 1980. The budgets for 1987, 1988, 1989, and 1990 were not problematic. Nobody was up to changing the provisions of the 1986 act and there were not enough votes to cut expenditures. In addition, given the growth of the economy, the deficit as a percentage of GDP had declined to manageable proportions.

Seven years of "Republican growth" came to an end in the second year of the Bush presidency. The Iraqi invasion of Kuwait was a precipitating event and the resultant rise in energy prices helped lead to a downturn in the economy. The slowing economy, along with the savings and loan crisis and bailout, caused consumers to delay purchases and markets to become cautious. With this general slowdown, government revenues also slackened, whereas expenditures continued to grow—unemployment compensation, food stamps, and other programs demanded the same if not higher levels of funding. It was clear by March 1990 that the budget deficit would be larger than predicted in the 1990 budget and larger than allowed under Gramm-Rudman-Hollings rules. This was the economic context of the budget crisis.

The original Gramm-Rudman-Hollings proposal of 1985 called for a balanced budget in 1991. In 1987 Congress revised this target year to 1993. The early-year targets were relatively easy to meet with the help of accounting practices and other tactics. But over time it became more difficult to meet the targets and, as the economy slowed in 1990, the projected deficits grew even larger. The Gramm-Rudman-Hollings target for 1991 was in fact a $64 billion deficit.

The downturn in the economy presented problems going into the 1990 elections. The economic slump and the ever increasing deficit meant that achieving Gramm-Rudman-Hollings targets would be difficult without substantial expenditure cuts and/or tax increases. The Republican experience of the early Reagan years had taught congressional members that opposition to taxes was good politics whereas cutting popular expenditures was bad politics. Democratic members knew that many government programs—Social Security and Medicare especially—were popular, but that raising individual income taxes was not popular. Thus, as Gary Jacobson (1990) argues, the public elected Republican Presidents committed to "no new taxes" and Democratic Senators and Representatives committed to increasing popular social programs. It is obvious that elections generating these kinds of preferences guaranteed continued deficits. If programs are popular and the taxes necessary to pay for them are not popular, the only way to have it both ways is to increase the deficit. In short, put off the tough decisions to the future, and certainly until after the next election. The Gramm-Rudman-Hollings solution to the problem was to set targets and, if they were not met, then cut spending across the board (excepting certain mandatory programs such as paying the interest on the debt) to satisfy the deficit reduction numbers. More importantly, this scheme allowed members to look like they were fiscally responsible—"I voted for and support Gramm-Rudman-Hollings"—while fighting to keep expenditures up in areas deemed important to their constituents.

President Bush's 1991 budget proposed expenditures of $1.23 trillion and revenues of $1.17 trillion for fiscal 1991, leaving a deficit of about $64 billion, right at the Gramm-Rudman-Hollings target. The Bush administration claimed that without this budget the deficit would be about $100 billion, and thus the need for $36 billion in deficit reduction. Bush proposed that $19.5 billion of this reduction should come from revenue increases, with the main increases coming from a reduction in the capital gains tax (thus inducing stockholders to sell shares, increasing their taxable income for 1991); user fees; and the imposition of Medicare taxes on state and local government employees. The rest of the $36 billion was to come from cuts in Medicare and entitlements plus a $4 billion cut in defense.

The Congressional Budget Office (CBO) released its own analysis, which differed greatly from the Bush budget. The CBO numbers showed a $161 billion dollar deficit for 1991. The difference in the budgets was due to the CBO's less-rosy assumptions about the state of the economy, and their inclusion of the savings and loan bailout in their calculations. Meanwhile, the Democratic House took up the budget issue and passed its own resolution 218-208, with no Republican voting in favor. The House resolution called for $1.24 trillion in outlays and $1.17 trillion in revenues, thus meeting the Gramm-Rudman-Hollings requirements. The House budget, however, differed greatly from the Bush budget in priorities. The Democratic Senate could not reach an agreement on a budget resolution and in frustration voted for the House resolution. Then both bodies told their Appropriations Committees to get to work.

Given the different preferences shown in the budgets, working out a solution would have been difficult under any conditions. The slowdown in economic growth exacerbated the problem and both sides agreed to a budget summit in May. Little was achieved as each side lectured the other on budget matters. Then, with the effects of the economic downturn becoming more obvious, on June 26, 1990, President Bush made his fateful reversal to allow tax increases as part of the budget deal. And on July 16, Richard Darman, the director of OMB, said that the deficit for 1991 could reach $231 billion.

Under these conditions, even with concessions on taxes from the President, the going was tough. Finally, on September 30, one day before $85 billion in automatic Gramm-Rudman-Hollings cuts were to kick in, the summit participants announced that they had made a deal. The agreement was a $500 billion deficit reduction package over five years beginning with $40 billion in 1991, and new budget procedures (mainly Pay-As-You-Go [PAYGO] and Budget Caps) to stop congressional backsliding on agreements.[3] Specifically, the deal would cut defense and discretionary (nonentitlement) expenditures by $182 billion over five years; cut entitlements and farm subsidies by $186 billion; and reduce interest payments on the debt by $165 billion by restructuring the debt. On the tax side, the deal would impose a 10 percent surcharge on earned income over $1 million; raise the top marginal tax rate from 28 to 33 percent; raise the alternative minimum tax from 21 to 25 percent; increase the Medicare tax base from $51,300 to $100,000; and forgo for one year the indexing of tax brackets mandated under Reagan's 1981 tax legislation. Thus the budget deal looked like a compromise—and it was. The negotiators were moderate Democrats, and they agreed to budget cuts and new budget procedures while the President and the congressional Republican leadership agreed to tax increases.

The fact that the leadership of both parties supported the compromise signaled that the majority-building strategy was to be bipartisan. Each party's leaders were to secure a majority of their congressional party in support of the bill, thus ensuring passage. As noted in the previous chapter, deficit-fighting coalitions took odd forms in 1982, 1984, and 1986. The need to raise taxes scares off the most conservative members, whereas some types of tax increases and spending cuts frighten away liberal members. Members of Congress look first to their home districts to see if they can afford to vote with their party. The right wing of the Republican Party was the first to react this time. They viewed the increase in individual taxes as a betrayal of all they had won under the original tax act of 1981. Liberal congressional Democrats were unhappy, too, over the regressive taxes on alcohol, gasoline, and tobacco, and over the cuts in Medicare. President Bush went public with a TV appearance à la Reagan, pleading for support. Public opinion turned against the President and the "Deal." Ed Rollins, a political consultant to the Republican Congressional Campaign Committee, advised Republicans to run against the President's deal. The Congress as an institution also suffered, with over 70 percent of the public disapproving of the Congress's role in budgetary politics.

It became clear, given the public reaction, that a majority of the Republicans in the House would not vote for the bill, at which point liberal Democrats also felt free to vote against it. The final vote was 254 against and 179 in favor. Of the Republicans, 71 voted yes whereas 105 voted no. On the Democratic side, 108 voted for and 148 voted against. Given our reasoning about gridlock, the opposition should be characterized by more conservative Republicans and more liberal Democrats voting no. Republicans voting against the budget had a mean ADA score of 15.4, while those voting for the budget had a mean ADA score of slightly over 20. Democrats voting against the budget had a mean ADA score of 75.9, while those voting in favor had a mean ADA score of 63.8. Thus the ideological wings of both parties voted down the compromise deal.

There were also district and electoral factors at play in the vote. Most importantly, the level of competition an incumbent faced for reelection was directly related to the vote, with those facing tough challengers more likely to vote against the deal (Jacobson 1993). Challengers to both parties' incumbents saw the deal as an important issue that they could use in their campaigns to unseat incumbents. Republicans challenging Democratic incumbents could claim that voting for the deal meant new taxes, whereas Democratic challengers could say that a "yes vote" cut popular programs like Medicare. A *Congressional Quarterly* survey found that over four hundred challengers said that they were opposed to the deal.

Following the budget deal's defeat, Congress sent President Bush a continuing resolution to keep the government going, and the President vetoed it, shutting down parts of the government and further angering the electorate. The Congress in haste reactivated the original House resolution, with majorities of Republicans in both the House and the Senate voting against it. In three weeks Congress put together a package that, after conference, dropped the 10 percent surtax (but in its place limited personal deductions), increased the top rate on taxes to 31 percent and not 33 percent, limited itemized deductions to 3 percent at the margin for top earners, and set the top capital gains rate at 28 percent. The new budget package cut popular programs less and counted on tax increases more than deficit reduction through cuts in entitlements. The new deal maintained many of the new budget procedures such as PAYGO and Budget Caps. The bill (H.R. 5835) passed the House by a 238-to-192 margin. The leftward shift of the second bill (more taxes, fewer cuts) resulted in liberal Democrats and moderate Republicans voting in favor. Democrats supporting the new bill had a mean ADA of 72.6 while those opposing were at 61.4. Republicans voting against the bill had an average ADA of 14.3 and those voting in favor had an average ADA of 32.1, though there were few Republicans voting yes. President Bush, falling in popularity and taking the blame for the government shutdown and budget deficits, signed the measure.

One obvious question arising out of the revolving gridlock framework is, given that the final deal shifted policy to the left of the original compromise, why didn't conservative Republicans vote for the initial deal, which was closer to their preferences? The answer lies in what is "revolving" about the revolving gridlock theory. Concisely, they *couldn't* vote for the early package. A vote for the initial compromise would have been a triumph over gridlock and would have secured a policy more to the Republicans' liking, but would have been opposed by their constituents and therefore would have led to their demise at the polls. Gridlock in budget matters occurs when there is lack of support among the electorate (and thus among the politicians) for any particular mechanism—tax increases or budget cuts—that would lower the deficit. Members of Congress who focus more on ending gridlock than on catering to their districts' preferences will lose their seats and thus will be unable to end gridlock in the long run. Those who prolong gridlock will be generally considered inept or self-serving and will debase the entire institution of Congress, but they will be viewed in a favorable light by their constituents and therefore will be reelected.[4] In 1990, President Bush focused on limiting budget deficits and ending gridlock. This meant breaking his promise to the American people and led to his electoral defeat in 1992.

Thus the events of the 1990 budget deal fit well with our scenario of preferences, supermajority institutions, and tough budget decisions. The 1988 election resulted in the victory of a Republican President and the continuation of a Congress that, since the 1986 elections, had been controlled by the Democrats and that was decidedly left of the President. President Bush's major domestic legislative achievements in 1989—the Americans with Disabilities Act and the Clean Air amendments—were both off-budget. With the rise in oil prices generated by the Gulf War, the economy stalled and the deficit grew. The President's original budget proposal met the $64 billion Gramm-Rudman-Hollings targets, but only by making rosy economic assumptions about growth. Then in the summer of 1990 the President called for a budget summit in which tax increases would be on the table. The summit—composed of Democratic congressional leaders, Republican congressional leaders, and administration officials—devised a five-year, $500 billion reduction package that increased taxes and cut expenditures (roughly equally divided). The legislative strategy was for a majority of both parties to pass the package, making the deal bipartisan and in the process protecting both the President and incumbent members of Congress. The right wing in the Republican Party objected strenuously to the deal on the grounds that tax increases betrayed the Reagan revolution of 1981. When it became clear that these conservative Republicans could not assemble a majority, they joined with liberal Democrats who were opposed to the cuts in entitlements to defeat the deal. The Gingrich-Dellums coalition, pairing the conservative Georgia Republican with the liberal Democrat from Berkeley, was indeed unlikely. However, this left-right coalition was anticentrist, capable only of voting against proposals. Clearly, they could work out no budget deal of their own; they were allied only because for their own reasons they favored the status quo over the proposed budget deal. President Bush's veto of a continuing resolution to keep the government running resulted in general opprobrium for the President and the Congress. The quickly-put-together budget that did pass emphasized taxes more than cuts in expenditures and was essentially passed by Democrats. Gary Jacobson (1993) has shown how both preferences and potential electoral vulnerability heralded the votes on the budget.

Explanations of Policy Outcomes

In the 1990 congressional elections nine Republican incumbents lost their seats, and in six open-seat Republican districts Democrats came away winners. With Republicans taking back fewer seats, the 102nd Congress was like the 100th and 101st—Democratic and to the left of the President. The domestic legislative agenda was characterized by inaction and presidential vetoes of congressional legislation. In all, President Bush vetoed twenty-four bills including two tax acts, the family leave act, a bill addressing China's most favored nation status, and campaign finance reform. Typically, Congress would pass legislation such as campaign finance reform and minimum wage increases that it knew the President would veto, and enough Republicans would then vote with the President to sustain his veto. In terms of the revolving gridlock theory, Congress passed legislation sufficiently left of the status quo point that was in turn vetoed by the President, and one-third or more (overwhelmingly Republican) members of Congress voted to sustain the veto, thus leaving policy at the status quo point or in gridlock.

Our interpretation of events from 1981 to 1992 is not unique. Many commentators and scholars have described the period in similar terms. Charles Stewart's analysis of tax policy (1991, 163–164) in the 1980s argues that:

> Tax policy in the 1980s was guided by the confluence of changing preferences and institutions. As the decade began, discontent with taxation had reached a high level, and a president was elected promising to cut taxes in a particular way. Uncertainty among congressional Democrats . . . along with Republican gains in both the Senate and the House, provided an influx of individuals . . . intent upon lowering taxes with

a supply side flavor. . . . After 1981 the story was completely different. While the 1981 tax cut was not a policy equilibrium, it was nearly so: given the configuration of policy preferences in the House and Senate, along with institutional vetoes, room to maneuver in negotiating tax policy had shrunk dramatically. . . . Stalemate in tax policy, which is half the stalemate in balancing the federal budget, is a product of the 1981 tax reform and the constitutional system of institutions sharing power.

Mathew McCubbins's analysis of U.S. budget deficits (1991, 103) tells much the same story. He concludes his analysis as follows:

Once the deficits of the 1980s were in full bloom, the check Ronald Reagan held over increases in revenue was sufficient to prevent Congress from enacting a tax increase. The compromise required to overcome the mutual checks held by the House Democrats and the Senate Republicans over each other's spending programs led to increased spending on nearly every function of government [in the post-1981 period]. Republican threats to veto tax increases will keep budget deficits in the headlines for some time to come.

Other work in regulatory politics (Romer and Weingast 1991) and welfare policy (Ferejohn 1991) share the same view. Namely, the 1980 elections yielded a congressional majority and a President intent on cutting personal income taxes, and this shift in member preferences resulted in a new tax policy. The shifts in 1982, 1984, and 1986 respectively increased corporate taxes, closed loopholes, and finalized the basic 1981 reforms. After the 1982 elections expenditures continued to rise (albeit at a slower rate) and the combination of congressional preferences and supermajority institutions yielded no major shift in budget policy. The rise in the deficit during the Bush presidency led Bush to agree to tax increases that were unpopular with much of his party in Congress, resulting in the fiasco of 1990. Ultimately, of course, the tax increases (especially in light of Bush's theatrical 1988 campaign promise of "no new taxes"), together with an anemic domestic program, led to Bush's defeat in the 1992 presidential election.

We do not disagree with other analyses demonstrating how various policies in the 1980s resulted from congressional preferences and institutional arrangements. Indeed, we have argued the same case. The details may differ—for example, we give Reagan a greater role than Stewart (1991) does—but the broad story is the same. We do, however, have a different emphasis. In all of these legislative matters, member preferences and constraining institutions such as the filibuster and the Presidential veto determine policies. Granted, party affiliation also plays a role. Democratic members of the House and Senate are generally more liberal than their Republican counterparts. However, our emphasis is less on the party affiliation and more on the policy preferences of the members; we do not care whether the 218th House voter is a southern Democrat or a northeastern Republican because in our view those members' positions and not their party determine policy.

This may not seem to be a significant difference, yet that is where the revolving gridlock theory truly begins to differ from the others. The major difference is that the election of a unified government—a Democratic President and Congress, for example—need not lead to policy shifts unless the election dramatically shifts congressional preferences as it did in 1980. In fact, as we argue in the next chapter, the election of Clinton in place of Bush was not accompanied by a correspondingly significant change in Congress, and the Clinton 1993 budget package—especially the tax increase—cost the Democrats their House and Senate majorities. Below, we briefly outline the reasons why scholars and other observers have believed that divided government causes gridlock, and why unified government ends it.

Studies of Divided Government

With the election of George Bush in 1988, the President was a Republican for the fifth time in the last six elections, whereas the House was still Democratic. Divided government had become the normal state of affairs in American politics. Electoral scholars were not surprised by the results because, as Rosenstone (1983) had shown, a generic Republican candidate would always beat a generic Democrat at the presidential level, and a host of congressional scholars, most notably Gary Jacobson (1990), have shown that Democrats will win House elections, ceteris paribus.[5] The Bush victory did, however, produce one surprise. Although divided government at both the federal and state levels had been common in the post–World War II era (Fiorina 1996), scholars and commentators began to see such government as a problem. James Sundquist (1988) was arguably the first to elaborate this theme by claiming that divided government was inefficient and irresponsible; and, because it was apparently here to stay, he further argued that we needed a new theory of governance. Other scholars followed suit, roughly divided into two groups: those who disliked and condemned divided government and those who more objectively examined why Americans elected divided governments and what it meant. The Committee on the Constitutional System, Lloyd Cutler (1988), and Ginsburg and Shefter (1990) fall into the former category. Cutler believed that divided government increased budget deficits whereas Ginsburg and Shefter partly attributed the deficit, trade and foreign policy problems, and increased congressional investigation of the executive to divided government. The *Congressional Quarterly* and the *National Journal* quickly picked up on this issue and other journalists followed suit. Thus by the time of the 1992 election divided government had become part of the normal vocabulary of American politics. In fact, in October 1992, a majority of Americans felt that a unified government would be better than divided government. (That the question was even asked demonstrates the attention now being paid to this issue.) Bill Clinton's victory in 1992 ended twelve consecutive years of divided government and the issue faded from the media spotlight, only to reemerge to some extent in 1995.

Leadership and Gridlock

Another tier of literature on the Bush presidency arose when scholars began to assess the lack of policy achievement during the Bush years. These reassessments focus on leadership, presidential style, and the organizational ability of the President. This kind of critique has deep roots in political science; leading works in the field are Richard Neustadt's *Presidential Power* (1960); Fred Greenstein's *The Hidden-Hand Presidency: Eisenhower as Leader* (1982); Tom Cronin's *The Presidency Reappraised* (1977) and *Rethinking the Presidency* (1982); and Terry Moe's work on the institutionalized presidency (1985, 1993). In all of these works the focus is on determining the bases of presidential power, the President's bargaining style, his standing in public opinion, and the way he organizes his White House staff and the cabinet. The sum of these various factors can in a sense give some indication of the quality of presidential leadership.

We do not deny that such variables have an effect on a presidency and on the President's electoral chances. We do, however, argue that most of these studies undervalue the role of the preferences of members of Congress and the use of supermajority institutions in determining presidential policy success. To be sure, most scholars adopting this approach mention that President Bush faced Democratic Congresses, and Neustadt goes so far as to point out that Presidents get elected on the basis of coalitions that have little to do with the policy problems they face. Heclo (1977), Greenstein, and Cronin point to the President's relationship to the bureaucracy as a crucial element in presidential leadership, and we do not deny a role for bureaucratic interests in determining policy. We differ in that our emphasis is on the President's role as a proposer of policy and as a frequent user, either by threat or action, of a supermajority institution—the veto. And we claim that congressional preferences, the location of the status quo policy, and the proposed policy's location are the more-important determinants of what is called "presidential success." Our argument is somewhat more consistent with Steve Skowronek's contention (1993) that the political opportunities of the time shape the President's policymaking ability; we differ in that we specify congressional preferences and supermajority institutions as the main variables affecting presidential ability. In this way, we are sympathetic to Charles Jones's work (1994), which seeks to place the presidency in the larger political context of a constitutionally separated system.

A good example of a work that has a different focus from our own is Bert Rockman's essay on the Bush presidency (1991). Rockman asks three questions in his essay: "First, what are a president's inheritances or legacies, and how do these constrain him . . . ? Second, how does the president relate to the presidency as a corporate enterprise? The third question asks how the president carries out his personal leadership role" (3). Answering these questions allows Rockman to assess the Bush presidency and to conclude that "George Bush showed himself to be an effective maintaining president" (31).

Other analysts of the Bush presidency speak of copartisanship (Jones 1991, 1994); the cooperative style of leadership (Quirk 1991); and the "Let's Deal President" (Campbell 1991). Each of these analyses starts with some form of the "President as leader" premise and each comments on the 1990 budget deal. We will turn to two of these explanations to show how they differ from ours.

Jones (1991), after reviewing the events leading up to the first Bush budget deal (the one that failed), argues: "Neither Bush nor congressional leaders were seemingly prepared for this outcome, in spite of signals that it might occur. . . . To propose increasing taxes and cutting programs is to touch the nerve ends of party differences. The achievement of getting a plan at all was overshadowed by its defeat on the House floor" (61). He concludes his analysis with: "Focusing only on the delay involved, or the compromise made, or the stalemate that results, fails to acknowledge the change in politics that has occurred" (64). Again we agree with much of what Jones has to say, especially the emphasis on the use of the presidential veto and the nature of the bargaining between the President and the Congress. The revolving gridlock theory, however, places a greater emphasis on the preferences of individual members and on the fact that the final policy is decidedly within the gridlock region. Moreover, the edges of this region were determined by conservative Democrats as part of a liberal coalition, once Bush had agreed not to veto all tax increases.

Colin Campbell (1991) attributes much of the budget debacle to the President's strategic errors, which were not simply errors in judging the preferences of the Republicans in Congress. "He [Sununu] then proceeded to fuel the suspicions of the Democrats who feared that the 'no preconditions' pledge might constitute a trap forcing them to come forward with proposals for new taxes that the administration would then bat down" (214). In short, the President's staff had not been unified and disciplined in regard to the 1990 budget; thus the debacle. Paul Quirk (1991) argues that: "The results on the deficit under Bush would indicate whether a moderate, pragmatic president pursuing a cooperative strategy would get a better result [than Reagan]" (77). Quirk argues that in the budget deal Bush was too flexible about ends while being rigid regarding means. Specifically, he argues that Bush was flexible about deficit reduction as an end and rigid in regard to the means, especially in regard to capital gains (75–77). "While seeking to achieve or at least project that reduction, Bush declined to modify his stand on taxes" (77). Quirk characterizes the final budget deal in this way: "Agreement had been reached, not by resolving differences in a manner that served long-term common interests, but by sweeping difficult choices under the rug" (79).

Note that in both Campbell's and Quirk's interpretations the President had made strategic errors in tactics (Campbell) and in bargaining (Quirk). Our view is that given the status quo on taxes and expenditures, especially entitlements, there was no majority in Congress for either serious tax increases or expenditure cuts, and thus interpretations using leadership strategies and tactics to explain the policy results are flawed. President Bush, given the preferences of his party, should have been even more rigid on the tax side as a means to deficit reduction. His flexibility on taxes cost him the original budget deal and left him with a party that was uncommitted to his candidacy during the 1992 election. The final budget deal was passed by the Democratic majority and emphasized tax increases over entitlement reductions. In short, our view is that leadership, although certainly an important concept, is hard to define and extremely limited as an explanatory variable once context has been taken into account. In regard to divided government, these leadership essays all focus on cooperation and either explicitly or implicitly argue that good choices can lead to results even under divided government.[6]

Given the above views regarding divided government and leadership, many political scientists, journalists, and insiders felt that electing a unified government with decent leadership would get the country moving. Those who had argued that divided government caused irresponsibility and was unrepresentatitive believed that the 1992 election would result in an end to gridlock. Clinton's campaign had featured an end-of-gridlock theme and his State of the Union Address in 1993 did the same. Democratic members of Congress hailed an end to gridlock; the result would be reduced deficits, fair and comprehensive health care policy, campaign finance reform, an increase in environmental legislation, tax cuts for the middle class, a family leave act, and many other cherished aims. Why did they believe that this would all happen? With the President and the Congress representing the same party, preferences are aligned, and both the legislative and executive branches have incentives to cooperate because policy success leads to electoral success. The veto pivot shifts to the "correct" side of the policy space (from right to left in 1992), and the President has the good fortune to lead a majority rather than a minority party. All this would be true if the election had resulted in the alignment of presidential and congressional preferences. If the preferences are not aligned and policy proposals are too far from the median voter's preferences, then the President's programs will fail and gridlock or the perceived failure of presidential leadership will result. Furthermore, if the preferences of Congress have not shifted and the President chooses to avoid proposing anything that a majority doesn't initially favor, gridlock again ensues. We claim in the next chapter that the congressional elections of 1992 did not shift preferences in Congress—and thus the likelihood of major policy change was slight, regardless of the fact of unified government.

Elections and Legislator Preferences

As we highlighted in Chapter 2 and have emphasized in Chapters 3 and 4, it is our belief that the preferences of members of Congress, along with the institutions in which they operate, determine policy outcomes at the federal level. The most effective way to change these preferences is by replacing the members themselves in elections. Elections give voters a chance to respond to the policies (or to the lack thereof) that legislators have enacted in the U.S. republican system. Only with major shifts in the preferences of congressional members can we expect breaks from gridlock.

One way to compare the membership of Congress over time is to examine how members have voted on a variety of issues in each Congress. As discussed previously, interest groups such as the ADA publish scores that demonstrate how liberal or conservative members are in a particular year. Because these scores are based on different votes every year, scholars have attempted to find ways to make vote comparisons over time. Keith Poole and Howard Rosenthal (1991a, 1997) have studied immense numbers of votes from all Congresses to gain some sense of voting over time. Groseclose, Levitt, and Snyder (1996) attempt to adjust the ADA scores to make them consistent over time. They generate what can be called "real" ADA scores.

In our Appendix, we include graphs of these real ADA scores over time for the House of Representatives. These scores are meant to provide a better picture of how elections and politics over time have led to congressional members' changing preferences. A quick glance across these graphs lends great support to the revolving gridlock theory that we have presented in the previous chapters. As the first graph (Figure A.1) illustrates, prior to the 1980 elections, the real ADA scores are seen to be basically flat, with legislators widely dispersed from liberal to conservative.

The 1980 elections featured a shift to the right (toward lower ADA scores). The 1981 budget deal divided the Democratic Party in the House, with southern Democrats supporting the Reagan budget. By 1982, the real ADA scores appear to be more bipolar than flat. There is a cluster of conservative Republicans at the low end, with liberal and moderate Democrats making up a second, though more diverse, lump on the high end. In between these two extremes are the moderate Republicans and conservative Democrats, typically from the South. In Chapter 3 we claimed that the conservative Republicans held together as a group whereas the Democrats were more divided; and some Republicans from moderate districts needed to support less-conservative positions in 1982 to retain their seats. This would explain the distribution of ADA scores shown in Figure A.2. The pivotal members necessary to break gridlock, given the bipolar nature of this distribution, are more spread apart than prior to the 1980 elections. This leads to a larger region of gridlock, where no policy changes are possible.

This bipolar distribution continues to be evident in Figure A.3, showing real ADA scores from 1984. Due to the lack of a center, it is not surprising that middle ground was difficult to find and that politics became more contentious. With the rise of budgetary politics, the liberal and conservative camps became more divided and pronounced. Some middle ground was found in 1986, as the tax laws were put into place, although this period is still shown to be somewhat bipolar by the real ADA scores (see Figure A.4).

As the figures in the Appendix illustrate, this divided and divisive period continued through Reagan's last years and through the Bush interregnum (1986–1992). In the next chapter, we will show how the 1992 elections led to very few changes in the preferences of members of Congress. Note the similarities between the distribution of real ADA scores in 1992 and those in 1993 (see Figures A.7 and A.8). With our contention that these preferences and the supermajority institutions of the veto and the filibuster help determine policy, it should then not be surprising that gridlock would continue into the Clinton presidency.

NOTES

1. See Cox and Kernell 1991, Jacobson 1990, and Fiorina 1996.

2. See, in particular, Cutler 1987 and 1988; Sundquist 1988, 1993, and 1995; Ginsburg and Shefter 1990; Mayhew 1991; and Jones 1994. On a more technical note, see Alt and Lowrey 1994, Krehbiel 1996, and Epstein and O'Halloran 1996.

3. The 1990 Budget Enforcement Act shifted attention from the Gramm-Rudman-Hollings fixed deficit targets to adjustable deficit targets. The idea was to treat deficit problems caused by the economy (downturns) differently than problems caused by legislation. Roughly, the three main features of this act were: (1) capping the discretionary budget (both authorities and outlays) through Budget Caps; (2) Pay-As-You-Go rules for revenue and direct spending; and (3) budget rules for direct and guaranteed loans. See Collender 1991 for additional details. For an excellent analysis of microbudgeting aspects of PAYGO and Budget Caps, see Cogan, Muris, and Schick 1994.

4. This is related to the phenomenon known as Fenno's Paradox (Fenno 1975). John Hibbing and Elizabeth Theiss-Morse (1995) present this type of argument in a more general form, leading to a judgment of Congress as a "public enemy," with survey analysis to support their case.

5. See also Erikson 1989 and Fiorina 1991b.

6. Hibbing and Theiss-Morse's recent work (1995) argues that citizens want leaders with strong principles, who are noncompromisers. Thus Bush would have been better off to not have compromised on the 1990 budget.

5

Unified Gridlock

Does unified government bring about policy change or unified gridlock? The theory laid out in Chapter 2 is strongly supported by the years of divided government of the Reagan and Bush presidencies. The institutional structures of government, including the filibuster and the veto, along with the individual preferences of members of Congress, have led to policy gridlock. This gridlock has been exacerbated by the specter of continued budget deficits. An analysis of the unified government of the Clinton administration and the Democrat-controlled 103rd Congress provides a more substantial test of the revolving gridlock theory, set against competing theories predicting that unified party control would be sufficient in its votes and vision to overcome partisan gridlock. In this chapter we will analyze the major policy proposals made by President Clinton in his first two years in office. We will focus on the gridlock region and the pivotal members of Congress, leading to firm predictions about the results of these proposals. Across the board, the compromises that were struck by congressional members and the final policy results provide strong support for the revolving gridlock theory.

We will analyze two types of policy that were proposed during the first two years of the Clinton presidency: (1) legislation in which only simple majority votes in the House and Senate are required and Clinton is to the left of the floor median; and (2) legislation in which the President is to the left of the floor median and a supermajority is required in the Senate. This second category is broken into two parts: old legislation in which a Republican veto kept the status quo policy to the right of the floor median, and new legislative proposals in which the status quo is defined to be the lack of the proposed programs. We will analyze the Clinton 1993 budget reconciliation proposal and the North American Free Trade Agreement (NAFTA) as examples of the first type of policy. We will analyze motor voter registration and family leave as examples of old legislation requiring supermajorities for passage. And we will investigate the stimulus package, national service, and health care as examples of new policies that also require supermajorities, in which the filibuster pivot voters are crucial. With the first type of legislation, we predict that the policy proposals will shift toward the floor median voter, whereas in each of the cases of the second type of legislation we predict that policy proposals will shift toward the filibuster pivot position. In a later section we will analyze the President's influence over votes. Because each of these predictions, as well as the question of the President's influence, hangs on first locating Senators and House members on a left-right scale, we first turn to establishing such a continuum.

Legislators' Preferences

Our strategy in previous chapters regarding a left-right continuum was to use the standard or adjusted Americans for Democratic Action (ADA) scores. In this chapter we will vary that strategy to show that our argument is robust. That is, if we use different measures of liberalism-conservatism and still get the same median Representatives and Senators, then (1) our use of ADA scores is justified and (2) our explanation holds irrespective of the measure used.

One non-ADA strategy for determining Senators' preferences is to choose a legislative arena—say, environmental politics—and to use the League of Conservation Voters index to array the members. We could repeat this procedure for other legislative arenas such as labor and small business. This method poses problems in that some legislation we might want to study encompasses several dimensions that cannot be isolated in any one vote or set of votes. Budget reconciliation, for example, features grazing rates, gas taxes, agricultural assistance, and many other policy arenas that are not voted on separately. Therefore we have arranged Senators and Representatives in two ways. First, we took the members' scores for eighteen separate ratings, converted them such that the lowest scores are conservative and the higher scores are liberal, and then averaged across all eighteen measures, ranking the members from conservative to liberal.[1] Second, we took the same eighteen measures, calculated which five or six Senators and Representatives were closest to the median on each rating scale, and tabulated the frequency of their median positions; for example, Charles Robb (D., Va.) was at or near the median on four of these issue measures. Tables 5.1 and 5.2 give these frequency measures for the 103rd Congress.[2] For the Senate we also calculated the filibuster pivot. Table 5.3 shows the liberal-to-conservative rankings of Senators in the 103rd Congress, based on their combined scores on these eighteen measures in the 102nd Congress. And Table 5.4 shows the liberal-to-conservative rankings of Senators in the 103rd Congress based on ADA scores, for a comparison.

The findings are hardly surprising to anyone familiar with the U.S. Congress. The Senate frequency measure in Table 5.1 reveals results one would expect to find in looking for median members of Congress. Democrats with three or more ratings as median were primarily from southern or border states (nine of twelve), with the others being from the Midwest (Nebraska) or the Southwest (Arizona and New Mexico). The four Republicans in this category were Packwood (Ore.), Cohen (Maine), Specter (Pa.), and Jeffords (Vt.). The most liberal and conservative Senators from Table 5.3 do not show up on the frequency scale.

TABLE 5.1   Frequency Indexed in Median Group (103rd Senate)

Frequency	Name
7	Nunn
5	Exon, Ford, Packwood
4	Breaux, Cohen, DeConcini, Heflin, Hollings, Johnston, Robb, Specter
3	Bingaman, Bumpers, Jeffords, Shelby
2	Boren, Bradley, Byrd, Chafee, Conrad, D'Amato, Hatfield, Pryor, Reid, Smith
1	Fourteen others

Frequency is the number of ratings in which this Senator appeared in the group of five to seven Senators at or near the median-rated member. Ratings used were: AAUW, ACLU, ACU, ADA, ASC, BIPAC, CCUS, CFA, COPE, LCV, NAM, NCSC, NEA, NFIB, NFU, PCCW, TEAM, UAW.

TABLE 5.2   Frequency Indexed in Median Group (103rd House)

Frequency	Name
9	Charles Wilson
8	Michael Andrews
7	Dave McCurdy
5	Sherwood Boehlert, Chet Edwards, Lee Hamilton, Joseph McDade, Stephen Neal, J. Pickle
4	Glen Browder, Robert Cramer, Dan Glickman, Timothy Roemer
3	Tom Bevill, James Bilbray, M. Carr, Gary Condit, George Darden, Glenn English, Larry LaRocco, William Lipinski, Marilyn Lloyd, Ronald Machtley, Constance Morella, Norman Sisisky, Ike Skelton, Christopher Smith, John Tanner
2	Cooper, Derrick, Dooley, Fish, Gibbons, Gordon, Leach, Moran, Murtha, Ortiz, Sarpalius, Slattery, Spratt, Whitten
1	Fifty-five others

Frequency is the number of ratings in which this House member appeared in the group of eleven members at or near the median-rated member. Ratings used were: AAUW, ACLU, ACU, ADA, ASC, BIPAC, CCUS, CFA, COPE, LCV, NAM, NCSC, NEA, NFIB, NFU, PCCW, TEAM, UAW.

As can be seen in Table 5.3, the averaged scores show that roughly the 38th to the 52nd Senators are in the interval from the filibuster pivot to the floor median. There are nine Democrats in this region: seven are from southern and border states, with one each from Nebraska and Arizona. The five Republicans come from Oregon (two), Maine, Pennsylvania, and Rhode Island. The most conserv-

TABLE 5.3 Preference Ordering of Senators (103rd), Liberal to Conservative (high numbers are more liberal, combining eighteen ratings)

Left of Median			Right of Median	
Wellstone	91.0		Johnston	61.5
Sarbanes	90.8		Nunn	60.7
Metzenbaum	90.6		Cohen	57.4
Leahy	90.5		Specter	56.5
Simon	90.3		Breaux	56.5
Levin	89.8		Packwood	53.7
Kennedy	89.2		Hollings	53.7
Harkin	88.6		Chafee	51.0
Akaka	88.4		Heflin	50.9
Moynihan	88.3	About 2/5th pivot →	Boren	47.3
Wofford	87.4		Shelby	46.8
Kerry	87.1		Durenberger	45.6
Mikulski	86.7		D'Amato	42.3
Riegle	86.5		Danforth	29.8
Lautenberg	86.1		Roth	29.3
Biden	85.7		Bond	27.5
Rockefeller	85.1		Murkowski	26.4
Pell	85.0		Gorton	25.8
Mitchell	84.9		Kassebaum	25.3
Glenn	84.9		Grassley	24.5
Sasser	84.7		Warner	22.8
Baucus	83.2		McCain	21.5
Bradley	82.6		Coats	20.6
Inouye	82.5		Thurmond	19.0
Dodd	80.6		Simpson	18.7
Daschle	80.5		Cochran	17.6
Kerrey	79.8		Brown	16.9
Byrd	78.9		Smith	15.9
Kohl	77.0		Mack	15.8
Bryan	77.0		Burns	15.5
Bingaman	76.9		Pressler	15.3
Graham	75.5		Lugar	14.9
Lieberman	75.4		Domenici	14.0
Reid	75.4		McConnell	14.0
Bumpers	74.3		Lott	12.9
Conrad	72.8		Hatch	12.3
Pryor	71.8		Dole	12.3
Jeffords	70.3		Craig	10.5
Robb	70.0		Wallop	10.4
Ford	69.0		Gramm	9.1
Exon	67.9		Nickles	8.3
Hatfield	62.7		Helms	7.1
DeConcini	61.6			

Ratings used were: AAUW, ACLU, ACU, ADA, ASC, BIPAC, CCUS, CFA, COPE, LCV, NAM, NCSC, NEA, NFIB, NFU, PCCW, TEAM, UAW.

TABLE 5.4   ADA Ordering of Senators (103rd), Liberal to Conservative (high numbers are more liberal, using 1993 ADA scores)

Left of Median			Right of Median	
Wellstone	100		Ford	60
Metzenbaum	100		Byrd	55
Feingold	100		Hollings	55
Sarbanes	95		Chafee	55
Leahy	95		Exon	50
Levin	95		Johnston	45
Lautenberg	95		Nunn	45
Kohl	95		Specter	45
Boxer	90		Roth	45
Kennedy	90	About 2/5th pivot →	Cohen	40
Harkin	90		Breaux	40
Akaka	90		Packwood	35
Moynihan	90		Heflin	35
Kerry	90		Shelby	35
Bradley	90		D'Amato	35
Murray	90		Danforth	35
Moseley-Braun	85		Kassebaum	35
Simon	85		Bond	25
Wofford	85		Stevens	25
Mikulski	85		Murkowski	20
Pell	85		Gorton	20
Mitchell	85		Grassley	20
Glenn	85		Coats	20
Baucus	85		Simpson	20
Inouye	85		Burns	20
Feinstein	85		Domenici	20
Riegle	80		McCain	15
Biden	80		Brown	15
Bumpers	80		Smith	15
Conrad	80		McConnell	15
Sasser	75		Faircloth	15
Dodd	75		Hutchison	13
Daschle	75		Warner	10
Kerrey	75		Thurmond	10
Robb	75		Mack	10
DeConcini	75		Pressler	10
Durenberger	75		Lugar	10
Campbell	75		Dole	10
Rockefeller	70		Coverdell	10
Bingaman	70		Gregg	10
Pryor	70		Helms	10
Boren	70		Bennett	5
Graham	65		Kempthorne	5
Lieberman	65		Lott	5
Mathews	65		Hatch	5
Hatfield	65		Craig	5
Dorgan	65		Wallop	5
Bryan	60		Gramm	5
Reid	60		Nickles	5
Jeffords	60		Cochran	0

ative Senators are to no one's surprise Helms (N.C.), Nickles (Okla.), Gramm (Tex.), and Wallop (Wyo.). The most liberal are all Democrats—Kennedy (Mass.), Metzenbaum, and Wellstone.

In Table 5.4, we included the same type of listing of Senators, this time using only ADA scores. The findings are remarkably similar. Again the same names show up as the most liberal and most conservative. And those near the filibuster pivot point are again Republicans and southern Democrats—Breaux (D., La.), Cohen, Heflin (D., Ala.), Packwood, and Roth (R., Del.). To calculate exactly how similar our combined measure of eighteen ratings was to the commonly used ADA ratings, we looked at the correlation between measures. The coefficient of correlation between our measure and the ADA measure over the same time period was 0.98 and between our measure and Roll Call was –0.82, where any numbers near 1 and –1 represent almost identical measures. Our ranking of Congress on a left-right continuum thus appears to be robust when tested against different measures of liberalism and conservatism.

It is not surprising that members of Congress can be aligned from liberal to conservative consistently across a broad range of topics. Poole and Rosenthal (1997) study every roll call vote taken in Congress and find that a single dimension can account for about three-fourths of all voting decisions. Krehbiel (1997, esp. chaps. 7, 8) gives an excellent review of why a simple pivotal voter model along a single dimension might not explain policy outcomes, due to factors such as partisanship, agenda setting, and presidential persuasion. His findings and his conclusion that the model predicts well in the face of many obstacles testifies to the robustness of the use of the single-dimensional model. These studies, along with our compilation and comparison of various rating systems, lends credence to the view that members of Congress can be modeled as having preferences along a single-dimensional continuum.

Given the establishment of such a continuum, we can begin to see who should be influential in making the deals necessary to break gridlock. Due to the election of a Democratic President, movement to the left on policy would be constrained in the 103rd Congress by those members at or near the two-fifths pivot, as shown in Tables 5.3 and 5.4. This represents a loosening of constraints due to the removal of the presidential veto—because Clinton would sign some legislation that Bush had vetoed. However, in order to secure major policy shifts, Bill Clinton would have had to come to office with like-minded members of Congress. This was certainly not the case given the 1992 elections. Figure 5.1 illustrates the changes in the gridlock region accompanying those elections.

The 103rd Senate had thirteen new members (including the winners of special elections like Senator Feinstein of California), seven of whom were Democrats and six Republicans. In the actual 1992 Senate elections, four seats changed parties—two Democratic incumbents were defeated, as were two Republican incumbents—with each party holding its open seats. Thus there was no change in party advantage—the Democrats went into the 103rd Senate elections with fifty-seven seats

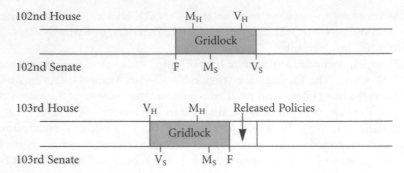

FIGURE 5.1   The 1992 Elections

and they came out with fifty-seven seats. The thirteen new members arrayed from left to right were two liberal Democrats (Boxer, Calif., and Moseley-Braun, Ill.); two moderate-to-liberal Democrats (Murray, Wash., and Dorgan, N.Dak.); two moderate Democrats (Feinstein, Calif., and Feingold, Wis.); and Ben Campbell (Colo.), the most conservative Democrat elected. The new Republicans ranged from moderate (Bailey-Hutchison, Tex., and Gregg, N.H.) to conservative (Bennett, Utah; Kempthorne, Idaho; and Faircloth, N.C.), with Cloverdell (Ga.) in between. Thus the thirteen new members fell on either side of Senator Campbell—who became a Republican in the next Congress—creating no shift right or left from the 102nd to the 103rd Senate. More importantly, given the institutional structure of the filibuster, all six of the newly elected Republicans looked to be to the right of the filibuster pivot (as shown in Table 5.4), and would therefore be a constraint on policy movements to the left. In sum, Bill Clinton would face a 103rd Senate not any more favorable to his position than the 102nd Senate.

In the House, even though Clinton beat Bush, the Democrats' percentage of all votes fell to its lowest level since 1980. In 1988 they won 53.3 percent of the vote, in 1990 they won 52.9 percent, whereas in 1992 they won only 50.8 percent, the lowest since the Reagan landslide. They won 59.3 percent of all House *seats*, again their lowest total since 1980. From the 102nd to the 103rd House, the Democrats lost ten seats. Forty-three seats changed parties as follows: sixteen Democratic incumbents lost to Republican challengers, whereas only eight Republican incumbents lost to Democratic challengers. Ten open Democratic seats went Republican, whereas eight Democrats took open Republican seats. The Democrats who lost or left Congress after the 102nd Congress had an average ADA score of 67, and on average they had supported Republican Presidents 32 percent of the time. Democrat winners had slightly lower ADA scores and had supported Bush 35 percent of the time. Thus the Democrats who left Congress were slightly more liberal than those Democrats who retained their seats. The Republicans who replaced these Democrats were on average very conservative, with ADA scores of 15 to 20, about 50 points more conservative than the people they replaced.

In all, the Senate in this first unified government in many years was about where it had been in the divided and gridlocked government that had preceded it; the 103rd unified House was to the right of the previous House. President Clinton faced a Senate perhaps more willing to filibuster moves to the left *and* a more conservative House with ten more Republican seats and conservative Republicans at that. The distribution of preferences given "real" ADA scores can again be found in the Appendix (Figures A.7 and A.8). As can be easily seen, no major shift in preferences came in 1993 or 1994, with the distribution maintaining the form it had prior to the 1992 elections.

Nevertheless, the 1992 elections gave hope to many political commentators, scholars, and politicians who believed that unified Democratic governance would end gridlock. The Committee on the Constitutional System and the Brookings Institution sponsored a conference on February 24, 1993, the results of which are compiled in James Sundquist's volume *Beyond Gridlock?* (1993). Whereas the participants were mixed in their predictions, a number of them believed that politicians were in the best position in a long while to break gridlock. Thomas Mann noted that "the return of unified party government is especially significant in 1992 as contrasted with 1960 and 1976. This time it follows an extended period of divided government—and conflictual divided government, which was really quite different from earlier experiences" (Sundquist 1993, 13). Explaining why there had been gridlock in the past, Barbara Sinclair argued: "The short answer is mostly divided government. . . . Obviously, hard choices do not become easy when one party controls both the presidency and the Congress, but the differences are likely to be less fundamental and, crucially, blame for not dealing with the problems is much harder to dissipate" (41). Sundquist shared Mann's "optimistic outlook," asking, "If the government cannot succeed in the present configuration, when can it possibly ever succeed? As Joan Quigley, the former official astrologer, might have said, the stars are really aligned right for the next four years" (25). The view from the White House representative, Howard Paster, Clinton's assistant in charge of congressional relations, was equally rosy: "That we can now, with a Democratic majority on the Hill and a Democrat in the White House, govern successfully, I think will be borne out" (15). And former Representative Thomas Downey noted what many of his former colleagues in Congress were saying: "We have a Democratic president and there is really not much that we have to do now. Now that we have eliminated divided government we will have eliminated gridlock" (45–46). Two years later, many of the same participants returned for another discussion to explain what had gone wrong (Sundquist 1995), with the theme now being *Back to Gridlock?*

In the following sections we will discuss the major legislation attempted by the 103rd Congress. This analysis serves two purposes: to show with concrete examples that congressional policymaking is determined by individual preferences rather than by strong parties; and to demonstrate *unified gridlock,* in which the policy changes that are made are at most incremental, always being drawn away from the original proposals of Clinton and median members of the Democratic party in order to capture the median floor voter or the filibuster pivot.³ One view of a strong party theory would argue that the names we would see in the press would be near the Democratic median. Senators such as Glenn (Ohio) and Sasser (Tenn.) would be engaged with the party leadership in attempts to hold the party together to get enough votes for the passage of legislation, and policy would be moved to their preference points. The revolving gridlock theory argues that the names we will run across will be those of the crucial members at the institutional pivot points: Breaux, Boren (D., Okla.), and Nunn (D., Ga.) will be key players in legislation requiring a simple majority, whereas Senators such as Durenberger (R., Minn.) and Specter will play pivotal roles in votes where the filibuster can be used to halt the passage of legislation. The latter of these two possibilities is what we see time and again in looking through the individual pieces of legislation: the bills must be changed to accommodate the median or the filibuster pivots. Those proposals that do not move sufficiently to the right do not pass. Those that pass hardly represent an end to policy gridlock.

Policies Needing a Simple Majority for Passage

The 1974 Congressional Budget and Impoundment Control Act and various "fast track" procedures have limited the ability of Senators to filibuster some budget and trade bills. When the President supports such legislation, the constraint caused by a reduced "gridlock region" is that of a simple majority in both the Senate and the House. The median voters are thus pivotal. In the analysis that follows, we argue that initial Clinton proposals on the 1993 Budget Reconciliation Act and NAFTA needed to be modified to the right to appeal to these constraining pivotal members.

The 1993 Budget Reconciliation Act

On February 17, 1993, in his first State of the Union Address, President Clinton proposed an economic plan containing a wide array of budget cuts and tax increases. The original plan spelled out the tax increases in greater detail than it spelled out budget cuts (*New York Times*, February 18, 1993). The media focused on the proposals for taxing the rich and for instituting the BTU (British Thermal Unit) energy tax as the highlights of the plan because these taxes, together with additional corporate taxes, would generate an extra $236.2 billion over the next five years (*New York Times*, February 18, 1993). The administration claimed that the reconciliation bill would reduce the budget deficit by $500 billion over the coming five years, with new taxes accounting for over half of the proposed deficit reduction. The Clinton proposal squared well with liberals in his party. Taxes on the upper 1 percent of income earners pleased liberals; the BTU tax on all fuels pleased environmentalists; and the increase in corporate taxes and limits on the tax deductibility of executive pay also pleased the liberal wing of the party. Moreover, the spending cuts came mainly from defense and the federal bureaucracy ($160.8 billion), with another $60.3 billion in savings theoretically coming from reduced health care costs at no loss in quality. The left wing of the Democratic Party had long favored defense cuts and a national health care system.

Thus the President's initial policy was clearly at or near the median Democratic Party position in both the House and Senate. Proponents of the theory of divided government featuring strong parties would have to predict passage of this plan with little modification. The Democratic Party could act en bloc to get the policy passed and signed. However, this is not what happened. The final reconciliation budget differed from the original, decreasing the tax hike and increasing spending cuts.[4] And the major players forcing these changes were moderate Democrats such as Breaux and Boren. In the end no Republicans voted for the legislation. The changes were thus meant to accommodate the moderate Democrats who could threaten to join the Republicans to defeat the measure.

Following the Congressional Budget and Impoundment Control Act of 1974, budget reconciliation bills in the Senate were considered using majoritarian procedures. Unlike most other Senate legislation, reconciliation rules allow a majority to write binding orders on committees, forbid filibusters, limit debate to twenty hours, and ban the addition of nongermane amendments and extraneous provisions. President Clinton's 1993 budget did not need to prepare for the possibility of a Republican filibuster; rather, fifty votes for his bill as proposed would have allowed passage in the Senate.

The President's original energy tax proposals charged different taxes on various fuels depending upon how efficient they were at using BTUs. The original energy proposals drew criticism from expected sources such as the American Petroleum Institute. By the end of April newspapers were reporting that the President would not "recognize large parts of this tax plan by the time Democrats in Congress finish with it" (*New York Times*, April 30, 1993). Among the first changes were the President's investment tax credit worth $28 billion and the proposed 36 percent corporate tax rate (a 2 percent increase). The Chairs of the House Ways and Means Committee (Dan Rostenkowski; D., Ill.) and the Senate Finance Committee (Daniel P. Moynihan; D., N.Y.) eliminated the investment tax credit and reduced the corporate tax increase to 1 percent. Rostenkowski said, "I'm not going to fall on my sword for an ITC that no one wants" (*New York Times*, April 30, 1993).

The energy tax turned out to be the most controversial part of the President's proposed tax increases. Energy taxes have differing effects over regions depending on the type of fuel used and produced in those regions. Senators and Representatives from the Northwest did not like fuel taxes on oil used for home heating, whereas farm-state Senators opposed fuel taxes on ethanol (made from corn) and western Senators opposed gasoline taxes because many of their constituents drove long distances to work. In addition, industries like aluminum that use large amounts of energy to produce their products organized in opposition to the BTU tax. In order to cope with the increasing opposition, the Clinton administration had by mid-May modified its plan in the following way: tax collection was shifted from utility to consumer, the farm use of diesel fuel was to be taxed at a lower rate, propane gas was to be taxed at a lower rate, and boat and jet fuel used in international travel were to be exempted. The hydroelectric power and oil industries, among others, were still seeking exemptions in early June.

The House passed a reconciliation bill in early June by a vote of 219 to 213, but many Democrats from energy and farm states voted for the bill only after being told that it would be amended in the Senate. These Democrats had good reason to believe that the bill would be modified there. On May 20, a bipartisan coalition led by Senator Boren and including the Democrat Johnston of Louisiana and the Republicans Cohen of Maine and Danforth of Missouri proposed an alternative budget plan that junked the energy tax. Thus going into the Senate the President's plan faced severe opposition first on the Finance Committee where Boren was a swing vote and then on the floor where it seemed quite possible that eight Democrats could side with the Republicans and vote down any bill that included a fuel tax. On June 7, 1993, the majority leader, Senator Mitchell (D., Maine), and the Finance Chair, Senator Moynihan, met with the President and told him that his reconciliation budget was in danger of being killed in the Senate due to opposition to the energy tax provisions. The next day Secretary of the Treasury Lloyd Bentsen revealed on the McNeil-Lehrer News Hour that the energy tax emerging from the Senate wouldn't be based on BTUs. By June 10 President Clinton was considering a proposal by Senator Breaux to replace the $70-odd billion energy tax with a $40 billion tax on gasoline and a $30 billion cut in Medicare. The $40 billion gas tax would be raised by taxing an additional eight cents per gallon. This new proposal immediately generated a reaction from the liberal wing of the party. Senator Rockefeller (D., W.Va.) and Representative Mfume (D., Md.), the head of the Black Caucus, objected to both the gas tax and the cuts in Medicare. Representative Waxman (D., Calif.) said, "It seems everybody is supposed to jump through hoops to satisfy conservative Democrats. But they have to face the fact that there are other Democrats who won't go along with more cuts" (1993 *Congressional Quarterly Weekly Report*, 1463).

While the energy tax bill was being jettisoned, there was activity across the board in the Senate on the President's reconciliation budget. Conservative Democrats were trying: (1) to decrease the individual tax rates for 1993; (2) to decrease the tax rates for Social Security recipients; and (3) to increase cuts in Medicare and Medicaid. The final package passed in the Senate represented moderate Democratic positions. The energy tax ended up as an additional tax on gasoline of 4.3 cents per gallon, which raised only $22 billion as opposed to the $72 billion proposed by the President's BTU tax. The President had proposed that Social Security payments be exempt from taxation on annual family incomes of $32,000 and under; Congress raised this to $40,000. The top individual income tax rate was set at 33½ percent, down from the President's 36 percent. In regard to spending, the Senate cut the provision for empowerment zones, cut Medicare payments to providers (for $67 billion in savings), did not ease the eligibility requirements for food stamps ($7 billion), and reduced Medicaid expenditures by $8 billion. In short, the Senate version of the reconciliation budget was more conservative than the President's bill—tax increases were significantly reduced while expenditures were cut deeper.

The House-Senate conference began work on the final reconciliation bill in June and completed its work in early August. The final package limited the energy tax to a 4.3-cent tax on a gallon of gasoline, made a $55.8-billion cut in Medicare payments, and raised the Social Security tax kick-in to $44,000 for couples and $34,000 for individuals. Thus moderate and conservative Democrats were able to eliminate the BTU energy tax and set limits on social spending, moving policy away from the President's original proposal. The Senate bill was more centrist than the final bill as liberals led by the Black Caucus, Bernie Sanders (Indep., Vt.), Henry Waxman, and others reinstated funding for enterprise zones, slightly reduced the Senate cuts in Medicare and Medicaid, expanded the earned income tax credit, and passed a $2.5 billion increase in food stamp funding. On the whole it seems clear that the final result was considerably more conservative than the President's original proposal.

The final bill that passed Congress and was signed by the President bore a remarkable resemblance to the bill that had passed in the 101st Congress in 1990. Both bills called for savings of half a trillion dollars over five years. Both contained tax increases on individual incomes in the highest brackets and spending cuts on defense. The same areas that were left alone in 1990 maintained their untouchable status in 1993. This is no surprise. Because the members of Congress and their positions did not change dramatically between 1990 and 1993, the bill outcomes are expected to be in the same range as before. The difficulty that Clinton faced, however, was that some of these tax increases and spending cuts were not merely extensions of the 1990 plan, but expansions of it. The taxing and spending cuts gouged deeper than before. As such, Clinton faced greater struggles in securing votes than would otherwise have been the case. Analysis of the 1994 election results shows that a vote for the Clinton budget deal was equivalent to the sacrifice of a congressional seat in a number of districts. Brady, Cogan, and Rivers (1995) find that those members in districts with low Clinton support in 1992 were severely hurt by casting votes in support of Clinton on the 1993 budget deal. These members were placed in a tight spot on the vote. If they voted against the President, the bill would be defeated and Democrats everywhere would be hurt for continuing gridlock.[5] If they voted for the budget, they could count on Clinton's support in the 1994 elections, if the President's endorsement could even be considered an asset in their reelection bids. As Clinton's popularity plummeted, the decision to vote against the majority of their constituents' preferences on the budget deal came to haunt these Democrats.

Without the support of most of the Democrats in Congress, Clinton's budget deal would have failed. The revolving gridlock theory predicts that without substantial changes in the preferences of members of Congress, major legislation is unlikely to succeed. In order to succeed, liberal or conservative proposals must be made more moderate by appealing to the preferences of Representatives and Senators in a narrow band near the median. Indeed, the 1993 budget proposals in the end were made more conservative than Clinton had initially intended in order to appeal to just these members. Nevertheless, the legislation was designed to make these members indifferent to voting for or against passage. They were made to gamble that a bid to support Clinton and bring an end to gridlock would make up for a budget vote that their constituents disfavored. The 1994 election results discussed in the next chapter show that this gamble did not pay off for many Democrats.

NAFTA

The North American Free Trade Agreement was negotiated by Ambassador Carla Hills during the Bush administration; thus the framework of the treaty had already been established when President Clinton took office. During his presidential election campaign, Clinton had said that he would support NAFTA if side agreements on labor and the environment could be reached. Clinton's original idea was to create North American labor and environmental commissions with the power to levy fines and sanctions. Under pressure from the Mexican and Canadian governments, the Clinton trade team relented and by mid-March Ambassador Mickey Kantor had told the Senate that the commissions should not have enforcement powers or extensive investigative authority (*Wall Street Journal*, March 15, 1993).

Clinton walked a tightrope on NAFTA; in order to pass the treaty he had to have Republican support, and such support would disappear if the side agreements on labor and environment were too tough. Even with the trade agreement being placed under the 1991 fast-track rules, thus eliminating the threat of a filibuster, the President was not guaranteed a simple majority. Yet without the tough side agreements, labor unions and environmental groups would oppose the treaty. The negotiations for side agreements began on March 17, 1993, and by mid-April Ambassador Kantor had agreed that the trinational commissions would neither have subpoena powers, nor be able to impose sanctions, nor have power to enforce their decisions. The commissions would serve as ombudsmen and work through moral suasion. This arrangement immediately met with opposition from the AFL-CIO and many environmental groups. Pressure from these groups led Mr. Kantor, in May, to propose trade sanctions as a last resort against persistent violators of laws protecting the environment and workers' rights. The Mexican and Canadian governments immediately rebuffed this proposal, claiming that such sanctions violated their sovereignty. On August 12, Kantor and the

Mexican and Canadian negotiators worked out a deal on the side agreements. The three countries agreed to create trinational commissions to deal with environ-mental and labor disputes. Disputes not resolved by the commissions would be forwarded to an arbitration panel with the power to recommend trade sanctions against Mexico and the United States. In the case of complaints against Canada, Canadian Courts would impose penalties.

Opponents led by Representative Richard Gephardt (D., Mo.) said that the side agreements: (1) failed to name a funding source for pollution cleanup along the U.S.-Mexican border; (2) did not go far enough to protect U.S. producers; and (3) did not include the possibility of trade sanctions against Mexico for failing to pay their workers a fair wage. The AFL-CIO president said that the agreements relegated workers' rights and the environment to commissions with no real power of enforcement (1993 *Congressional Quarterly Weekly Report*, 2212). It was clear from the reaction of Representative Gephardt and the AFL-CIO that the President had chosen a strategy to keep Republican votes and pick up moderate Democrats, rather than appeal to the Democratic party median.

In the weeks that followed, questions of funding border cleanups were an-swered and the amount and source of monies for worker retraining were debated. At one point President Clinton proposed a tax to provide the billions necessary for worker retraining. Minority whip Newt Gingrich (R., Ga.) immediately sent the President a note saying that House Republicans would not support NAFTA with such a provision in the enabling legislation, and the plan was dropped. In the crucial House vote, 132 Republicans voted for NAFTA along with 102 Democrats. The point is quite clear—Clinton's early support hinged on the cre-ation of the trinational commissions with subpoena powers and sanctions, and such a policy was not acceptable to the Republicans. At every stage of the game, from renegotiating the NAFTA treaty to the side agreements to funding pollution cleanup and worker retraining, Clinton and Kantor took positions that diverged from the center of their party in an attempt to keep the support of the Republicans and the moderate-to-conservative Democrats. The final treaty and the final vote clearly reflect this appeal to the floor median member's preferences.

In both of our cases addressing majority-win institutions—the 1993 budget reconciliation and the North American Free Trade Agreement—the President's original policy inclination was to the left of the floor median. In both cases the final policy output was close to the median floor position, with the President call-ing for support of these centrist policies. The budget proposal, which featured a $72 billion BTU energy tax, a 36 percent corporate tax rate, and relatively small spending cuts, was modified by eliminating the BTU tax and replacing it with a gasoline tax (raising only $22 billion), by cutting in half the corporate tax rate in-crease, and by greatly reducing Medicare and Medicaid payments. In both the House and Senate the crucial votes came from Senators and Representatives at or about the median—Breaux, Boren, Johnston, and DeConcini (D., Ariz.) in the Senate; and Stenholm (D., Tex.), Wilson (D., Tex.), and other conservative

Democrats in the House. When the Senate version of the act passed, it was liberals such as Rockefeller, Waxman, and Mfume who objected to the reduced taxes and decreased expenditures. The final bill gave liberals some cover by adding enterprise zones, additional food stamps funding, and an $8 billion cutback from the Senate's Medicare cuts, but the overall result clearly shows a rightward policy shift toward the floor median.

The negotiations on NAFTA followed the same pattern. The Clinton administration: (1) proposed, then rejected renegotiating NAFTA; (2) proposed creating trinational commissions on environmental and labor issues that had subpoena powers as well as the ability to apply sanctions and enforce them, then dropped meaningful sanctions, allowing Canada out completely; and (3) proposed a tax for funding worker retraining, and then also dropped that idea. At each stage pressure from Republicans, who asserted that they could not vote for a NAFTA with strong trinational commissions and new taxes, brought the policy closer to the floor median. On the final vote, Clinton sided against a majority of his party in order to get NAFTA through the Senate. On the budget vote the battle was solely within the Democratic Party, and the centrist Democrats—Breaux, Johnston, and Nunn—got most of what they wanted. On the NAFTA vote the treaty was made acceptable to Republicans and the winning votes came from moderate Democrats. In both cases it was the preferences of Senators and Representatives at or about the median that carried the day. Later in this chapter we will analyze the votes further to test this general thesis.

Old Legislation Vetoed by Republican Presidents

It is relatively easy to predict the outcome of legislation for which there exists a majority favoring the policy but not a supermajority sufficient to override a veto. For House members, the election of a Democratic President eliminates the veto threat for bills like family leave and motor voter registration; thus these bills will most likely easily pass. The Senate presents a more interesting case because there is still a filibuster pivot (i.e., a three-fifths supermajority is necessary), thus keeping the policy from drifting too far left. Here we would predict that if the President's policy is too liberal there will either be a filibuster or the credible threat of one, and the policy will have to be modified to break the filibuster.

Family Leave

The Family and Medical Leave Act (H.R. 1, S5) was introduced in the Congress on January 5, 1993; and on February 5, one month later, President Clinton signed the bill into law. The eight-year history of the bill is of some interest. Five times Senator Dodd (D., Conn.) had reported family leave laws from his committee and two of these had reached the White House only to be vetoed by President Bush. The original bill applied to businesses with as few as fifteen employees and granted leaves of from eighteen to twenty-six weeks. The first bill to make it to the White House (1990) raised the minimum number of employees to fifty (which exempts 95 percent of U.S. companies but covers about one-half of the work force) and reduced allowable leaves to twelve weeks. President Bush vetoed the bill and neither the House nor the Senate had enough votes to override the veto. In the 102nd Congress a bipartisan effort sponsored by Senators Dodd and Bond (R., Mo.) changed the family leave legislation to make it attractive to moderate Republicans. The deal exempted the top 10 percent of employees in each company, covered only workers who had worked over 1,250 hours the previous year, and allowed employers to demand medical opinions and certifications regarding leave. This bill passed the House and Senate, but was again vetoed by President Bush. The Senate overrode the veto 68 to 31, whereas the House narrowly sustained the veto 258 to 169.

The family leave bill introduced in 1993 thus had majority support in the House and a supermajority in the Senate sufficient to overcome a possible Republican filibuster. The Senate passed a bill similar to that of 1992 by a vote of 71 to 27, and the House approved the Senate version by 247 votes to 152. Democrats like Pat Williams (Mont.) claimed that passage signaled an end to gridlock. Note, however, that the bill had already been amended to accommodate moderate Republicans, and that the 1993 bill kept all those Bond-Dodd compromises and thus enjoyed the same amount of support as in 1992. Because the bill already had majority support from the previous Congress, the only question was whether a filibuster was possible, and given that the Senate had overridden the Bush veto in 1992 it was clear that a family leave law would pass. The only change from 1992 to 1993 was that the veto pivot had changed dramatically from anti–family leave to pro–, such that the House could pass the legislation with a majority and the Senate could invoke cloture and pass the legislation with sixty votes. Clearly the institutional arrangement allowing a two-thirds majority to override a veto affected results. The surprising result is that the bill wasn't strengthened again to the level of the bill that found its way to the White House in 1990. No longer were the changes between 1990 and 1992 needed to override a veto. The Family and Medical Leave Act had been modified to bring along Republicans in the previous Congress, and Clinton submitted that modified bill rather than a more liberal bill featuring lower numbers, longer leave, and paid leave, as many in his party would have preferred.

Motor Voter

On July 2, 1992, President Bush vetoed the so-called Motor Voter Registration Act, and on September 22 the Senate failed to override the veto. The newly elected 103rd House immediately reintroduced approximately the same bill (H.R. 2) and on January 27, 1993, the House Administration Committee cleared the way for floor consideration. The House voted for final passage on February 4, 1993, by a vote of 259 to 160. This bill made voter registration easier by tying registration to driver's license applications. In addition, the bill required states to provide uniform voter registration through the mail, and its most controversial proposal required that registration forms be made available at various state and federal offices that provide public assistance, such as welfare and unemployment outlets. Republicans in the House objected to the bill on the grounds that it would cost states money to administer the act, that the bill encouraged the registration of illegal aliens, and that the availability of registration materials was targeted to register potential Democratic voters.

The swift passage of the Motor Voter Registration Act in the House was not to be duplicated in the Senate, where the Republicans could threaten a filibuster. Democrats in the Senate led by Senator Ford (Ky.) claimed they had enough votes to cut off a filibuster, because they had garnered sixty-two votes in the attempt to override the veto in 1992. However, this time around Republican Senators knew that there would not be a Presidential veto to back them up. Republican leaders made good on their filibuster threat on March 5 when they mustered the votes to delay debate on the bill (52 to 36). The only Republican to vote to cut off the debate was Senator Hatfield (Ore.), who was a cosponsor. Ford was counting on moderate Republicans—Specter, Durenberger (Minn.), and Jeffords—to vote as they had in 1992, thereby providing the necessary cloture votes. Instead these Republicans, joined by Packwood, voted on March 9 to continue the debate. Over the eight days to final passage, Republican moderates won important concessions; the provision to require registration at welfare and unemployment offices was dropped as was a provision requiring the registration of some welfare recipients. With this reform won, five moderate Republicans supported the bill, and it passed the Senate 62 to 37.

The concession to the Republicans generated opposition from the head of the National Association for the Advancement of Colored People (NAACP), who said, "We can not support this bill now. No way" (1993 *Congressional Quarterly Weekly Report*, 664). House sponsor Al Swift (D., Wash.) regarded the concession as gutting the heart of the bill. Thus House-Senate negotiations over motor voter in conference began with a House bill to the left of the Senate version and a key provision of the bill in dispute. Key backers of the House bill threatened to withdraw support if the House conferees went along with the Senate version (1993 *Congressional Quarterly Weekly Report*, 837). The League of Women Voters and the American Civil Liberties Union voiced opposition to the Senate version of the bill. The only Republican threat, nevertheless a serious one, was that without dropping the public agency section the Republicans would be able to filibuster the bill, thus killing its chance for passage. Attention then turned to Senator Durenberger, who offered a "noncoercion clause" to satisfy his and other moderate Republicans' concerns about passing out registration forms at agencies dealing with the disabled and welfare recipients. The Senate version of the bill dropping the requirement for registration at unemployment compensation offices was retained. Thus the final conference version moved back toward the original House bill but not nearly as far back as the bill's sponsors preferred. To pass the legislation over a Senate filibuster, the Democratic leadership modified the bill to accommodate Republican Senators at the filibuster pivot. Thus it was Specter, Durenberger, Jeffords, and others who were able to move the bill toward their preferred position because of the filibuster. If Senate Rule XXII did not allow members of a minority to filibuster, the final Motor Voter Registration Act would clearly have been closer to the House version. Again we have a case where policy moves to the preferences of the key voter—in this case the group of Republican filibuster pivot voters.

New Legislation Requiring Supermajorities

In the case of both family leave and motor voter legislation, previous Congresses had passed bills only to see them vetoed by President Bush. Congress had previously modified the bills to meet pivotal voter preferences, and they became law under Clinton due to the loosening of institutional constraints. These circumstances, however, do not necessarily apply to new legislation introduced by President Clinton. We now turn to an analysis of the stimulus package, the national service bill, and health care to show that, even with new legislation, preferences and constraining institutions determine policy results.

The Jobs Bill

Shortly after his inauguration, President Clinton began to hint at a jobs stimulus package designed to get the economy going. The President's early discussion of the bill was not specific, and estimates of its costs ranged as high as $60 billion, as proposed by James Tobin, a Nobel economist working for the Clinton administration. In early February Secretary of Labor Robert Reich said there *would* be a stimulus package costing between $15 and $20 billion. During his State of the Union Address in 1993, President Clinton proposed a $16.3 billion package, with $4 billion going to unemployment benefits, $3 billion to highway programs, $2.5 billion for block grants to state and local governments, $1 billion for a summer youth program, $500 million for Head Start, and the rest for miscellaneous programs under $350 million apiece. The House immediately went to work on the Clinton "jobs bill," which moved forward as a supplemental appropriations bill. On March 9, 1993, the House Appropriations Committee passed the Clinton plan virtually unchanged. Conservative Democrats led by Stenholm met with the President to ask for a leaner package. Speaker Tom Foley (Wash.) called a March 11 meeting of the Democratic Caucus and after the meeting told the press that there was strong opposition to delaying or downsizing the jobs bill. The House voted on March 19 to approve the jobs bill at $16.3 billion; House leadership gave

Clinton credit for hardballing the conservative Democrats' attempts to change the bill (1993 *Congressional Quarterly Weekly Report*, 649).

The bill's fate in the Senate was another story. Even before the House had passed the bill, Senator Simpson (R., Wyo.) had promised that Republicans would filibuster the bill unless changes were made. Senator Byrd (D., W.Va.) made it clear that he would strongly defend the President's package; however, Democratic Senators Boren and Breaux were pushing to modify the President's proposal. Senator Byrd used an unusual tactic to wrap the bill in a suit of amendments by "treeing" the bill such that amendments to the bill could only be offered after the bill had been defeated. This maneuver clearly upset Republicans and kept Senate Democrats like Boren from proposing amendments to the bill. By late March the President had two problems: (1) moderate Democrats did not like the bill as it was and were being prevented from amending it, and (2) Republicans were united in opposition to the bill. The President responded by speaking out against Democrats who were overly concerned with the deficit (*Wall Street Journal*, March 24, 1993). During the period before spring recess, Republicans attacked the bill as pork for urban Democratic constituents; Byrd and liberal Democrats countered by railing against Republicans, whereas moderate Democrats sought compromises to ensure the bill's passage.

On March 25, 1993, Byrd offered his "tree" amendments, which essentially would have passed the Clinton proposal less $110 million for the Internal Revenue Service. This tactic put the jobs bill in the strongest position. If Republicans filibustered or if Democrats voted against Byrd they would appear to be directly opposing a new President, and thus continuing gridlock. Senator Boren responded by filibustering for more than four hours, keeping the bill from being voted on that week. Mitchell met with moderate Democrats on March 26, and after the meeting Boren and Breaux said that they could vote for the bill with administration assurance that some spending would be delayed. Other Democrats, however, were working to change the package, and the threat of a filibuster by the Republicans still loomed. A motion to table a Republican amendment cutting $104 million was defeated with help from Senator Kerry (D., Nebr.), clearly signaling to Mitchell that the bill was in trouble. This defeat led Senator Byrd to withdraw his "tree amendments," which opened the way for new amendments to pare the bill back. The question was, what would the compromise look like? All parties agreed on $4 billion for unemployment benefits; however, beyond that issue, nothing was clear. Democratic Senators Nunn, Kerry, Boren, and Breaux, among others, did not favor the $2.5 billion targeted to urban areas. Republicans were also divided on what a compromise bill should look like. On April 2, the Republicans, unhappy with the jobs bill as it was, filibustered and proceeded two more times to block Democratic attempts to move the bill to the floor. Democratic leaders threatened to keep the Senate in session until the bill got to the floor. The President appealed to the media, claiming that Republican gridlock was thwarting the economic recovery. For eight days the filibuster held, and on

April 6 the President sent word to the Hill that Mitchell could strike a deal that would drop the $1.8 billion in the package for Pell grants (*New York Times*, April 6, 1993). The liberal wing of the House responded by saying that they were wary of concessions to the moderate Senate Democrats.

The White House targeted three Republicans—Specter, D'Amato (N.Y.), and Jeffords—for wooing; but then, after finding that these stalwarts couldn't be wooed, blamed them for a faltering economy. By April 13, the President stepped up his attack on the Republicans, claiming that children's immunization programs were being lost because of the filibuster (*New York Times*, April 14, 1993). Three days later the President said he would be willing to compromise, and Senator Dole (R., Kans.) called Clinton to talk about the jobs bill. Mark Hatfield attempted to introduce a compromise package but the Republicans rejected it, and on April 20 a pared-down $15.4 billion jobs bill only garnered 52-to-46 approval with five Democrats defecting. It was clear that the new bill could not achieve the sixty votes necessary to beat a filibuster. President Clinton gave up on the bill on April 22, 1993, settling for a $4 billion extension of unemployment compensation.

The point is again clear—the President proposed a bill too far to the left of the filibuster pivot to pass. The ultimate result was that the bill pleased neither moderate Democrats nor the filibuster pivots. They preferred the status quo (the absence of a jobs bill) to the liberal jobs bill that had been proposed. Senator Byrd's attempt to maneuver the bill through the Senate solidified Republican opposition and disturbed key Democrats. Again, we have seen how preferences and constraining institutions are the primary factors responsible for policy results. Despite both the President's and Senator Byrd's many appeals for party unity, a strong partisan Congress did not emerge to support the jobs bill.[6]

National Service

Turning to national service legislation, we see the filibuster pivots demanding the same types of compromises to the right as we found with the jobs bill. During his presidential campaign, Clinton had promised to establish a national service program in which college graduates could pay off their loans by working in various service sectors. No one pressed the Clinton campaign team for the specifics of the plan, so the team used rhetoric such as: "Everyone will be able to get a college loan as long as they're willing to give something back in return" (Bill Clinton, Candidacy Announcement Speech, October 3, 1991).

After the election, the transition team began to work out the details of the plan. In an ambitious attempt to match the campaign rhetoric, the team initially developed a program that would give about $10,000 per year in educational awards to each participant. The program would start out with 25,000 participants at a projected cost of $650 million the first year, growing to cover over 100,000 participants by 1997. But in this time of budget cutting, the program was to be scaled back several times. In February, the OMB called for a 40 percent reduction to the program. In meetings with Democratic Representatives and Senators over the next few months, the discussions focused on how big a national service program would be likely to pass through Congress. Some Democrats voiced concerns that this program would undermine other federal education and aid programs. Veterans' groups argued that the size of the educational awards should not be higher than those given under the GI Bill. Because Clinton was already facing hostility from the military (due to his policy on integrating homosexuals into the military and to his own lack of service), a compromise was reached cutting the loan repayments to $5,000 a year.

When the national service bill was introduced in Congress and sent to committee in June, the program had already been cut to $389 million for 25,000 participants in the first year, with a slowly growing five-year authorization and a maximum loan repayment of $5,000 a year. The bill breezed through the House (275 to 152). But this toned-down program was still too liberal for many Republicans in the Senate, where the threat of a filibuster was frustrating the bill's supporters. When the bill reached the Senate floor, Nancy Kassebaum (R., Kans.) proposed an amendment that authorized the program for only two years at $100 million a year. To back up their position, Senators Dole and Kassebaum led a filibuster in late July. On July 29, a cloture vote showed that supporters were one vote short of ending the filibuster (59 to 41).

Bad publicity led some moderate Republicans (Packwood, Chafee [R., R.I.], Hatfield, and Specter) to move against the filibuster the following day. But this did not occur before a compromise was struck to appease these filibuster pivots. The national service program that passed the Senate on August 3 had been cut even further than the House bill. The Senate reduced the size of the education award to $4,725 a year, cut the initial number of participants to 20,000 at a first-year cost of $300 million, and authorized the program for only three years, down from the original five. The conference committee quickly agreed on the Senate bill as the compromise that would be able to get through both houses of Congress. It passed, and Clinton signed the bill into law as the National and Community Service Trust Act on September 21, 1993.

Had a strong-party model of legislative action been in effect, Clinton's meetings with median Democratic members would have led to a bill acceptable to the Democratic Party, and there would have been a filibuster standoff with the Republicans. Only after deals with the Republican leadership had been struck would the legislation pass. As an indication of the weakness of the parties, however, the deals were struck not with the Republican leadership but with the filibuster pivots. The compromises were just sufficient to gain the votes of a few filibustering Senators, those needed to give the sixtieth cloture vote.

The final piece of legislation to be examined in this chapter is that of health care.

Health Care[7]

The Clintons hoped that health care legislation would be the crown jewel of their early achievements. President Clinton involved First Lady Hillary Rodham Clinton in gathering information and formulating policy, using horror stories about the uninsured to make the case for the need for reform. Clinton argued that the objective of a balanced budget could only be achieved by controlling health care costs through a major overhaul of the health care system. The combined efforts of the first family brought the issue of health care to the forefront of the American agenda for several months. As with most of the Clinton policy proposals during the 103rd Congress, the proposal for health care reform seemed significantly more liberal than the median member of Congress would have desired. The highly regulatory Clinton plan established universal coverage of all Americans as its major goal. As the plan was brought into light, it became quite evident that the trillion-dollar Clinton proposal was far out of line with the preferences of the average American, as well as of the median members of Congress. Vote counters noted that the plan would have received only a handful of supporters in Congress.

Although the health care plan never made it to the floor of Congress, the committee debates and backroom dealings are well documented (Brady and Buckley 1995; Broder and Johnson 1996; Hacker 1997; Matsui 1995; Skocpol 1996). Hacker argues that Clinton and his advisers naively thought that managed competition would appear liberal to liberals and moderate to moderates. Skocpol argues that Clinton's health care plan failed because of Reagan's antigovernment legacy, the deficit, and the fact that Clinton spent critical time and energy on NAFTA (an issue that antagonized liberals and labor groups).[8] Broder and Johnson provide an excellent description of the policy process but conclude (wrongly in our view) that the political system cannot handle such major reforms. Although these studies are valuable in their attention to detail, they are crucial in showing how politicians, scholars, and journalists can miss the broader policy picture. For a Clinton proposal to be successful, it must appeal to conservative Democrats and moderate Republicans at the filibuster pivots. Thus any focus on the loss of liberals and labor groups shows how far off the mark the discussions and proposals were.

As with other major legislation in the 103rd Congress, more conservative plans would need to be considered to appeal to the median members and to overcome potential conservative filibusters. The policy proposals of President Clinton and members of the 103rd Congress gave different emphases to the three issues of cost, quality, and coverage. Each of the plans is located on the liberal-conservative scale in Figure 5.2. For illustration, we focus on the Senate. The proposals are differentiated specifically according to *how many* people are covered and *who* is expected to pay for care. On the left of the continuum is the most liberal of the pro-

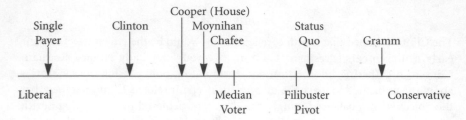

FIGURE 5.2   Health Care Proposals in the 103rd Senate

posals, the single-payer plan, which would cover all Americans by a direct cost to taxpayers. On the far right of the continuum is the Gramm plan, which does not increase coverage and serves basically as a minimal reform of the insurance industry. In the figure, the status quo is at or near the filibuster pivot in the Senate, with about 85 percent coverage via Medicare and Medicaid programs and private insurance companies, with emergency access for all.[9]

Given the position of the status quo, a successful proposal could not be to the left of the median voter. The Clinton plan was just that. Universal coverage was the major goal of Clinton's strongly regulatory plan. The expansion of coverage to include the last 15 percent of the public essentially would be paid for by an indirect tax on employers—the so-called employer mandate. The combination of universal coverage and employer mandates locates the Clinton plan to the left of the median voters. When the Congressional Budget Office (CBO) reported the cost of the proposal, and hearings further exposed the estimated numbers, it was clear that the Clinton plan was going nowhere. With maybe thirty votes at its peak of success, the Clinton plan failed to accommodate the preferences of conservative Democratic members at the median (let alone moderate Republican filibuster pivots), and represented a far-too-costly alternative to the status quo.

Representative Cooper's (D., Tenn.) plan was at least closer to the preferences of House moderates than was the Clinton proposal. The Cooper bill eliminated employer mandates (and thus universal coverage), but increased coverage by taxing deductibles and health care benefits. After the CBO estimates on Cooper's plan were released, the costs again proved prohibitive, and like the Clinton proposal the Cooper plan had no chance of passing. With the failure of the two most prominent plans, the pressure was on House committees to produce legislation. At this point, however, the House Ways and Means Chairman was being indicted, and potential proposals would never induce moderates in the committee, such as Representative Andrews (D., Tex.), to vote for them (Broder and Johnson 1996, 430–435; Matsui 1995, 30–31). The Energy and Commerce Committee, under the liberal leadership of Chairman Dingell (D., Mich.), proved too fragmented to produce a moderate proposal. Not only were the individual House committees unable to bring bills to the floor, but Representatives were reluctant to vote on health care prior to the more-conservative Senate. House members did not want to repeat their performance on the budget bill, when they were forced to vote on the BTU tax only to have it later stricken from the Senate version. Given the dim prospects for passing health care legislation in the House, attention turned back to the Senate.

The Senate Finance Committee was expected to produce the bill with the greatest chance of success. This committee, chaired by Senator Moynihan, was viewed as the most representative of the Senate, including both moderate Democrats and Republicans—the key to building a majority. Moynihan's attempt, put forward as a Chairman's mark, was a diluted version of the Clinton plan: a 45 percent increase in the tobacco tax, full deductibility for the self-employed, a requirement that insurance companies cover preexisting injuries and persons who change jobs, and increases in the number of pregnant mothers and children covered by Medicaid. The Moynihan plan sacrificed universal coverage, but increased the funds available to the plan through taxes and greater costs to employers. As information became available on the cost and complexity of Moynihan's plan, it too was also eliminated as a viable challenger to the status quo. In many ways, it appeared as if no plan stood a chance of actually passing through Congress.

As the chances of passing a health care bill in the 103rd Congress diminished, Majority Leader Mitchell called for a bipartisan coalition to salvage reform. The group of moderates, headed by Senator Chafee, proposed expanding coverage without requiring employer mandates. Even this bipartisan compromise failed to make it to the floor. The Chafee plan may have been more attractive to the median voters in Congress than the other proposals, but two factors ensured its defeat: (1) the pro-business filibuster pivot voters in the Senate, and (2) the plan's late entrance into the debate. By the time the Chafee bill had been introduced, members were uncertain whether voters even wanted substantial reform. In late 1994, after a year of debating the Clinton plan and its less-complicated alternatives, Congress officially abandoned health care reform without so much as a floor vote.

Aggregate Analysis

Table 5.5 surveys the results of the legislation we have analyzed. In the case of each proposal requiring only a simple majority for passage, the policy moved toward the floor median. News stories on the budget act featured moderate Democrats such as Boren, Breaux, Nunn, Johnston, and DeConcini; and House Democrats such as Stenholm, Wilson, and Andrews, as the major determiners of the final product. On legislation where supermajority institutions came into play, the names most frequently mentioned were Republicans—Specter, Cohen, Chafee, Packwood, Hatfield, Jeffords, and Durenberger—who of course controlled the filibuster pivot. On motor voter, the job stimulus package, and health care the difference between victory and defeat was in large part due to the compromises made on motor voter, which passed, and the lack thereof on the jobs bill and health care, which failed. The family leave bill passed most easily, largely because the President submitted the compromise worked out in 1992. Had the President submitted a bill

TABLE 5.5 Summary of Legislative Changes

Type of Legislation	Bill	Presidential Proposal	Provisions	Changes	Pivotal Members
Majority only	1993 Budget Act	Left of floor median	1. BTU energy tax 2. Not many cuts 3. 36% top rate on individuals	Eliminate BTU $60 billion in cuts 33.5% top tax rate	Breaux Boren Nunn
	NAFTA	Left of floor median	1. Renegotiate 2. Trinational commission sanctions 3. Tax for worker retraining	Not renegotiated No real sanctions Dropped	Johnston DeConcini Stenholm Wilson
Supermajority					
Old	Family Leave	Republican filibuster point	1. 12 weeks coverage 2. Companies >50 employees 3. Exempt 10% 4. Full-time employees	None; the President supported a package worked out in 1992	Bond
	Motor Voter	At floor median	1. Registration required in welfare offices	Dropped/modified	Durenberger Specter
New	Job Stimulus	Left of floor median	1. Urban spending 2. Youth summers 3. Pell grants 4. Unemployment	Dropped Dropped Dropped Passed	Boren Breaux
	National Service	Left of floor median	1. $650 million 1st year 2. 5-year authorization 3. $10,000 education awards	$300 million 3 years $4,725	Chafee Kassebaum Packwood
	Health Care	Left of floor median	1. Universal coverage 2. Employer mandates	Dropped Dropped	Cooper Andrews

further to the left as with the 1987–1988 bills, Senators would have filibustered to pull the legislation rightward. And national service legislation passed only after shifting far enough to the right to appease the moderate-to-conservative Senators. In sum, the examination of the major legislation attempted during Clinton's first years has shown two things: (1) the bills that pass Congress are characterized by their appeal to the preferences of institutionally placed pivotal members, and not by their partisan appeal; and (2) gridlock continues under unified government in the form of significant limits on change away from the status quo.

It is also evident that budget divisiveness played a huge role in producing unified gridlock. No Republicans supported the 1993 budget deal, and conservative Democrats forced a number of concessions before they went along with the package. Family leave and motor voter legislation passed the costs off to business and to state and local governments. The programs that would be costly to the federal government were scaled back or killed: the job stimulus package proposed at $16.3 billion was reduced to a $4 billion unemployment compensation extension; the national service program projected initially at $650 million with costs rising annually for five years was cut to $300 million for the first year and authorized for only three years; and the health care bill, argued at one time to cost one trillion dollars, was abandoned entirely.

Switcher Analysis

Thus far we have considered the possibility that policy is the result of parties, preferences, and institutions. We have argued that members' preferences in combination with the supermajority institution of the filibuster largely accounted for policy results in the early years of the Clinton presidency. Partisanship, here defined as the attempt to enact legislation at the median party position, did not seem to influence policy results. In majoritarian issues (the budget act and NAFTA implementation) the policy moved toward the median voter, whereas in nonmajoritarian issues policy moved further to the right in order to secure the cloture vote of the filibuster pivot. Additionally we found that the initial Clinton proposals were to the left of the floor median or the filibuster pivot, and that policies move toward pivotal voters because members' preferences on issues dominate.

However, as is well known, Presidents and others can and do offer congressional members benefits unrelated to the issue at hand in order to gain the members' votes on the pertinent issue. During the final week preceding the NAFTA vote, stories about President Clinton "buying" votes via the treasury were common. It is clear that Presidents and party leaders can offer congressional members policy concessions and favors unrelated to the issue at hand to get them to vote their way. Snyder (1991), Groseclose (1995), and Groseclose and Snyder (1996) have modeled this process and shown that optimal vote buying is characterized by the proximity of the legislation's position to that of the *legislator's* preference. The President or party leader will focus efforts on members at (or close to) the floor median (and pivotal positions) rather than on those strongly favoring or opposing the policy in question. Efforts targeted at legislators close to the pivot are more likely to succeed in changing the vote because of the near indifference of these members, whether the deal entails changing the bill or making off-issue compromises. Accepting this reasoning allows us to test the revolving gridlock theory more generally on legislators who, in the course of decisionmaking, first vote one way but later switch to the opposite position. There are numerous kinds of votes, such as successive cloture votes, pre- and postconference votes, and successive votes on rules, where "switchers" can be identified.[10]

We wish to test the hypothesis that in the 103rd Congress the switchers were those members near the predicted pivot points. On the budget vote, because this vote was majoritarian in both the House and the Senate, we expect those changing their votes to be located at or near the middle of the left-right continuum, rather than at the *party* medians. Concretely, this means that David Boren and John Breaux are more likely to switch than Carol Moseley-Braun. Furthermore, because the filibuster pivot is crucial to our theory as it relates to most other legislation, we expect that switchers there will tend to be to the right of the floor median in the Senate, and specifically at (or near) the three-fifths filibuster pivot. That is, because coalition building in the Senate is a supermajoritarian process, the President and party leaders will have to reach across the partisan divide to obtain the sixty votes necessary to overcome a filibuster.

Using Roll Call's ranking of Senators in the 103rd Congress, Figure 5.3 graphs switchers in 1993.[11]

Three things are clear. First, although a baseline model of random switching might predict that this graph would be flat because everyone is equally likely to be the target of a buying effort, the actual graph is remarkably peaked. Switchers are much more likely to be moderates than extremists. Second, as predicted, most of the switchers are to the right of the Senate median. Clinton cannot simply count on a Democratic majority; he must make concessions or otherwise induce moderate Republicans such as Specter, Jeffords, and Hatfield to vote with him. Third, this pattern of switchers near the filibuster pivot holds for both Democrats and Republicans.

Switching Across Time

Although the foregoing analysis is specific to unified government and to the 103rd Congress, a similarly revealing exercise can be conducted in the few cases where nearly identical pieces of legislation were addressed by successive Congresses. Of these, the most salient is undoubtedly "fast track" and NAFTA.

In spring 1991, President Bush was pushing for an extension of the fast-track procedures for trade bills. The only major trade bill looming on the horizon was NAFTA, and the discussion thus focused on the use of fast-track procedures for the NAFTA trade negotiations. Without fast track, negotiators would be unable to make

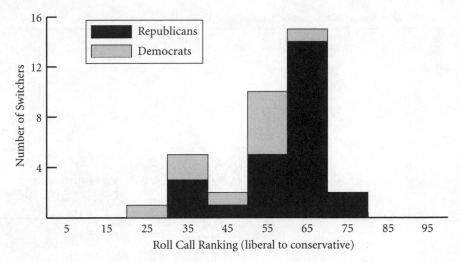

FIGURE 5.3   Switchers in the Senate (1993)

the binding agreements necessary for progress toward NAFTA. Supporters of fast track argued that NAFTA would die without these procedures, and many opponents voted against it for just that reason. However, on May 23, 1991, the House voted 231 to 192 to extend the fast-track procedures, and the Senate followed suit on the following day. As the votes in 1991 seemed to be based on the positions congressional members took on NAFTA generally, a comparison with their votes on the passage of NAFTA in 1993 does not seem unreasonable. The actions leading up to the mid-November votes have been discussed above. The resulting votes were both pro-NAFTA: 234 to 200 in the House and 61 to 38 in the Senate.

The crucial consideration in the use of the trade bill as a test of partisanship versus preferences is that the party leader, Clinton, lined up in opposition to the preferences of many members of his own party in the final vote. Had the Democratic President taken a typical Democratic position, party and preference would have remained aligned and no test could be constructed that would discriminate between the two hypotheses—a preference-driven Congress or a partisan one.

The comparative ability of partisan versus preference concerns to describe the patterns in the two NAFTA-related votes can be determined via simple crosstabulation. Institutional mechanisms such as the filibuster do not play a role here because the votes were filibuster- and veto-proof. For Democrats and Republicans alike, any of four vote combinations (two nays, NN; two yeas, YY; or a mix, NY or YN) may, and in fact did, occur. A simple first pass at the votes, shown in Tables 5.6 and 5.7, asks: what percentage of vote combinations are consistent with the hypothesis that voting on these free-trade issues is based on preferences? The assumption is that solid free traders (YY) and strong protectionists (NN) qualify,

TABLE 5.6   Cross-Tabulation of Senate Trade Votes (Democrats)

1993 NAFTA Vote

	No	Yes		
No	20	7	27	7/27 = 26% Attraction
Yes	4	16	20	4/20 = 20% Nonretention
			47	

1991 Fast-Track Vote

whereas legislators switching away from Clinton (YN) or toward him (NY) were near the point of indifference and thus susceptible to influence by the President, interest groups, shifts in constituency opinions, and so on. The answer is found on the diagonals of the two tables: 77 percent (36/47) of Democrats' vote combinations and 79 percent (30/38) of Republicans' vote combinations can be attributed to consistent preferences alone. Votes on NAFTA in 1993 followed votes on fast track in 1991 quite closely.

This need not be an argument for preferences and against parties, as party and preference are correlated. The question is: Can a partisan-based theory or a preference-based theory better predict the behavior of those who did not vote consistently—the switchers over time? If unified government breaks "partisan gridlock," as these theories claim, then it must be because an executive in unified government is better positioned to harness his party's strength in the Congress. More specifically, the switching behavior that we observe on the off-diagonals in Tables 5.6 and 5.7 should be *significantly* asymmetric. For example, focusing on Democrats, a partisan-based unified government theory predicts that, with the unified government of 1993 (as opposed to the divided government of 1991), Bill Clinton—as President, party leader, and free trader—should pick up a much greater percentage of erstwhile Democratic protectionists than he should lose of erstwhile free traders. The former (nay-yea, or NY voters) are rallying to the cry of their party's standard bearer who at long last occupies the White House. The latter (YN voters) are deserting him in a time of need, and to make matters worse they had *not* deserted Republican George Bush two years earlier.

We can make such comparisons of switchers in two ways: within the President's party and across parties. A partisan-based theory would predict that within the

TABLE 5.7   Cross-Tabulation of Senate Trade Votes (Republicans)

1993 NAFTA Vote

		No	Yes		
1991 Fast-Track Vote	No	3	3	6	3/6 = 50% Attraction
	Yes	5	27	32	5/32 = 16% Nonretention
				38	

Democratic Party Clinton's *attraction* rate (percentage of former Ns to switch to Y) would exceed his *nonretention* rate (percentage of former Ys to switch to N). Additionally, across the parties, a partisan-based theory would predict a higher attraction rate among Democrats than among Republicans, and a higher nonretention rate among Republicans than among Democrats. These three comparisons can be made in both the House and the Senate, for a total of six comparative tests of the partisan theory on this issue. As will soon be shown, none of these provides firm evidence of partisan-based vote switching.

The data for Democratic switchers on NAFTA provide the only bit of support for the partisan-based theory. Bill Clinton's attraction rate was an unimpressive 26 percent; only seven of twenty-seven Democrats switched to their President's position. And his nonretention rate, counting the Democratic switchers to protectionism, was nearly as high: four of twenty (20 percent). The predicted asymmetry appears, but ever so barely. It appears that the effect here of having a Democratic President is a gain of one or maybe two Democratic votes in the Senate. One more defector would have put these percentages at nearly identical levels—about one in four would switch each way.

The cross-party comparisons are no more supportive of the partisan-based unified government theory than were comparisons within the President's own party. Clinton's attraction rate among Democrats was significantly lower than that among Republicans. He picked up *half* of the Republicans who had opposed fast track under Bush, but only had an attraction rate of 26 percent within his own party. And his nonretention rate was actually *higher* among Democrats than among Republicans. Tables 5.6 and 5.7 show Clinton losing 20 percent of previous Democratic trade supporters, whereas he only lost five of thirty-two

Republicans (or 16 percent) who had supported fast track. Both of these sets of results run counter to the partisan theory.

For both Democrats and Republicans, the same analysis was replicated for the House. The results are almost identical. Democratic switching differences are even closer to zero in the House than in the Senate; Republican switching differences run contrary to what the partisan-based theory of unified government predicts. Of the six comparisons made in both the House and Senate, none provided strong support for the partisan model and a few even ran counter to that model. As we mentioned above, depending on the positioning of the President and the status quo, it is often not possible to discern partisan voting from preference voting, because the two may be in alignment. With this test we have the forces of party and preference in conflict, and no asymmetrical partisan switching is found. This raises doubts about the use of party affiliation as a standard by which to predict voting patterns, beyond knowing the preferences of the legislators.

Finding no support for the strong partisan-based model, we are left to question who these switchers are. We know that a group of switchers does not gain its direction or size based on the party of the legislators, but can we say any more than this? A preference-based model actually does allow further explanation of this switching phenomenon. As in the case of switching votes during the course of legislative action on the individual bills noted above, these across-session switchers are also those who are near the pivotal median point. Whether they were the easiest to buy one way or the other, or whether their constituencies were fairly equally balanced and just tipped in one direction or the other, these switchers fall squarely between the solidly anti-NAFTA and solidly pro-NAFTA legislators. The mean ADA score for the free traders (YYs) in the Senate was 41.0, for the protectionists (NNs) 72.5, and for the switchers 60.1, just about the median member's score.[12]

The logic here seems very straightforward. Clinton takes a position that runs counter to the preferences of many members of his party. The party isn't strong enough to carry the necessary votes, so Clinton must appeal to members of Congress who are closest to his position. Thus these switchers are both the moderate Republicans and moderate Democrats who are nearly indifferent to voting for or against NAFTA. So, although the partisan theory lacks predictive power in this switcher analysis, the preference-based theory again indicates where to look for this type of switching behavior.

This type of cross-temporal analysis is not limited to the case of trade. Whenever similar bills are found in unified and divided governments, and the President takes a position not aligned with the preferences of his party, these types of tests can be constructed. As such, we can also look at the switching that took place between the 1990 Bush budget deal and the 1993 Clinton budget reconciliation package.

On November 5, 1990, President Bush signed the 1991 Budget Reconciliation Act, thus breaking his "no new taxes" pledge to the American people. The similarity between this 1990 budget deal and the deal that passed the 103rd Congress

TABLE 5.8   Cross-Tabulation of Senate Budget Votes (Republicans)

1990 Budget Vote

		No	Yes		
1993 Budget Vote	No	18	16	34	16/34 = 47% Attraction
	Yes	0	0	0	No calculation
				34	

in 1993 is remarkable. As mentioned above, the 1993 budget deal called for $493 billion in savings over the following five years; likewise, the 1990 deal called for $496 billion in savings over five years (1990 *Congressional Quarterly Weekly Report,* 3710–3717). Both were formulated under the rules for reconciliation, which do not allow filibusters. Both measures increased the income tax on the highest bracket; both raised gas taxes by nearly five cents a gallon. Both budget deals cut significant portions of the defense budget, among other areas. The proposals in 1993 that would have led to a different type of energy tax or different proportions of cuts were all batted down.

The comparisons of voting in Congress seem a little more abstract than those we made on NAFTA, however, as Bush was the President aligning himself *against the perceived preferences* of members of his party. As Tables 5.8 and 5.9 show, we are making our comparisons in an anachronistic fashion. Here a YN is a switcher who voted for the Clinton budget but against the Bush budget. As with the trade votes, most of the voting (58 percent) is consistent with fixed preferences; these voters are either solid budget supporters (YYs) or budget detractors (NNs), seen along the diagonals in the tables.

Of the remaining Senators, the strong partisan-based theory would predict that the switching toward the Bush budget should be among Republicans, whereas the switching away from the Bush budget should be among Democrats. Again, we compare the attraction and nonretention rates within the President's party and the cross-party comparisons of these two rates. Unfortunately, such a comparison is not feasible for the nonretention of Republicans as the pool for that possibility is zero (no Republicans supported the Clinton budget).[13] Thus our remaining comparison is the attraction rate across parties. The strong parti-

TABLE 5.9   Cross-Tabulation of Senate Budget Votes (Democrats)

1990 Budget Vote

	No	Yes		
No	3	3	6	3/6 = 50% Attraction
Yes	15	25	40	15/40 = 38% Nonretention
			46	

1993 Budget Vote

san–based theory predicts that a larger percentage of Republicans voting against the Clinton budget would be attracted to the Bush budget than the percentage of Democrats switching to support Bush. The results are slightly opposed to this hypothesis. Although Bush was able to attract 47 percent of the erstwhile skeptics of tax-and-spend budgets within his own party, his attraction rate among Democrats was 50 percent. Again, these results provide no support to the partisan-based theory.[14]

These comparisons for both the trade and budget votes are summarized in Table 5.10. Column I shows the President's attraction rate within his own party, while column II shows his nonretention rate also within his own party. These two comparisons of attraction and nonretention rates within the President's party take place with Clinton on the trade issue. Neither comparison supports the strong partisan–based theory of unified government. Columns III and IV show these rates, respectively, within the opposition party. There, in all four cases, the President is more likely to gain than to lose members of the opposing party.

Four further comparisons can be made of the President's attraction rate within his own party as opposed to that in the opposition party. Contrary to the partisan-based theory, three out of four such comparisons show a greater attraction rate among members of the opposition party (compare columns I and III). The data on NAFTA show Clinton with a greater attraction rate among the Republicans than among the Democrats in both the House and the Senate. Bush had a higher attraction rate among members of his own party than among the Democrats when we look at the House data on the budgets, but no difference is found between these rates in the Senate. The final set of comparisons can made between Columns II and IV, which show the nonretention rates. In this case, the

TABLE 5.10   Comparison of Attraction and Nonretention Rates

		President's Party		Opposition Party	
		I Attraction Rate	II Nonretention Rate	III Attraction Rate	IV Nonretention Rate
Trade	Senate	0.26	0.20	0.50	0.16
	House	0.23	0.23	0.39	0.14
Budget	Senate	0.47	—	0.50	0.38
	House	0.77	—	0.47	0.21

partisan theory predicts that the desertion of the President's position would occur at a higher rate among those outside of the President's party than among those within his party. Once again, the two comparisons that are possible (those on the trade issue) run counter to the partisan theory in both cases. In short, given the sets of votes we analyze, a total of twelve comparisons can be made (two within the President's party, four within the opposition party, and six across parties). Only one supports the strong partisan-based model, whereas the other eleven either show no evidence of partisan switching or even run counter to the partisan-based hypothesis.

As was the case with trade, the switchers on the budget can best be accounted for with a preference-based theory. Although those sticking with their pro– or anti–"Democratic budget deal" principles hold extreme preference positions, the switchers are much closer to the median pivot points. In the Senate, the mean ADA score for budget supporters (YYs) was 84.0, for budget detractors (NNs) 20.9, and for switchers 53.8.[15] Table 5.11 summarizes these preference scores for both the budget and trade votes. As with NAFTA, the budget vote unfolded as follows: President Bush takes a position opposed by members of his own party; the party isn't a strong enough institution to carry enough votes for passage; so the President has to turn to the other party for votes. And which members can he win over? Those moderates closest to his own position.

In both of these cases of vote switching over a period of time, the crucial ingredient for our testing was to find the President endorsing a policy that did not comport well with his own party's preferences. Most members of Congress stuck to their original positions, not being swayed by a change in party stance. Those who did switch did not do so in a noticeably partisan fashion. Rather, they did so due to a change in preferences caused by their near indifference, changes in their constituents' leanings, off-issue bargaining, or other concerns. These switchers were those members near the relevant pivot points, the voters who have been found to be most crucial to determining the fate of all the legislation discussed in this chapter. The switcher analysis, combined with our discussions of particular bills, elaborates on our argument: (1) legislators switch their positions over time due to various incentives or changes in the bills; (2) this switching behavior is not

TABLE 5.11   Preference Scores for Switching over Time

		Mean ADA Scores		
		Consistent Support	Switching	Consistent Opposition
Trade	Senate	41.0	60.1	72.5
	House	33.3	51.6	77.1
Budget	Senate	84.0	53.8	20.9
	House	80.1	53.3	17.6

due to partisan leanings, but rather to preferences and constraining institutions such as the veto or filibuster; (3) because the crucial members of Congress gain their power by their preferences and by these institutions, their positions of power do not change with a change in the party of the President; and (4) as a result, gridlock under divided government will continue under unified government, with the crucial voters now being those needed to invoke cloture rather than those needed to override a veto.

How did this system of relationships evolve, whereby members of Congress at the floor median, the filibuster pivot, or the veto pivot determine policy? Has it always been this way, and have we just failed to notice the significance of these members because the overlap of parties and preferences has masked the true preference relationship? These questions lead to the all-important question—just what is a political party? In the weakest sense, a party is simply the aggregated preferences of members, where members with liberal preferences are the party of the left and those with conservative preferences are the party of the right. (In systems with multiple parties there would be center, center-left, center-right, and other more finely honed parties as well.) In the strongest sense, a party as an institution would have sanctions such that members would feel compelled to vote for legislation contrary to their personal preferences. In short, in a strong party system the institutional arrangements give party leaders the ability to enforce decisions.

A major dispute in the recent literature on political parties concerns their significance—Cox and McCubbins (1993), Rohde (1991), and Aldrich (1995) are on one side, and Krehbiel (1993) is on the other. Although the dispute raises many issues, here we are concerned only with the relationship between party and preferences. Krehbiel's view, in simplified form, is that a party is the aggregation of induced preferences. Thus when parties are separated we call them strong; when they overlap we call them weak. Roughly speaking, for Cox and McCubbins, Rohde, and Aldrich, parties are more than the mere aggregation of preferences; they tie together voters, elections, institutions, and strategy. For example, Cox and McCubbins argue that party leaders dispense favors such as committee assignments based, in part, on party loyalty. We cannot resolve these differences here (or perhaps anywhere). But, for our purposes, it is enough that Cox and McCubbins, for their reasons, and Krehbiel, for his reasons, would agree that parties are weaker at the end of the twentieth century than they were during earlier periods of American history, and thus that preferences matter more—especially the preferences of those at or around the median.

How party systems change over time is a much-studied and, in our view, little-known phenomenon. For example, in the U.S. Congress, the heyday of the strong party system was the 1890–1910 "Czar" period. Surely Czar Cannon[16] was a product of a strong party system, where the party as an institution meant something. Yet, reading Cannon's comments on the "strong" party system he ran, one can also imagine a party as an aggregation of preferences, as a homogeneous and bipolar system in which the Speaker is simply a coordinator. In order to answer questions about why and how this system of individual preferences evolved, more work along the lines of John Aldrich's *Why Parties?* (1995) will have to be done. Suffice it to say that, for our purposes, the old post-1938 New Deal alignment (Democrats divided between North and South wings and Republicans operating as the presidential party with a permanent House minority) has been changed in part by the budget crises of the late 1970s and early 1980s, in which votes became zero-sum.

Conclusion

By studying the continuation of policy gridlock through the unified government period of the 103rd Congress, we find that the revolving gridlock theory of preferences and institutions influencing policy outcomes still holds. Those who claimed that divided government caused gridlock either explicitly or implicitly argued that giving one party control of government would lead to an end of gridlock—to nonincremental policy shifts. Our argument was that it is not parties that cause gridlock; rather, it is preferences of the members of the House and Senate in combination with supermajoritarian institutions like Senate Rule XXII that cause gridlock. A brief review of the major pieces of legislation proposed by President Clinton showed that in each case his proposals had to be acceptable to either the floor median voter or the filibuster pivot voter in order for the proposal to pass. We applied two tests of this thesis and both confirmed our interpretation of preferences and institutions as the proximate causes of gridlock.

If the preferences of key members of Congress essentially drive policies, what further conclusions can we draw? The first is that the President's powers are generally overrated by some scholars and the media, and that Congress ultimately determines policy results. Gridlock objectively means that neither conservative nor liberal Presidents can pull or push policy far away from where Congress wants it. Unified government gridlock simply means that policy change will be held back by the filibuster pivot Senators, rather than by the members needed to override a veto. In short, in order to get any kind of legislation from budgets to civil rights acts passed, Republican Presidents are forced to move their proposals to the left whereas Democratic Presidents must move theirs right. Second, since policy is maintained within a narrow band controlled by moderate Democrats and Republicans, gridlock occurs under both unified and divided government. Third, the key to understanding what will happen to today's proposed policies is determining median floor preferences, filibuster preferences, and veto pivot preferences. If they are to pass, policy proposals must be modified to accommodate these key members.

Finally, it is important to note that we have not claimed that this process yields good (or bad) policy. We have simply claimed that policy results can best be explained by looking at members' preferences and constraining institutions rather than at partisan variables. Ultimately the important questions are: what is the degree of agreement between key members' policy preferences and the public's preferences; and does the congressional system of representation of local and regional interests rather than national interests yield viable long-term policies?

Those who believed that the 1992 elections would bring an end to gridlock focused on the return of unified government and, with it, the advancement of a Democratic agenda (Sundquist 1993). The 1994 elections showed that the public found the Clinton policy direction to be inappropriate. Democrats from conservative districts who voted for Clinton's policies were defeated (Brady, Cogan, and Rivers 1995). In the words of V. O. Key (1964, 544), "The vocabulary of the voice of the people consists mainly of the words yes and no; and at times one cannot be certain which word is being uttered." Clearly the electorate seemed to say "No!" to President Clinton, but was there also a "Yes!" for Republican governance?

The press treated the 1994 election results with astonishment, referring to the Republican victories in terms traditionally reserved for natural disasters and acts of god—as a "tsunami," as the most dramatic congressional landslide in forty years or more. Walter Dean Burnham, the eminent scholar on realigning elections, wrote the piece "Realignment Lives: The 1994 Earthquake and Its Implications" (1995), asking, "What kind of event was the 1994 election? Very probably the most consequential off-year election in (exactly) one hundred years" (363). In the previous century, the 1894 election brought the Republicans to control in the Congress. Two years later, the 1896 elections kicked off fourteen consecutive years of unified Republican government, ushering in policy changes in the areas commonly associated with turn-of-the-century capitalism—the gold standard, protective tariffs, and foreign expansionism.

Was the 1994 election a precursor to (or part of) another realignment? The realignments of 1894 and 1930 were both immediately followed—in 1896 and 1932—with unified party control and new agendas (Brady 1988; Burnham 1965, 1970; Glad 1966; Key 1955). Linking this election to those would indicate that the Republicans would control the agenda in the 104th Congress, and that a Republican challenger would easily beat President Clinton in 1996—if he were so bold as to run again. The alternative, however, is that 1994 was just a return to divided government. Thus we would be "back to gridlock," to use Sundquist's term (1995), or simply continuing "revolving gridlock," as we refer to it.

NOTES

1. The ratings used were AAUW, ACLU, ACU, ADA, ASC, BIPAC, CCUS, CFA, COPE, LCV, NAM, NCSC, NEA, NFIB, NFU, PCCW, TEAM, and UAW.

2. The rankings were based on votes in the 102nd and previous Congresses. Therefore, new members are not listed in Tables 5.1, 5.2, and 5.3. The point is that we want to analyze the Congress as though it were new. Thus by taking returning members' scores and looking at their replacements (by party), we can guess whether congressional preferences shifted. This assumption is nonheroic in that a rich literature shows that members vote extremely consistently across time. Members who are liberal in their first Congress will be liberal in their tenth. See Kingdon 1973; Poole and Rosenthal 1991a, 1991b, 1997; and Groseclose, Levitt, and Snyder 1996.

3. As mentioned previously, our notion of parties is not incompatible with either Cox and McCubbins's theory of parties (1993) or the theories of Rohde (1991) or Aldrich (1995). In Cox and McCubbins's view, the party leadership focuses on shaping committee appointments early in members' careers, and the connection between policy results and elections is loose. Our view allows for *some* party influence over member preferences, but brings district responsiveness and electoral success to the fore.

4. In a later section we will make a comparison of this budget reconciliation with that under the Bush administration in 1990. Both called for $500 billion in savings over five years by cutting defense and other areas, imposing a gas tax, and increasing individual income tax rates for earners in the highest bracket.

5. Note that we are clearly *not* saying that members of Congress have no concern for their party or for the public's perception of them via their party. It is in this sense that we are not making any argument against the "parties matter" camp. Clearly concern for the party does have an influence on an individual's preferences, but what matters in the end are district preferences and reelection, not just the party.

6. Although some might claim that the Democrats as a party could not pass legislation against a strong filibustering Republican Party, it should be noted that even Democrats defected from the President's position. Additionally, the other examples show that appealing to the filibuster pivots, whether Democrats or Republicans, can get these key members to change their votes.

7. Part of this section is drawn from Brady and Buckley 1995.

8. Skocpol comes close to getting it right when she argues in her final chapter that program costs killed both the Clinton and Cooper plans. It is important to note, however, that she writes from the perspective of one who favors national health care and focuses more attention on liberals than on the moderates who would be needed to cast the crucial votes.

9. That the status quo was to the right of the filibuster point was in question as of 1994. It seemed that nothing could pass, and yet, in the 104th Congress, the Kennedy-Kassebaum bill succeeded.

10. For "switching" behavior in the context of bill copartisanship, see Krehbiel 1995.

11. We used Roll Call because it allowed us to use all 100 Senators, while ADA and other scores had not yet been updated by the time of our first writing of this chapter. Analysis of switchers using ADA scores mirrors these results, showing three times as many switchers to the right of the median as to the left.

12. For the House, these figures were 33.3, 77.1, and 51.6, respectively, again with the switchers falling right in the middle. There is an additional separation between switchers

toward Clinton and those away from him, with the switchers moving against the President (YNs) having a lower mean ADA score, but we do not speculate on this distinction here.

13. We concede that the fact that no Republicans voted for the Clinton budget has a partisan flavor to it. Unfortunately, this is again a case where preference and party are aligned. Did Democrats vote for the bill because they were liberals, or did liberals vote for the bill because they were Democrats?

14. This test run on the House data provides the only support of the partisan model in this chapter. There, Bush appears better able to attract Republicans than Democrats.

15. In the House, these figures were 80.1, 17.6, and 53.3, respectively. Again, there was a further distinction between YNs and NYs.

16. Joseph Gurney Cannon was a Representative from Illinois who served as Speaker of the House from 1903 to 1911. Speaker Cannon along with Speaker Reed (R., Maine) were called "czars" by the press because they were so powerful.

6

The Republican Congress

On September 26, 1994, Senate majority leader George Mitchell (D., Maine) declared health care legislation dead—thus, for all practical purposes, ending the 103rd Congress. The first unified government in twelve years began with high hopes and ended with little of its agenda passed. Health care, campaign finance reform, term limits, environmental legislation, and middle-class tax cuts had all failed to pass. Public opinion, favorable early in 1993, had turned against the Congress and the President. The 1994 congressional elections brought divided government back to Washington, though in the unfamiliar garb of a Republican Congress and a Democratic President. Not since Harry Truman and the "do nothing" 80th Congress (1947–1949) had Washington seen such an arrangement. Given our approach emphasizing preferences and supermajority institutions, what could one expect from the 104th Congress?

Our position has been that from 1975 to the present, the federal budget has come to dominate the congressional agenda. Certainly by the end of the Carter presidency politicians were faced with hard choices regarding taxing and spending. The 1980 election had sharply shifted the preferences of the Congress and the President to the right. The result was a decrease in individual income tax rates and a lower marginal tax rate; these changes were formalized in 1986. The new equilibrium on taxes meant that, without a major shift in the preferences of members, anyone trying to raise taxes to deal with the deficit would find little support. Expenditures were another story. Though the *rate of growth* in expenditures had slowed during the Reagan years, governmental expenditures continued to rise. Reconciliation instructions and the Gramm-Rudman-Hollings rules had failed to stem the growth of expenditures, largely because Presidents Reagan and Bush did not have the votes in Congress to balance the budget through cuts in expenditures and liberals did not have the votes to raise taxes, especially over presidential vetoes—threatened or used.

When Clinton took office in 1992, a number of bills that had been held up by Republican Presidents' vetoes were signed into law. New proposals were more difficult to achieve, because no major shifts in the positions of key members of Congress accompanied Clinton's victory. The President's proposals were scaled back or shifted to the right in order to secure majorities and to beat filibusters.

Those programs—like health care—that were not scaled back sufficiently did not receive enough congressional support, thus making the federal government appear to be in gridlock again. On the budget, the concessions that Clinton was forced to accept moved the bill back to the right, to about the position of George Bush's 1990 budget bill. Nevertheless, the 1993 budget savings came on top of the 1990 savings, making the cuts tough to bear. Realizing that this would lead to difficult votes for the Democrats, no Republicans voted for the 1993 budget deal. Democrats from conservative districts—mainly in the South—did indeed face a tough choice: either vote with their constituents' preferences and be associated with the perpetuation of gridlock under a unified government, or vote with the President and risk their individual seats. Just enough Democrats went along with the 1993 budget deal for it to pass. After that vote, Clinton had run out of favors from Congress and fallen from the good graces of the American people. In 1994, many of those Democratic budget supporters from conservative districts would be voted out of office.

The major effect of the 1994 election from our perspective was that it shifted the Congress to the right. The newly elected Republican majority in the House had run on the strength of the "Contract with America," which promised major government reforms and substantive changes that would give America a balanced budget while cutting taxes. Tax cuts decrease governmental revenue, and thus the cuts in expenditures would have to be large in order to balance the budget—in short, entitlements would have to be on the policy agenda. With the shift in congressional preferences to the right, the President's veto point on the left became a real and relevant constraint. The Republican-led 104th Congress had run on and would propose an agenda that was to the right of the status quo—there were now at least 218 House votes and 51 Senate votes that favored shifting public policy to the right. In short, the median voter in the House and Senate was (on most issues) a Republican who favored less government.

If the U.S. government was based on a parliamentary system, we would expect policy shifts to the right, such as cuts in welfare and entitlements and the loosening of regulations, because there are few if any supermajority institutions in a parliamentary system. That is, without the threat of a filibuster or a presidential veto, a new majority can enact the policies it prefers with 50 percent plus one of the legislature.[1] The American system, however, features the veto and the filibuster, which allow the President and minorities in Congress to extract policy shifts from the majority. A liberal President willing to veto conservative legislation can either keep the policy at the status quo or induce the majority to shift proposals toward the left. After the previous chapters' argument that gridlock is not necessarily linked to divided government, it may seem surprising that we argue that gridlock would predominate under this again-divided government. But the new situation is simply a continuance of the same interplay of preferences and institutions. As Reagan and Bush did with the Democrats, Clinton would remind Republicans of the power of the supermajority institution known as the presidential veto.

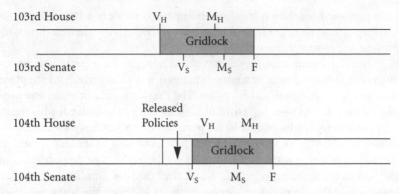

FIGURE 6.1   The 1994 Elections

The 104th Congress, especially the House of Representatives, came to Washington intent on shifting policy to the right. As Figure 6.1 indicates, they had good reason to believe that such shifts could be enacted, given that the released policies are on the left. President Clinton was now clearly left of the median voters in the House and the Senate. His veto threat defined the gridlock region on the left. In addition, the filibuster pivots in the Senate were now moderate Republicans like Jeffords (Vt.), Specter (Penn.), and Cohen (Maine). The Republican agenda was set out in the Contract with America and it was clear that the new Speaker of the House (Newt Gingrich, Ga.) would have a majority for most of the agenda. In the more moderate Senate, the majority leader (Bob Dole, Kans.) faced a serious problem in that he was running for the Republican nomination for President and would have to deliver the votes for the Contract agenda. His problems were that: (1) the Senate was more moderate than was the House; (2) President Clinton's veto pen was ready and waiting; (3) proposals that the President found too politically costly to veto could be filibustered by moderate Democrats; and (4) failure to deliver on the Contract would generate intense criticism from more conservative Republican presidential candidates such as Phil Gramm (Tex.) and Pat Buchanan.

President Clinton's life in one sense became much easier than it had been in the 103rd Congress. No longer would he be an agenda setter; rather, he would become responsible for moderating the Republican agenda. His congressional party may not have delivered majorities for him on his health care and campaign finance reform proposals, but they would stick with him on vetoing Republican legislation that was far from their preferences. In short, Clinton could now either take moderate positions and have the support of the moderates in his party or take liberal positions and count on enough Democrats to back him by sustaining a veto. He had gone from trying to build policy coalitions to acting with the automatic support of a blocking coalition. Note that this new situation hangs on the difference between the Republican proposals needing to focus on capturing Democratic members' support (at the veto pivot on the left), rather than on the

President's proposed legislation needing to appeal to moderate Republicans (at the filibuster pivot on the right). Neither task is easy, especially when dealing with issues with severe budget consequences.

For a numerical example, suppose that the status quo on a particular policy was at fifty, the Democratic congressional median was thirty-five, and the floor median in the 103rd Congress was fifty-two. The President cannot make any proposals that have a shot at winning without looking too conservative for his party, and if he proposes legislation closer to his party's median, say forty, then his proposal would fail and the press would portray him as lacking in leadership ability. Consider the effect of the shift in Congress to the right. The Republicans in Congress now become the agenda setters, and they propose a policy at a median of, say, seventy. If the Democratic median remains at about the same position, and Democrats constitute about 45 percent of the legislature, then, when the President vetoes the Republican policy, he should have no trouble finding enough support in his party to sustain the veto because most Democrats prefer the status quo (fifty) to the Republican proposal. The President can now claim that he vetoed the policy because it is too conservative—that it harms children, that it is too hard on the poor, that it provides tax benefits to the rich—and his veto will be sustained. He can argue in the upcoming campaign that he protects Medicare, Medicaid, education, and the environment. Under these new circumstances Clinton suddenly becomes leaderlike, his party approves of his vetoes even though he can't help them achieve their ideal policies, and the press portrays him as a President with strength and principle.

The political interpretations of the President's actions would change dramatically. In the first scenario, where Clinton is the agenda setter, he does not have the support to propose policies that will change the status quo by much; thus he is vulnerable to charges of ineffectual leadership and of forgoing his party's liberal principles. In the second scenario, in which the President resists rightward shifts, his party and the media treat him as a principled leader standing foursquare for fair policies. Nothing changed except the position of the median voter in the Congress. The President's positions are the same and his personality is the same, yet political commentators and scholars will talk and write about him in an entirely different fashion. In that sense the Republican takeover of the Congress surely made President Clinton's task easier than it had been when his role was to bring about policy change. Now he had only to oppose change as the Republicans did in the 103rd.

A good share of the Contract with America involved governmental reform: a line-item veto, a balanced budget amendment, term limits, campaign finance reform, and internal congressional changes such as reduced staffs. Many of these items had been on the agenda of the Democratic freshman class of 1992, and they were popular with most segments of the American public. Under these conditions we would predict success for some of the reforms with bipartisan support. Those requiring a two-thirds majority (amendments to the Constitution) would have, naturally, a smaller chance of success. The real test for the Republicans would come when their substantive policies came to be incorporated in the budget.

We have argued that since the 1970s, the budget has basically dominated congressional politics. Thus it is reasonable to expect that Republicans would have some successes early in the 104th Congress especially on governmental reforms but that the real test would occur over budget issues, and here the veto power of the President is crucial. In short, in the 104th Congress the supermajority institutions of the filibuster and particularly the veto shift policy away from the Republicans' preferences. Moreover, it is only when the real budget numbers are put on the table that the politics becomes painful—when members must vote to cut entitlement benefits for the elderly and the young, for example.

In this chapter we will: (1) briefly review the results of the 1994 election; (2) describe the fate of various Republican proposals including government reforms and other items in the Contract with America; and (3) show how the reconciliation budget was shaped and finalized, given the shift in preferences, by the threat and use of the presidential veto.

The 1994 Elections

When the 104th Congress convened in January 1995 it was the first Republican-controlled Congress in forty years. No Republican in the 104th House had ever been in the majority—none had ever been Chair of a committee or a subcommittee. The Republicans' majority status was a novelty to the members and a surprise to most analysts. We know of no well-known pollsters or pundits who had predicted a Republican victory in the House. Leading Democratic pollsters like Peter Hart and Republican pollsters like Bob Teeter were predicting a 20- to 25-seat Republican gain, about 20 seats short of what they would need to become the majority party. The conventional wisdom was that Republicans would gain House seats but Democrats would remain in the majority as they had been for forty years. The results in the Senate were not as surprising because the Republicans did not need to gain many seats there to become the majority party, and they had recently been the majority, from 1980 through 1986. What accounted for the Republican victory, especially in the House?

Postelection analysis revealed that Republicans won control of the House by capturing 22 of 31 open-seat Democratic districts (the 31 districts in which a Democrat had retired after the 103rd Congress) and by defeating 34 of the 225 Democratic incumbents seeking reelection. This gain of 56 seats was only offset by Democrats capturing 4 open Republican districts, giving Republicans a net gain of 52 seats. Part of the reason for all of these Republican wins was that the contested districts were moderate or conservative to begin with. That is, Republican gains came in districts where neither Bill Clinton nor Michael Dukakis had done particularly well. If we take the percentage of the vote for Clinton in 1992 to represent the preferences of the voters, the results show that where Clinton was weak in 1992, Democrats stood a good chance of losing the seat in 1994. In the 31 previously Democratic open-seat districts, the Republicans won every seat where President Clinton had won *less* than 56 percent of the two-party vote and they lost every seat where Clinton had received *more* than 56 percent of the vote. The successful Republicans in these elections made Bill Clinton and his policies the issue. The editors of *Congressional Quarterly*'s preelection issue demonstrated this point. In North Carolina's second district, they note, "Funderburk has been using the familiar GOP tactic of linking the Democrat with President Clinton" (1994 *Congressional Quarterly Weekly Report*, 3042). In North Carolina's fifth district, "Here again, the Clinton card is played early and often. Burr claims Sands is just like Clinton" (3042). In Indiana's second district, the editors indicate that the Republican "has focused almost exclusively on President Clinton." In Arizona's first district, the Republican candidate Salmon aired a television advertisement in which a computer "'morphs' a photograph of Blanchard (Dem.) into Clinton" (3043); this technique was used by other Republican candidates as well. And so it went in the open-seat districts. In essence, in conservative-to-moderate districts with open Democratic seats, the Republican candidates won. In territory more liberal and therefore more friendly to Clinton, they did not.

The Republican victories over incumbent Democrats are more interesting be-cause the famous "incumbency advantage" should have protected Democrats (Erikson 1976; Jacobson 1981; King and Gelman 1991; Alford and Brady 1993); yet thirty-four, including the Speaker of the House Tom Foley (Wash.), lost. We can account for the Republican takeover of the House by comparing district pref-erences with the candidates' support for President Clinton. Thus we should ex-pect that Republican wins over incumbent Democrats should come in moderate-to-conservative districts where the incumbent voted with Bill Clinton.

The case of Democratic Representative David Mann (Ohio) is a good example. Congressman Mann represented Ohio's first district, marginally Democratic in each of its last three House elections. In 1992, the district split its Presidential vote evenly between Bill Clinton and George Bush (43 percent each, with 14 percent going to Ross Perot). In 1988, George Bush had beaten Michael Dukakis by 25 percent in the old first district, which was not much changed by redistricting be-fore the 1992 election. Despite the district's conservative tendencies, Congressman Mann voted with President Clinton 81 percent of the time. By November, however, despite being a Democrat, Mann was scrambling to distance himself from the Clinton agenda, running what was perhaps the campaign's most eyebrow-raising advertisement: "Clinton and the Congressional leadership's tax increase—**against**. Clinton and the leadership's $18 billion pork barrel pro-gram—**against**. Clinton government takeover of health care—**against**."[2] Despite his strenuous assertions, Mann lost his reelection bid to a county official whose campaign pursued a familiar theme: "Mann's pattern of support for President Clinton explains why President Clinton is fighting so hard to help Mann in

TABLE 6.1   Percentage of Democratic Incumbents Defeated, 1994

| 1993 Presidential Support | 1992 Clinton Vote in District | | |
	Less than 40%	40% to 50%	Greater than 50%
Less than 60%	0% (5)	0% (4)	0% (0)
60% to 75%	27% (15)	7% (27)	0% (9)
Greater than 75%	63% (19)	22% (65)	1% (80)

SOURCE: Brady, Cogan, and Rivers 1995. Cell entries are percentages of incumbents in the given category to have been defeated in 1994. The total number of incumbents in a particular category is given in parentheses.

Congress," ran one advertisement (1994 *Congressional Quarterly Weekly Report*, 3043–3044).[3]

With respect to the big picture, the question remains: How important was support for the President's legislative agenda in contributing to the large loss of Democratic seats among House incumbents? We claim that support for the President's policies affected election results differentially depending on district characteristics. The more moderate to conservative the district, the more a pro-Clinton voting record hurt. Table 6.1 shows the percentage of incumbents defeated in three categories of districts and for three levels of pro-Clinton voting. District preferences are based on the 1992 presidential vote, with our inference being that the higher Clinton's share of the vote in that race, the more liberal (or Democratic) the district. Table 6.1 shows the percentage of the district vote for Clinton in 1992 by the level of legislative support for the President as measured by *Congressional Quarterly*. The entries in the nine cells are the percentages of incumbents in that category who were defeated. Thus, for example, in districts where President Clinton received less than 40 percent of the three-way vote (Perot's share included) in 1992, no Democratic incumbents who supported him less than 60 percent of the time were defeated in 1994, whereas 63 percent of incumbents who voted with Clinton more than 75 percent of the time were defeated. These results dramatically show that in moderate-to-conservative districts Democratic representatives who *supported* the President were much more likely to lose than were their colleagues from moderate-to-conservative districts who voted *against* Clinton's policies.

The results are quite clear. Where Clinton ran poorly in 1992, Democratic incumbents with a pro-Clinton voting record in Congress were much more likely to be defeated than those with lower levels of support for the President. In districts where Clinton won less than 40 percent of the actual vote in 1992 (which we dub "conservative" districts), the higher the incumbents' pro-Clinton voting records, the greater the percentage of defeats. In the most marginally Democratic districts, *no* incumbents with a low Presidential support score were defeated, but a *majority* of those who had been highly supportive of the Clinton program lost. In districts where Clinton got 40 to 50 percent of the 1992 vote ("moderate" districts), the percentage of incumbents losing was lower than in the conservative districts, but, again, the more pro-Clinton an incumbent's voting record, the higher the probability that incumbent would be defeated. Where Clinton did well in 1992—winning a clear majority of the total vote—only one Democrat was defeated.[4] This pattern is robust to different choices of thresholds between categories.

This is the same pattern we note with regard to congressional elections during the Reagan-Bush years.[5] Members of Congress must be careful to represent their districts, even at the expense of their party, if they hope to be reelected. This finding is not new. Fenno (1978) emphasizes members' "reelection constituencies" to which they must appeal, and whose support they can maintain from one election to the next if they vote with their districts' preferences. Gilmour (1995) argues that actions that satisfy these constituencies often undermine the negotiations and compromise necessary to overcome political stalemate, leading to extreme proposals that have little chance of passing. Although we agree that district preferences and institutional structures lead to gridlock, we note that occasionally the desire to overcome gridlock puts members' seats at risk. In an attempt to please the party and the President and to end gridlock, Democrats from conservative districts voted in ways that were considered too liberal at election time. This accounted for the Republican landslide in 1994.

In January 1995, the new Republican Congress (especially the House) came to Washington with the belief that they had received a clear mandate for change. Not only had their victories come over incumbent Democrats who had supported the President, but they had also signed a "Contract with America" promising a reduced and reformed government and a balanced budget. Before we proceed to evaluate the Republicans' progress with these goals, a further look at the principal actors' changed positions on the gridlock scale would be useful.

Prior to the election President Clinton's policy agenda was left of the floor median in the House and Senate, and close to or roughly at his party's median. The failure of health care, campaign finance reform, and the stimulus bill and the rightward adjustments to the NAFTA and BTU tax bills testify to the President's position. The President in this situation was not *vetoing* legislation but was rather trying to build *majorities* for legislation. In fact, his threatened use of the veto unless Congress gave him a health care bill with universal coverage had hurt the chances for the bill because there was no majority for universal coverage. The election results indicated that the American public was to the right of both the President and the Democratic 103rd Congress.

The Republican House would now set the agenda for the 104th Congress, and a fundamental question became: How far to the right would their proposals be? On issues of political reform—a balanced budget, term limits, reduced congressional staffs, and the line-item veto—our view is that the new median member of the *entire* Congress was not far from the American public's preference, but that the median member of the Republican Party (and especially of the freshman class) was too conservative for the American people. If the Republicans held together as a party and made proposals to dramatically cut expenditures, especially entitlements, then the nature of the political situation would shift tremendously. A substantial Republican agenda too far to the right of the public would put President Clinton in the position of being able to veto such legislation in the name of moderation, placing him in a favorable light and leaving the Republican Congress in the unenviable position the President had been in a year earlier—too far away from the center. In the discussion that follows we shall argue that this is exactly what happened. Republicans were largely successful in passing governmental reforms (indeed often with Democratic support). However, when it came time to vote for entitlements cuts to balance the budget, the President was able to position himself as the moderate. This is not to say that on certain issues such as aid to agriculture and environmental legislation some moderate Republicans did not intervene to shift policy proposals back to the left. Rather, we argue that in general a unified Republican majority proposed and passed a budget that was "perceived" as being harsh (i.e., right of center), thus giving President Clinton the middle ground between the liberals in his own party and the Republican majority.

The Republican Agenda

The Republicans in the 104th Congress were committed to political reform. Among other reforms, the Republicans sought to reduce congressional staffs by one-third, restructure the committee system, eliminate the use of proxy votes in committees and subcommittees, restrict the number of terms a member could chair a committee, and limit the number of terms Speakers could serve. They also sought: (1) a balanced budget amendment, (2) an amendment limiting the number of terms Representatives and Senators could serve, (3) a line-item veto for the President on budget issues, (4) an end to unfunded mandates, and (5) campaign finance reform. Of these reforms, all were majority-vote items in the House (if they received presidential support), except the two amendments regarding a balanced budget and term limits. With regard to the two Constitutional amendments, both the House and the Senate would have to deliver two-thirds of their membership in order to start the amendment process. Thus on both these items Republicans needed Democratic support in order to gain the necessary votes. All the other reform proposals would only require a majority in the House; however, in the Senate the Democrats could use the filibuster to move policy in their direction, and the presidential veto could provide an even greater constraint. Such were the constraints on other Republican proposals as well, including ending unfunded mandates and turning welfare programs over to the states. Table 6.2 shows the major proposals of the 104th Congress and their resolution.

As Figure 6.1 made clear, whether the battles were framed by the need for two-thirds support to propose a Constitutional amendment, an identical supermajority to override a presidential veto, or three-fifths support to overcome possible fil-

TABLE 6.2 Major Legislation in the 104th Congress

Type of Legislation	Bill	Initial House Proposal	Provisions	Changes	Pivotal Members
Constitutional Amendments	Balanced budget	Right of median	1. 3/5ths vote on tax increases 2. Balance by 2002	1. Stripped 2. Still lost in Senate	Bingaman (D., N.Mex.) Daschle (D., S. Dak.) Dorgan (D., N. Dak.)
	Term limits	Right of median	1. Three two-year terms	1. Six two-year terms 2. Still defeated	Senior Democrats and Republicans
Supermajority Legislation	Line-item veto	About median	1. Enhanced rescissions	1. Weakened slightly 2. Dole pressure	Breaux (D., La.) Heflin (D., Ala.)
	Unfunded mandates	Right of median	1. 3/5ths point-of-order override 2. $50 million on private business	1. Stripped 2. $100 million on private business	Conservative Democrats
	Budget	Right of median	1. Cut $894 billion in spending 2. Reduce increases in entitlements, e.g., Medicare, Medicaid 3. Reduce taxes $245 billion 4. Balance by 2002	1. Smaller cuts 2. Abandoned 3. Abandoned 4. Abandoned	Multiple coalitions attempted and abandoned
	Welfare	Right of median	1. $82 billion in savings (six years) 2. AFDC to states 3. Medicaid to states 4. School lunches, food stamps options to states	1. $54 billion in savings 2. Retained 3. Abandoned 4. Abandoned	Moderate Democrats up for reelection

ibusters, the constraint would be in the more-moderate Senate. The Republican revolution may have captured the House by storm, but the battle lines would be drawn in the Senate.

Proposed Constitutional Amendments

We begin with the two constitutional amendments. The balanced budget amendment preferred by House Republicans required a three-fifths majority of both bodies in order to raise taxes to balance the budget. This was not surprising given that Republicans generally prefer a smaller government, resulting from reduced taxes and spending. Liberal Democrats, of course, would not support such an amendment; thus, in order to garner the two-thirds vote necessary to propose the amendment, attention focused on moderate, conservative, and southern Democrats like Charles Stenholm of Texas. The Conservative Democratic Caucus favored a balanced budget amendment that did not include the three-fifths tax requirement. Without these Democratic votes it was clear that the amendment would not pass the House. What was unclear was whether, if conservative Democrats' only choice was to vote for a balanced budget amendment that included the three-fifths tax requirement, they would vote for it over the status quo (no amendment). If the Republican leaders could be certain that these Democrats would vote for their amendment over the status quo, they could have the Rules Committee report out a rule requiring an up-or-down vote on only the Republican amendment. Stenholm was the primary spokesman for the conservative Democrats, and he went to great pains to say that the Caucus (about seventy votes) would not vote for the Republican amendment, thus ensuring its defeat. Stenholm, on the other hand, felt sure that the Republicans, if faced with a majority-rule amendment or no amendment, would vote for his alternate balanced budget amendment, which did not include the three-fifths tax condition. This was a case in which uncertainty about members' preferences would act in favor of the status quo.

The problem was resolved when the Rules Committee issued a "Queen of the Prom" amendment that allowed each alternative to be voted on against the status quo.[6] The first vote was to be on the Republican amendment and, if it passed, it would be the new status quo against which the Stenholm amendment would be pitted. If the Republican amendment collected two-thirds of the vote, then the Stenholm amendment would fail because Republicans would vote against it. If it failed to get these necessary votes, then the Republicans would have to choose between the status quo (no amendment) and the Stenholm amendment. The conservative Democrats were betting that the Republicans would vote with them on this latter vote. In the first vote on the Republican amendment the conservative Democrats voted no, thus killing the three-fifths tax clause amendment. The vote on the Stenholm amendment forced the Republicans to choose between either a failure to get *any* amendment or a balanced budget amendment that was not as strong on taxes as they preferred. In the end, the Republicans voted for the Stenholm amendment, as did more than seventy Democrats, which yielded the necessary two-thirds majority. Clearly, the supermajority Constitutional requirement forced a change in policy from what the majority preferred, and the policy had to be shifted left toward conservative and moderate Democrats in order to pass.

The Senate presented a different story. Because the Senate was more moderate than the House and Senators had not endorsed the Contract with America, the likelihood of passage was smaller. The chance that the Senate would pass an amendment with a three-fifths tax requirement was nonexistent, and thus they would clearly be voting on the Stenholm amendment. Furthermore, the Republican majority faced a worthy adversary in Senator Robert Byrd (W.Va.), a former majority leader and a master of Senate rules, who led the battle against the amendment. As in the House, the crucial votes necessary for passage of the two-thirds majority were southern and moderate-to-conservative Democrats. Media accounts of key voters featured the names of moderate Democratic Senators like Nunn (Ga.), Ford (Ky.), Hollings (S.C.), and Bingaman (N.Mex.). These Senators were presented as moderate Democrats on the various preference rating scales in the previous chapter. Nunn and Ford were classified as median members on more rankings than any other Senators (Table 5.1). Bingaman is only slightly more liberal, positioned at about the veto pivot in the 104th Congress, given the shift to the right in the 1994 elections.

The Senate had voted on balanced budget amendments in 1986 and 1994, and in each case the amendment had failed. The sweeping nature of the Republican victory in 1994 gave the amendment's backers their best shot at victory. For five weeks the Senate debated the amendment, which called for a balanced budget every year starting in 2002, unless three-fifths of both Houses voted to suspend the requirement. It was clear that the amendment was supported by a majority in the Senate and in the country as a whole. Opponents of the amendment needed cover, and they found it in Social Security. As the Senate vote neared, opponents argued "that Social Security was somehow threatened, on the basis that the surplus revenue from the payroll tax used to pay for the program is being used to mask the size of the deficit" (1995 *Congressional Quarterly Weekly Report*, 673).[7] Several swing Democrats said that they would vote for the amendment if Social Security were exempted (which would mean that the unified budget that includes Social Security would no longer be the standard accounting mechanism). In the final vote, fourteen Democrats voted with fifty-one Republicans for the amendment, for a total of sixty-five votes.[8] Of these fourteen Democrats, seven were up for reelection in 1996, and three, Baucus (Mont.), Biden (Del.), and Harkin (Iowa), changed their votes from 1994. Of the thirty-five Democrats voting against the amendment, six changed their 1994 "yes" votes to "no"—Bingaman, Daschle (S.Dak.), Dorgan (N.Dak.), Feinstein (Calif.), Ford, and Hollings—and none of them were up for reelection in 1996. Thus, once again, a balanced budget amendment had failed and the key was that moderate Democrats who were not up for reelection chose to vote against the amendment.

Because limiting the terms served by House and Senate members would necessitate a constitutional amendment, this reform also requires a two-thirds vote. The odds for passing it in the Senate were low given the Senate's more moderate nature, and passage of the amendment in the House was problematic because key Republicans like Bill Archer (Tex.; Chair, Ways and Means) and Henry Hyde (Ill.; Chair, Judiciary) were opposed to term limits. A majority of the congressional Democrats were also opposed, and the combination of Democrats and senior Republicans opposing the amendment was formidable. The freshman Republicans were adamant, however, and insisted that the House at least *vote* on the issue. The Judiciary Committee held hearings and reported out a bill limiting House members to six two-year terms (twelve years total) and Senators to two six-year terms. The only bargaining point was how many terms members should be limited to, with some freshman Republicans advocating three two-year terms. It was obvious that the greater the number of terms allowed, the greater the chance of passage, and thus the Judiciary Committee's bill was offered as a less-constraining alternative to freshmen desires. The hearings and the debate did little to change preferences. In the vote, the combination of senior Republicans and Democrats was enough to keep the amendment from receiving the necessary two-thirds supermajority. The final vote tallied 40 Republicans and 187 Democrats opposing—enough to defeat the Amendment. The correlation between seniority and the vote was high (over 0.7), indicating that recently elected House members were in favor of term limits whereas senior members were inclined to oppose. In fact, 30 of the 40 Republicans voting against the amendment chaired a committee or subcommittee. The issue was not likely to have much of an electoral effect because seniors like Archer and Hyde would be reelected in spite of their "no" votes, while freshmen who had campaigned for term limits could use this to their advantage in their reelection bids.

As can be seen, constitutional amendments fit well into the revolving gridlock model, along with statutory lawmaking. Proposed amendments that have too conservative a flavor must be tempered to gain votes. But the two-thirds voting restriction is very constraining, and thus most proposed amendments (even after moderation) will fail against the formidable status quo position of the unamended U.S. Constitution.

Reforms Under Less-Restrictive Rules

Neither of the two amendments to the Constitution, which required supermajorities, had passed. In the House the balanced budget amendment received the necessary two-thirds vote only after the original Republican amendment had been modified. The failure of the bill by a single vote in the Senate killed the amendment, although in a parliamentary move Senator Dole voted against the bill to preserve the right to bring it up again. The budget crunch in late 1995 turned attention away from the amendment, reducing the likelihood of passage later in the session. The Senate Judiciary Committee reported out a term limits bill, but the odds that Senator Dole could bring it successfully to passage by a two-thirds majority were low. Governmental reforms needing only a simple majority vote (or facing only filibuster possibilities) fared better. On January 4 and 5 the House passed a rules revision and a congressional accountability act. Congressional staffs were cut by one-third, committees were rearranged, Chairs' terms were limited (as was the Speaker's), proxy voting was ended, and House members were no longer exempt from federal laws. On January 11 the Senate passed the congressional accountability law. In these internal reform measures, majorities of House Democrats supported Republican rule changes; for example, term limits for the Speaker and committee Chairs passed 355 to 74. Pat Williams (D., Mont.) summed up many Democrats' feelings when he said: "A lot of what the Republicans are doing is good. Democrats should have done this if we could have, but we couldn't. . . . We had a stake in continuing the status quo" (1995 *Congressional Quarterly Weekly Report,* 13).

By March 7 the House and Senate had passed a paperwork reduction bill, the main feature of the bill being the reduction of paperwork requirements on business. The legislation authorized an annual 10 percent across-the-board decrease in paperwork and reauthorized the Office of Information and Regulatory Affairs (OIRA) in OMB to oversee the reductions. The vote in the House was 418 to 0 and the Senate passed the bill 99 to 0.

Line-Item Veto.   The President's line-item veto for budget matters was more controversial, especially because the President was a Democrat. Nevertheless, by the end of March 1995, both House and Senate had passed a line-item veto. Technically the bills passed were not line-item vetoes, because such a bill would require amending the Constitution (and many still argue that the bill passed is unconstitutional). Rather, the House and Senate bills increased the President's authority to propose spending cuts. The House bill extended the President's "enhanced rescissions" power to cut spending out of appropriations bills that had become law and allowed the President to target tax breaks going to fewer than one hundred individuals. As it was, the President could request rescinding expenditures but Congress was free to and did ignore such rescissions. The new "line-item veto" required that when the President proposed rescissions they take effect unless Congress were to block them via a complicated process requiring a two-thirds vote. The essential idea behind the veto is to curb the congressional tendency to slip "pork barrel" projects into appropriation bills that the President has to sign (in toto) or veto (in toto).

Critics argued that the bill tipped power too much toward the President, and that aggressive Presidents could rewrite appropriations bills wholesale to punish opponents and reward supporters. In voting for this bill, the House rejected a

Stenholm "expedited rescission" bill that had passed in 1994. In addition, they rejected other Democratic amendments such as a proposal to allow the President to "veto" any tax bill benefiting the top 10 percent of taxpayers. The Republican bill passed 294 to 134, with 71 Democrats voting in favor. Note the difference between this bill and the balanced budget amendment. When the Republicans needed a two-thirds majority, they ended up supporting the Stenholm amendment that weakened their preferred proposal. Here, however, they rejected the Stenholm plan and passed their preferred plan; this was possible because they needed only a simple majority, 218 votes, to win. Democrats who favored "enhanced rescission" were forced to choose between the status quo (no veto) and the Republican plan, and most of these Democrats voted for the Republican plan—reversing the votes cast in the balanced budget amendment that included the three-fifths tax clause.

Senator McCain (R., Ariz.) introduced a line-item veto bill much like the House version, but difficulties soon arose and a substitute proposal was put forward. The version that was finally accepted mandated that, after appropriations bills were passed, any new legislation regarding spending or taxing must be broken down into literally hundreds of smaller bills, and it is these bills that the President may "veto." In effect the Senate bill gives less power to the President because it specifies which items the President may veto. The compromise passed the Senate 69 to 29, with nineteen Democrats voting "yes." Those voting in favor were the usual set of moderate Democrats—Breaux (La.), Ford, Heflin (Ala.), and others—plus some liberals up for reelection like Harkin.

It is not surprising that the bill proposed by the Senate provided a weaker form of a line-item veto. It is unlikely that a President would veto any legislation giving him extended powers. As such, the supermajority constraint on this legislation comes in the form of the Senate filibuster. In order to provide a line-item veto acceptable to more than sixty Senators, the bill needed to be weakened, and it was.

The two Houses had passed different versions of the line-item veto. Neither had tried to pass a constitutional amendment, given the strict two-thirds voting rule required by the amendment process; rather, in their bills, both had focused on procedures allowing the regular appropriations process to go to completion and then, and only then, allowing the President to move to cut appropriated moneys. The House procedure limited the President's line-item veto powers, but less so than the Senate version. Having passed two different versions, Congress sent the legislation to a conference committee. Getting a compromise bill would have been difficult even under ordinary circumstances, and as time progressed the differences on the reconciliation budget between the President and the Republican Congress left the Republicans with little reason to hurry the line-item veto conference toward resolution. In other words, as it became clear that President Clinton would veto the *entire* Republican budget, Republicans were not anxious to hand him a new tool to aid him in his dispute with Congress. Regardless, by that point, it was clear that the line-item veto would not be allowed to go into effect until after the 1996 elections. Throughout the 1995–1996 budget fight, the conferees sat on the "line-item veto," keeping it locked up in the conference committee.

In late March 1996, a year after the initial proposals had been adopted, an agreement was reached in conference. Bob Dole had captured enough support in the primaries to be confident of his nomination as the Republican Party's candidate for President. He now turned his attention to passing some major legislation in the Senate. As such, he put pressure on Senate Republicans to support the stronger rescission provisions of the House's line-item veto proposal. Although the bill was weakened somewhat for the less-conservative tastes of the Senate, much of the language of the House bill was retained by the conference committee. In the end, it all came down to "whatever Bob Dole wants to do," as Thad Cochran (R., Miss.) put it (1996 *Congressional Quarterly Weekly Report*, 780). Dole was able to gain the support of fifty Republican Senators, with nineteen Democrats joining in passing the conference report, on March 27. The following day, the House followed suit by a vote of 232 to 177.

Unfunded Mandates Limitations. The unfunded mandates bill passed the Senate on January 27, 1995. This bill was designed to curb the imposition of new requirements on state and local governments that cost these governments money to meet the requirements. Any federal legislation that would impose costs of more than $50 million on state and local governments would be subject to a "point of order." Once a point of order had been moved, majorities in each chamber would have to vote to waive it; if waived, the legislation would be sent to the floor. Bills relating to civil rights, national security, and disaster relief were exempt from this legislation. The Congressional Budget Office (CBO) was tasked with estimating the costs of bills, amendments, and conference reports that would impose the mandates. The idea behind the bill was that by forcing representatives to vote on mandates, there will be fewer of them. Previously such unfunded mandates were routinely buried in bills, and members were not held accountable for them.

In a previous chapter we showed how, given budget constraints, the Congress and the President had increased the passage of off-budget legislation, which pushed costs onto state and local governments, businesses, and consumers. The Americans with Disabilities Act is a case in point. That legislation requires governments, businesses, local schools, and other bodies to, among other things, provide special access to disabled persons. These kinds of renovations obviously cost money, and they are not funded by the federal government that required them in the first place. The increase in such off-budget items generated opposition from state and local government officials, who favored the unfunded mandates legislation.

Passage of the bill in the Senate was not easy. There were fifty-nine hours of debate on the bill and forty-four roll call votes before it finally passed, 89 to 10, with all dissenting votes coming from Democrats. The final arrangement was a compromise because Senator Gramm's amendment to require a three-fifths majority to override a point of order was withdrawn due to lack of support and a threatened filibuster. Democratic opponents failed in their attempts to amend the bill by exempting mandates that involved the health of children, pregnant women, and the elderly; public health and welfare; radioactive substances; and so on.

The House passed its version of the unfunded mandates bill on February 1, 1995. The House version, like the Senate bill, required a point of order on any mandate costing over $50 million. The same set of issues—civil rights, national security, and disaster relief—was exempted. The House bill differed in that it exposed federal agencies to lawsuits if the agencies fail to perform cost-benefit analyses or do not consult local officials. The House bill also required a point of order on unfunded mandates of over $50 million on *private business,* whereas the Senate version set the limit on businesses at $250 million. The conference committee faced some difficulties resolving these differences, which mirrored, of course, the difference between a more conservative House and a more moderate Senate. It is important to note that in the debates on unfunded mandates, the Americans with Disabilities Act and the Clean Air amendments of 1990 were most frequently mentioned as those acts that the new legislation was trying to correct. Democratic Senators were especially worried that, because federal agencies were still formulating the rules for enforcing the Clean Air Act (PL 101-549), the unfunded mandates bill might be used to restrict the Clean Air Act. An amendment to include revisions of previous mandates in the unfunded mandates bill was voted down as being too conservative for even the House.

Passage of the act in the House was not easy, with well over a hundred amendments proposed on the floor tying up the bill for two weeks. The opponents' strategy was to add public health, environmental, and labor laws to the exempted requirements. On average, about eighty Democrats joined Republicans in voting down these amendments. The eighty were conservative and moderate Democrats from southern, border, and midwestern states. The conference committee compromised on the House-Senate differences by setting a $100 million cost limit on private sector mandates and by requiring federal agencies to consult with local officials before passing mandates. Conservatives such as Phil Gramm felt that the bill was not strong enough, whereas liberals felt that it went too far. The President signed the bill on March 22.

Other Reforms. Other reforms such as registering lobbying groups and consolidating regulatory agencies moved through the 104th Congress. In the end, the record on reform was mixed. The internal reforms were passed early and did not require the President's signature. Unfunded mandates, lobbyist registration, and a gift ban passed and became law. The line-item veto passed both Houses but was still in conference when the budget battle began. And both constitutional amendments—term limits and the balanced budget amendment—had failed to get the two-thirds vote necessary for passage. One important reform popular with the American public—campaign finance reform—had not been considered.

Campaign finance reform is an interesting issue in that, during the Bush administration, the Democratic Congress had passed a bill secure in the knowledge that the President would veto it. The election of a Democratic President might have signaled to some that the Democratic bill of 1992 would become law; however, without the veto threat and subsequent ability to blame the President, Democrats failed to get a bill in the 103rd Congress. Public concern over the role of money in campaigns continues to be high, and interest groups like Common Cause and Ralph Nader's organizations (such as his state-based Public Interest Research Groups) continue to push for public financing. Despite the public pressure, campaign finance reform is a hard issue to promote in Congress.[9] Republicans, who had suffered since at least 1978 because of the greater funds available to Democratic incumbents (Jacobson 1981), had wanted reforms prior to the 104th; whereas the majority of Democrats had enjoyed a monetary advantage and thus were reluctant to give it up. With the Republicans now in the majority and Political Action Committee (PAC) money flowing their way, the Republicans in the 104th Congress were slow to move. Nevertheless, given the public pressure, President Clinton and Speaker Gingrich shook hands on June 11, 1995, sealing a promise to create a commission to explore changes in the way campaigns are financed. Little occurred after the handshake. Clinton issued a statement detailing how the commission should be structured, while Gingrich admitted that the issue was complicated and said that he would develop a position paper.

Activity in the committees focused on two main proposals. In the House a bipartisan group of Representatives put forward a bill making modest changes in PAC donations and banning member-run PACs. In the Senate there was a bipartisan plan to control campaign spending and eliminate PAC donations to Senate candidates. The Senate plan set voluntary limits based on voting populations and provided free TV time and reduced postage rates to candidates who abided by the limits. In addition, 60 percent of expenditures were required to be raised in-state, and higher expenditures were allowed for candidates running against self-funded opponents. Prospects for passage did not look good because the Republican point man in the Senate—McConnell (R., Ky.)—threatened to filibuster a Clinton independent commission arrangement. In short, whereas some preferred public financing, others preferred less restricted monetary limits à la pre-1974 rules, and still others preferred minor rather than major changes. Given these varied preferences, plus the importance of the issue to incumbents, there was no majority for any specific change, and campaign finance reform remained in the gridlock region.

The bills that did resurface from committees in 1996 had little chance of success. The bipartisan bill in the Senate was indeed filibustered and declared dead by the end of June after a failed attempt at cloture, losing by six votes, 54 to 46. With the bipartisan bill failing to gain the necessary supermajority in the Senate, partisan and electoral politics came into play. Bills drafted by each party were considered in the House in July, with both the Republican and Democratic proposals going down in defeat.

The Republican agenda had also called for passage of crime legislation, civil litigation overhaul, changes in product liability legislation, and welfare reform. Moreover, the Contract with America had proclaimed that this legislation would be passed in the House within the first one hundred days, and to a large extent the House succeeded. Between February 7 and 14 the House passed six new crime bills; by February 24 they had passed a moratorium on federal regulations; and by March 10 they had passed a civil litigation bill and a product liability act. Within a week the House had passed a welfare overhaul bill. Scholars "[were] amazed by the House Republicans' ability to keep the Contract with America on its steady 100-day time table" (1995 *Congressional Quarterly Weekly Report,* 909). The agenda setter was clearly the Republican House, not the President. One scholar, David Mayhew, went so far as to say: "Not only is the President not taking a major part, he is largely on the other side" (1995 *Congressional Quarterly Weekly Report,* 911). Other scholars compared these hundred days to the 1867 period when the Radical Republicans set the agenda and neutralized President Andrew Johnson by impeaching him. Professor James Thurber felt that the Republicans were "cutting back the scope of government rather than defining problems and finding solutions" (1995 *Congressional Quarterly Weekly Report,* 912). Regardless of their views about the desirability of the policies, they agreed that there were few precedents for the achievements of the 104th Congress.

In spite of these comments, by the end of the first session, exactly two of the Contract's ten provisions had been signed into law. One was the requirement that the Congress end its own exempt status from eleven workplace laws. The other was the above-mentioned unfunded mandates bill and a bill to reduce federal paperwork. Still unfinished were a major telecommunications bill, a final version of the line-item veto, an intelligence authorization bill, a defense authorization bill, the product liability bill, a significant banking reorganization act, some nonreconciliation farm matters, the Superfund toxic cleanup act, and the regulatory overhaul bill, among others. What accounts for the end-of-session malaise on substantive legislation despite the House's success after one hundred days?

The primary explanation is that the Senate had failed to pass the House legislation, as in the case of the balanced budget amendment; to pass the *same version,* as in the case of the line-item veto; or to act on the legislation at all. Considering just the items in the Contract, as of mid-December 1995 the Senate still had in committee House crime legislation including required restitution to victims (H.R. 665), modification of the exclusionary rule (H.R. 666), and block grants to give communities control over funds (H.R. 728). The national security legislation passed by the House (H.R. 7) had not been reported out by a committee. The parts of the Contract covering civil law and product liability (H.R. 988) had not passed out of committee, and the Senate had not yet considered term limits (S.J. Res. 21). On those Contract items where the Senate had acted, they had passed or were about to pass legislation that differed from the House versions. As a result, legislation involving the line-item veto, welfare (H.R. 4 and H.R. 2491), tax credits, Social Security benefits, capital gains cuts, and frivolous suits against companies were all in conference.

The major reasons for the Senate's inaction were as follows: (1) Senate rules allow individual Senators more influence, which leads to delays; (2) the possibility of a filibuster by the Democratic minority or of a presidential veto increases uncertainty over what will pass; and (3) the median Senator was clearly left of the median House Republican. In order for Senator Dole to win even a majority vote he had to have the votes of his party's moderates: Chafee (R.I.), Cohen, Specter, Kassebaum (Kans.), Jeffords, Campbell (Colo.), and others. In order to beat a filibuster he had to have all these votes plus the votes of moderate Democrats like Heflin, Nunn, Breaux, and Johnson (La.). And to override a presidential veto— well, that didn't seem likely at all. Thus getting major policy shifts passed was a delicate task given that the Senate was more liberal and that the rules prohibited speedy expedition of legislation.

Passing major policy shifts that downsized government would have been difficult under any conditions, but the actions of House Republicans, especially the freshmen, exacerbated the problem. In their fervor to "keep faith with America," the freshmen, who were unaccustomed to the give-and-take of politics, tried to push the Senate into action by attaching riders to bills they had passed. For example, House Republicans attached to the appropriations bill for housing and other domestic programs a set of provisions that stripped the Environmental Protection Agency (EPA) of its power to regulate and enforce major sections of the air and water pollution laws. In another bill they attached a rider allowing exploratory drilling in the Alaska National Wildlife Refuge. These environmental riders went to the Senate Environment and Public Works Committee chaired by Senator Chafee, who refused to consider the House legislation, saying: "The so-called clean water bill they sent over went way beyond what was acceptable to me and way beyond what was acceptable in the Senate as a whole" (1995 *Congressional Quarterly Weekly Report*, 3712–3713).

The Republicans in the House had held together remarkably well throughout the first year, although some moderates had shifted policy to the left on the environment and on tax cuts for "the rich." Overall, although there were some splits, the congressional Republican Party remained largely unified. The seventy-three first-term Republicans generally pulled the party to the right across a whole set of issues. They believed that they had been elected to transform American politics by downsizing the role of government as regulator, provider of entitlements, and tax collector. All year the Republican leadership had tried to carefully shift the status quo across a set of policies without moving so far that they would not be able to achieve their policy objectives. Internally they were divided over how far to go, with some arguing that being timid put them at greater risk with voters than did boldness. Freshman Republican Senator James Inhofe (Okla.) summed up this position when he said: "The old way of negotiating [splitting differences] and giving in is not what we want" (1995 *Congressional Quarterly Weekly*

Report, 3709). Activist Republicans referred time and again to the policies of George Bush, especially his 1990 budget deal. By mid- to late October it became clear that in spite of the Senate's moderation the country's public policies were being shifted to the right—and thus away from the status quo.

A summary of Republican legislative action in the 104th Congress typically boils down to a single question, as suggested by the revolving gridlock theory: How great of a supermajority constraint is institutionally imposed on the passage of particular pieces of legislation? The 1994 elections were indeed remarkable— the Contract with America attests to numerous policy areas where new majorities for change have been established in the Congress. Yet, with the need for sixty votes in the Senate to overcome possible filibusters, much of the House legislation has been held up or toned down. More significantly, where two-thirds supermajorities are needed—for the constitutional amendments balancing the budget and imposing term limits, and for vetoed legislation like the Republican budget and welfare plans—the proposals are stopped dead. The gridlock region in these cases truly does result in gridlock. The newly Republican Congress will not move policy to the left, and movements to the right that don't meet Clinton's approval will result in sustained vetoes.

In an election year these battles are played out in the public view, with extremely high stakes. If the Republican proposals are "too conservative" for the public, the President can veto legislation and seize the middle ground. By laying claim to the moderate agenda, Clinton won the battles over environmental protection and other issues and was able to lay the blame for the government shutdowns on the Republicans; his 1996 State of the Union Address set forth this moderate agenda. However, if certain Republican proposals are considered "moderate" by the public, the President will be inclined to sign them, rather than veto and appear too liberal. Yet by signing such "moderate" Republican legislation the President would be upsetting the liberal wing of his own party. Nowhere did this conflict provide public drama better than in the 1995–1996 debates over the budget.

The 1995–1996 Budget Standoff

Many of the substantial changes in policy passed by the Republican House (and sometimes the Senate) had budgetary implications. Welfare reform, for example, had such implications: How should states receive federal moneys for Aid to Families with Dependent Children (AFDC) and how *much* should they receive? Likewise, how much should the EPA receive, given that the Republicans wanted fewer regulations? As the end of the fiscal year (October 31) approached and much of the "Contract" (and other substantive legislation) was still in Senate or conference committees, the reconciliation budget loomed larger. Most professional Washington observers expected a clash over the budget. The differences between and within the parties had slowed down the reconciliation process. Under "normal" conditions, when a final bill is not finished on time, Congress passes and the President signs a continuing resolution to keep the government running until the final reconciliation has been worked out.

In 1995 the Republican strategy was to deny the President a chance to veto the reconciliation bill and the spending bills without simultaneously shutting down the government. Given that the Republicans knew that they would not have all thirteen appropriations bills ready by the end of fiscal year, they passed and sent to the President two budget-related bills. The first was a stopgap spending bill, the second a short-term borrowing extension for the Treasury. Both bills contained "poison pills," measures that the President had promised to veto. From November 8 to 13 the House and Senate—in party-line votes—passed the stopgap appropriations bill and the debt limit bill and sent them to President Clinton. On November 13, 1995, the President vetoed both bills and on November 14, 800,000 "nonessential" federal workers were sent home. On November 15 the House and Senate passed another continuing resolution funding the government through December 5, 1995, and on November 17 the House and Senate (again in party-line votes) passed a reconciliation budget that cut taxes and balanced the budget by 2002. Thus, as had been true since at least 1981, the budget reconciliation act came to dominate congressional politics. Smaller government, lower taxes, less regulation, shifting control of government back to state and local levels—all Republican issues in 1994—boiled down to the central questions of what to cut and how much.

The newly elected Republican majorities had "promised" Americans that they would both reduce taxes and balance the budget by shrinking the size of the government. The vehicle for accomplishing this was the standard reconciliation budget. The basic steps in the reconciliation process are: (1) the passage through both Houses of a budget resolution that contains the economic assumptions, the tax component of the budget (reduced as in 1981 or raised as in 1993), the cuts in expenditures (discretionary and entitlements), and the instructions to the relevant authorizing committees in regard to the amounts (though not in regard to how to meet the reconciliation targets); (2) the passage through regular means of the tax bill and the thirteen appropriations bills; and (3) after the House-Senate conferences, the passage of a final reconciliation package.

In all of the major budget and tax reforms since 1981, the support of the President has been crucial. With no public consensus about how to address the deficit, gaining even bare majorities has been difficult. President Reagan played a crucial role in the budget and tax reforms of 1981, and then went along with some forms of tax increases in 1982 and 1984. Increases that he opposed stood no chance of passage. In order to deal with deficits in 1990, President Bush had to break his promise of "no new taxes" and go along with the Democrats. In 1993, President Clinton secured a budget deal with the barest of majorities, and with the support of only Democrats. In 1995, the Republican congressional majorities had three possible strategies with regard to the budget package: (1) to forge a budget deal that the President would sign; (2) to attempt the unprecedented (and highly unlikely) maneuver of gaining the two-thirds necessary to override a veto of a budget bill; or (3) to score some political points by proposing a major budget bill and having the President veto it, despite being unable to override the veto.

With the Congress to the right of the President, and with the House of Representatives being more conservative than the Senate, the battle lines were drawn. The House budget resolution had deeper cuts in taxes and spending than did the Senate budget resolution. In conference, the difference in tax reduction was split down the middle, while the House expenditure cuts were tempered by the more moderate Senate cuts. In the Senate, not only were the Republicans more moderate, but the rules allowed the Democratic Senators more room to maneuver to block the "harsher" aspects of the House resolution. The joint House-Senate budget resolution essentially claimed that it would reduce taxes by over $200 billion while promising to achieve a balanced unified budget by the year 2002. The "unified budget" includes the Social Security Trust Fund and other nondiscretionary budget items in its accounting. The last unified balanced budget had been in 1969—thus the budget resolution of 1995 promised to end twenty-six consecutive years of unbalanced budgets.

Budget resolutions are not binding and, as happened in 1981, authorizing committees can report bills that do not meet reconciliation targets, thus creating final budgets that are larger than intended. In short, the hard work begins after the passage of the budget resolution. Over the next few months debates about how to balance the budget were prominent in the government and in the media. Moderate and conservative Democrats joined by some moderate Senate Republicans suggested eliminating the tax cuts in order to more easily balance the budget. Representatives from agricultural districts fought to keep the cuts in their areas from being too deep. On occasion, moderate Republicans voted with Democrats to prevent even deeper cuts in environmental programs. Opponents of welfare reform fought to keep federal standards for welfare policy. And so it went—there were battles in committees over the extent of cuts in federal programs and in Ways and Means over the depth and type of tax reduction.

The major problem for the Republicans was that given the reductions in federal revenue from the tax cut, the expenditure cuts had to be large, and the major entitlement expenditures were for popular programs such as Social Security and Medicare. One of the new majority's earliest positions was to take Social Security off the table ("building a firewall around it"), meaning that the largest entitlement program could not be touched. In order to achieve a balanced budget over seven years the Republicans were left with reductions in Medicare and Medicaid as viable vehicles for reconciliation purposes. It is important to note that the budget calculations made under reconciliation follow base-line spending. That is, if a program now spends $100 million annually and five years in the future is projected to cost $150 million, and the new budget authorizes spending $125 million in five years, the $25 million shortfall is treated as a cut. Thus if Medicare is projected to grow by 10 percent annually over the next five years and the rate of growth is slowed to 6 percent, the difference is counted as savings. In short, the disagreements between Democrats and Republicans and between the Congress and the President with regard to Medicare, Medicaid, and other issues are about cuts in the rate of growth and not about overall reductions. This does not mean that these are not real cuts because most of the projected growth in programs like Medicare comes from increases over time in the numbers enrolled in the programs.

The dilemma for the Republicans was that they could not reach a balanced budget by 2002 without cutting some entitlements, and with Social Security off the table Medicare and Medicaid were the most likely targets. Cutting into Medicare would be especially hard given the popularity of the program and given the fact that the elderly are well represented by interest groups like the American Association of Retired Persons (AARP). Through the summer of 1995, news stories featured various proposals for cutting taxes, with the flat tax making a comeback, and, more importantly, the battle to frame the Medicare question. Opponents of the Medicare cuts argued that Republicans were shredding the safety net for the elderly. Republicans got a break when the Social Security Trust Commission (a bipartisan commission) issued a report stating that Medicare would be broke sometime early in the twenty-first century. The Republicans tried to frame the issue by claiming that their policy proposals were intended to save Medicare.

In addition to Medicare, welfare reform loomed large. Republicans sought to turn the programs back to the states, whereas Democrats claimed that millions of children would be hurt by these Republican proposals. As votes on the individual appropriations occurred, various coalitions formed and re-formed. Conservative Republicans, especially from the freshman class, bolted over abortion issues to vote with liberal Democrats against a defense bill. This coalition was reminiscent of the Gingrich-Dellums liberal-conservative coalition of the 1990 Bush budget negotiations. Sometimes moderate Republicans voted with Democrats to temper conservative proposals as in the above-mentioned environmental legislation. The House-Senate differences also played a role in that the Senate bills were in general more moderate than the House bills.

Given the fundamentally different approaches of Democrats and Republicans, the House-Senate differences, and the fact that a Democratic President could veto legislation, the reconciliation process ran behind schedule—as it usually does. In the past the problem of the lack of appropriations bills before the end of the government's fiscal year has been solved by a continuing resolution allowing the government to continue spending, usually at the previous year's level. In addition, the government at this time would ordinarily seek an increase in the debt limit to borrow money to pay off the federal deficit. In 1995 the continuing resolution question, the extension of the debt ceiling, and the final reconciliation budget all needed to be addressed simultaneously in early November.

The reconciliation budget that was passed by Republicans in Congress would cut $894 billion from projected federal spending by 2002, producing a $4 billion surplus. The bill proposed entitlement reductions as follows: welfare, $82 billion; Medicare, $270 billion; Medicaid, $163 billion; and the paring back of agricultural subsidies with the ultimate goal of eliminating them. In addition, the reconciliation bill reduced taxes by $245 billion over seven years. The presidential vetoes of the stopgap and debt limit measures signaled his intention to use the veto to force Republicans to compromise on their reconciliation package. The President said that he would veto any "bill that requires crippling cuts in Medicare, weakens the environment, reduces educational opportunity or raises taxes on working families" (1995 *Congressional Quarterly Weekly Report*, 3505). Moreover, Clinton said that he would not sign any bill with cuts too large, even if it takes "90 days, 120 days, or 180 days" (CBS Evening News, November 15, 1995).

The battle lines were clearly drawn, and they delineated the major differences between the parties over the role of the federal government. The President's position was that the economic assumptions of the Republican bill (the CBO estimates) were too pessimistic; he preferred to use his own (OMB) estimates that predicted greater growth and less inflation, thereby decreasing expenditures and raising revenues over the coming years. The rosier assumptions meant that the cuts would not have to be as deep; these assumptions, combined with a smaller tax cut, allowed the President to project a balanced budget with less pain.

Given the shutdown and the Republicans' inability to override the President's veto, both sides compromised on a continuing resolution, which passed on November 20 and kept the government going until December 15. The President agreed to a balanced budget by 2002 as scored by the CBO, and in return Republicans agreed to have the CBO reestimate the effects of their budget given the stronger-than-expected growth in the U.S. economy in 1995. The new CBO estimates yielded about $130 billion more than the original estimates—a combination of lower expenditures and slightly higher corporate tax revenue given the balanced budget. Thus by December both sides could sit down and compare on an "oranges-to-oranges" basis the effects of their proposals (both tax cuts and expenditures) on the deficit.

Normal politics, however, was not to be. The President's strategy of criticizing the Republican budget as being too harsh and thus "against our [American] values" appeared to be winning the battle for public opinion. President Clinton's approval ratings climbed over 50 percent for the first time in more than a year. Moreover, the President and the Democrats had a 23 percent margin over Republicans in public opinion polls asking who could better handle the deficit— a major reversal from the early days of the 104th Congress.[10] Republicans insisted that the President keep his promise and bring to the negotiating table a CBO-scored budget that would eliminate the deficit by 2002. The December 15 continuing resolution deadline came with no agreement and once again parts of the government closed down. The President and the Democrats argued that it was the ideological freshman class of 1994 that was responsible for shutting down the government. Republicans insisted that the President was not to be trusted because he had not yet presented his balanced budget. On January 6, 1996, the ball began to roll again. The Republican Congress passed and the President signed a series of continuing resolutions to keep parts of the government operating through September and all of it through at least January 26, 1996. The President submitted a budget (using CBO scoring) that would be balanced by 2002. At last, two budget proposals were on the table that could be compared.

The President's proposal differed significantly from the Republican budget. Cuts in Medicare, Medicaid, and welfare were about one-half the size of the Republican cuts. The Clinton budget included tax cuts in the form of a $500 child credit plus a mild capital gains cut, and in addition there were proposals to raise taxes on corporations (either tax increases or the closing of tax loopholes, depending on one's position). Specifically the Clinton balanced budget proposal projected savings of $102 billion in Medicare, $52 billion in Medicaid, $43 billion in welfare, $296 billion in discretionary spending including national defense, $60 billion from closing corporate loopholes, and $87 billion in tax cuts, for a total savings of $526 billion. This plan projected an increase of $97 billion in savings over Clinton's December proposal. The President's tax cut was over three years, with the possibility of renewing the cuts if the economy performed well. The cuts in discretionary spending, Medicare, and Medicaid were back loaded such that the brunt of the cuts would be felt in the last two years—2001 and 2002. For example, $185 billion of the $296 billion in discretionary cuts were scheduled for the last two years. Agricultural programs and student loans were spared in the President's budget. The Republican plan cut $99 billion more in Medicare, $65 billion more in Medicaid, $88 billion more in discretionary spending, $37 billion more in welfare, and a whopping $154 billion more in taxes. In sum, there were major differences between the President's budget and the Republican Congress's budget.

The initial Republican reaction was to try to portray the Clinton budget as more tax-and-spend liberalism. The Democrats, on the other hand, portrayed their budget as a responsible plan that put the burden of payment where it belonged while preserving the social safety net. The Republican leadership in the House was seriously negotiating with conservative and moderate Democrats (who had earlier proposed their own balanced budget) in an attempt to put forward a budget that was closer to their initial proposal and for which they could garner significant bipartisan support. The Senate Republicans were imitating their House counterparts by negotiating with conservative and moderate Democrats to find common ground on a balanced budget. The politics of this strategy should by now be familiar. One possible solution was similar to the 1981 Reagan strategy—to build a coalition of Republicans and conservative Democrats. The problem with this strategy was that the Republican leadership could not achieve a two-thirds majority for the original Republican reconciliation bill. Unlike in 1981, the pivotal voter was at the veto point rather than the median, and was thus solidly in the liberal wing of the Democratic party.

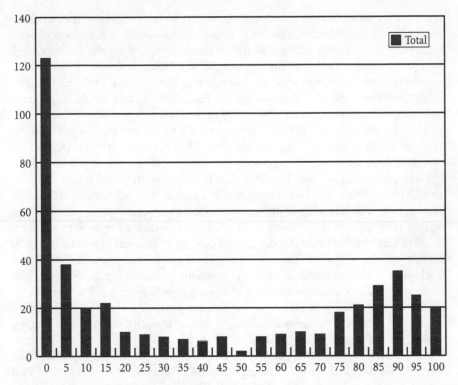

FIGURE 6.2   Raw House ADA Scores, 1995

Another strategy was to compromise with the conservative and moderate
Democrats by reducing the amount of the tax cuts, thus reducing the need to cut
into Medicare and Medicaid as sharply. This was not an unreasonable strategy because in an earlier vote, forty-eight moderate-to-conservative Democrats had
voted with them and against the President. The pitfall was that as policy moved
away from the Republican bill, there was a danger that the conservative wing of
the congressional Republicans would defect and the President could still veto the
bill. In short, there was the decided possibility that the 1990 Bush debacle could
be repeated. The other possible alliance was a center-out coalition that would include the President, moderate-to-conservative Democrats, and about one-half of
the congressional Republicans. This coalition seemed unlikely given the preferences of the median Republican in the House. The bipolar distribution of preferences noted in the Appendix was significantly shifted toward the conservative
end of the spectrum by the 1994 congressional elections. Figure 6.2 shows that
the conservative pole greatly outnumbered the liberal pole (with more than 120
Representatives voting conservatively on all twenty votes analyzed by the ADA).
Thus the median voter in the House had an ADA score of about 20 while the veto

pivot was a Democrat with an ADA of about 75. Obviously, those in the middle—from 25 to 70 in ADA score—were not numerous. Given this distribution of preferences, finding middle ground would be hard, especially on the all-important budget. Moreover, the reconciliation bill that the House had passed was already viewed as a major compromise by many House Republicans, and much movement away from their bill and toward the President's budget would cause mass defections among Republicans, especially in the House.

Some Democrats in Congress were pushing the President to let the government close rather than give in to the Republicans. They reasoned that the Democrats' strongest issue from a public relations standpoint was that the Republican budget was too harsh and that their best shot in the 1996 presidential and congressional elections was to be tough regarding Republican cuts in Medicare, Medicaid, and welfare. The left wing of the congressional Democrats stood ready to vote against the President if he moved too far toward embracing Republican numbers on Medicare and Medicaid. Moderate and centrist Democrats favored a balanced budget but one with fewer tax cuts and lower reductions in the safety net. Thus, both parties, their leadership, and the President had different preferences, and finding a majority solution would not be easy especially given that 1996 was a presidential election year. There was a distinct possibility that the negotiations would not achieve a consensus that could deliver majority support in Congress and secure the President's signature.

On January 8 and 9, 1996, each side moved somewhat toward the other. The Republicans dropped Medicare savings to $168 billion and also moved Medicaid and welfare toward the President's position. The President's team agreed to somewhat higher tax cuts and higher savings on discretionary, welfare, Medicare, and Medicaid. However, by Tuesday both sides were reporting that there was no more room for movement without abdicating their principles, mandates, and values. Talk of a one-year reduced continuing resolution with both sides taking their case to the electorate in November became common.

The President seemed to have won the day in that the government shutdown was blamed on the Republican Congress, and especially on Speaker Gingrich. Prior to the government shutdowns, the *Wall Street Journal*/National Broadcasting Company (WSJ/NBC) poll put Speaker Gingrich's job approval rating at plus 11 in early 1995 (46 percent approval, 35 percent disapproval).[11] The first government shutdown occurred on November 14, 1995, and on November 19 Speaker Gingrich's public approval rating was minus 33 (27 to 60). The WSJ/NBC poll continued to ask about the Speaker, and the results were not encouraging to him. The early December WSJ/NBC poll put the Speaker at minus 24, and in mid-January 1996 the result was minus 28.

In contrast, the President's approval ratings shot up. From January 1995, shortly after the Republican sweep in November, through April, the President averaged plus 4 over four WSJ/NBC polls. These numbers were historic lows for a President presiding over a relatively strong economy. From June through October,

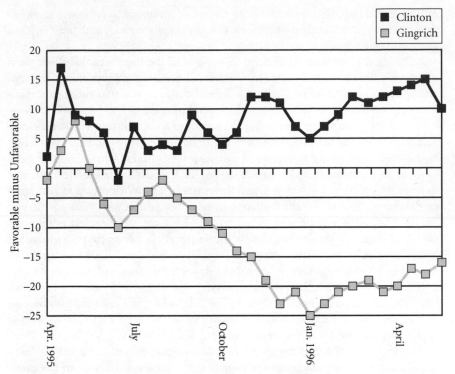

SOURCE: Compilation of polls from a variety of agencies, all listed in detail by Politics Now (1996) at http://www.politicsnow.com/resource/polltrak.

FIGURE 6.3   Polls for Clinton and Gingrich

in two WSJ/NBC polls, the President was plus 3 and plus 4. Five days after the first shutdown (November 19, 1995), the President was plus 7 and by the first week in December he was plus 11. The poll results for mid-January showed the President back at plus 3 but still 31 points higher than Speaker Gingrich—a reversal of over 40 points within a period of six to seven months. This growing gap is demonstrated across a wide variety of polls, as is illustrated in Figure 6.3.

January through March yielded almost a dozen stopgap spending bills as the President and the House battled for public opinion. By March 30 the Congress had passed and the President had signed appropriations bills funding Agriculture; Energy and Water Development; Foreign Operations; Transportation, Treasury, and Postal; legislative branch appropriations; military construction; and general government. Defense appropriations had become law without the President's signature. The President had vetoed appropriations for Commerce, Justice, State, and Judiciary; Interior; Veterans Affairs and Housing; and Urban Development. The Republican House had failed twice to override Clinton's veto. Given its more liberal composition and its supermajority requirements, the Senate did not vote on the vetoed bills. On April 25, Congress passed an omnibus appropriations bill that rolled together all appropriations not previously passed, and the President signed it the next day.

Although the omnibus act of April 25 was not all the Republicans had sought, it did mark a significant first step. The bill covered domestic appropriations and represents approximately 16 percent of the federal budget, but it is a crucial part of the budget given that it pays for most of the federal bureaucracy and just about everything else the government does other than defense and cash transfers. Republicans sought policies and budget numbers to the right of the President, who vetoed bills he did not like, believing that he could win the public opinion battle. Thus, the policies and the numbers moved left, back toward the President. The President was able to protect education, job training, and the environment. With regard to education and training, Clinton got the Congress to keep his AmeriCorps National Service Program (albeit at a 30 percent reduction) and his Goals 2000 project in the budget. With regard to the environment, Clinton forced Congress to drop provisions and riders that he viewed as detrimental, such as proposals to change wetlands policy and to allow salvage logging. As for the Republicans, they had wrung a 9.1 percent reduction in domestic appropriations over the 1995–1996 period, or approximately a $22 billion cut in expenditures. The original Republican proposals for cuts in Medicare, Medicaid, and other entitlement programs were left stranded because the President's veto could not be overridden.

This sequence of events matches well with the examples of the previous chapter. Significant policy changes were proposed by a zealous Republican Congress. The supermajority constraint of the presidential veto became real and relevant. Proposals that were shifted back to the left passed; those that could not be shifted far enough were vetoed and left in gridlock. Table 6.2 summarizes the results of the major legislation of the 104th Congress.

Because 1996 was an election year, everyone claimed victory. The President claimed that the omnibus bill was both good policy and bipartisan. "We have shown we can work together, and that when we do, we can get results that are good for the American people. . . . But when the leadership of Congress insists on going it alone, one party alone, we get gridlock, stalemate, vetoes, government shutdowns" (*New York Times*, April 26, 1996). Representative Livingston (R., La.) the Chair of the House Appropriations Committee, called the bill "a monumental change in the way that the government does business," while his Senate counterpart, Mark Hatfield (R., Ore.), said: "Everybody got something, everybody gave something."

The passage in April of H.R. 3019, which passed seven months late, put to an end a long debate over appropriations. There had been fourteen partial spending bills, two government shutdowns, and almost infinite amounts of endgame politics. The 1997 budget was for all practical purposes put on the back burner because by April 25 the contest for the presidency was in full bloom. Clinton's strategy was to claim that he was a check on the right wing of the Republican Party. He characterized himself as defending Medicare, Medicaid, education, and the environment, while at the same time reducing the deficit and balancing the budget by 2002. The strategy appeared to be working. The March, May, and August WSJ/NBC polls showed the President with job approval ratings of plus 12, 14, and 18, respectively. In contrast, Speaker Gingrich continued to be unpopular, with between minus 15 and minus 20 approval ratings.

The Unraveling of Proposals: Welfare Reform

The Republican Congress had wrapped together hopes for major changes in welfare, Medicare, Medicaid, tax cuts, and a balanced budget in their initial budget package. When it was clear that their budget was not going to pass, the package came apart, leaving many proposals to pass or fail on their own merits. One such proposal that continued its journey through Congress in 1996 was that of welfare reform. Given popular opinion against the present welfare system, the fact that it was an election year, and the President's promise to "end welfare as we know it," it seemed that something might pass.

Initial welfare proposals in the Republican House had been part of the overall budget package. Programs such as Aid to Families with Dependent Children (AFDC) and Medicaid would be turned over to the states in the form of block grants. Congress would also give states more control over food stamps, school lunch programs, foster care, and nutritional assistance programs. Welfare recipients would be required to find work within two years and would be limited to five years of benefits. Savings from welfare, Medicaid, and Medicare would amount to about half a trillion dollars over seven years. This package of reforms was vetoed by President Clinton when he first vetoed the budget reconciliation bill on December 6, 1995. Popular opinion fell on the side of the President. Thinking that welfare reform by itself might be a winning issue, Republicans passed the welfare legislation on its own, no longer coupled to the budget package. Again Clinton vetoed the proposals, claiming that they cut far too deep, ended essential services, and would be a step in the wrong direction. The President called for Democratic participation in the drafting of new proposals.

Over the next few months, the welfare proposals were indeed modified, although they still represented a shift to the right. Savings on welfare were decreased, such that federal spending on the programs was still expected to rise at a rate well above that of inflation. The transfer of control to the states of a number of programs such as Medicaid, food stamps, and school lunches was abandoned. Nevertheless, $54 billion in savings was still achieved and AFDC was still to be turned over to the states, ending its automatic entitlement status and leaving many eligibility requirements to be decided by state governments.

President Clinton announced in July that he would overlook his objections and sign this modified bill. By that point, the bill had already been weakened enough to have the support of supermajorities sufficient to override a Presidential veto. The conference agreement was passed on July 31 by a vote of 328 to 101. The Senate cleared the legislation the following day, 78 to 21. It clearly was an election-year attempt at change, with the very liberal Paul Wellstone (D., Minn.) being the only Senator up for reelection to vote against the bill. Given the electoral popularity of reforming the welfare system, it appeared that some change would need to be made. And given the vast shift to the right in the 1994 elections, it was clear that the shift on welfare would be to the right. As Representative Robert Matsui (D., Calif.) asked, "How do you move to the left in a period when the country's moving to the right?" (1996 *Congressional Quarterly Weekly Report*, 2196).

Although the welfare bill represented an area in which an agreement could be reached, other issues were left unresolved by the unraveling of the many parts of the Republican budget reconciliation package. Forecasts continue to show that the Medicare program must be changed over the next few years to avoid financial crisis. Entitlement spending is still rising faster than the rate of inflation. The tax code is still essentially frozen into the framework secured in 1986. And, above all else, tough budget decisions are here to stay.

Little Stories That Make Up the Big Picture

The big story of the 1995 budget was, of course, the President's veto of the Republican version of that budget. Because the veto point was to the left of the Republican reconciliation bill, the veto pulled the final budget outcome to the left. In addition to this big picture, there are hundreds of local stories at the district level that also demonstrate a pull toward the status quo and gridlock on the budget proposals; we cannot cover all of these stories or even any one in great detail. Funding for the Los Alamos laboratories in New Mexico was in part protected by Senator Domenici (R., N.Mex.) who in general favors smaller government. This is not an uncommon story. Barry Goldwater (the former Republican Senator from Arizona and Republican presidential nominee in 1964) was known as "Mr. Conservative," yet he favored funding the Central Arizona Water Project because, without the Colorado River water, Arizona's population growth was limited. In short, no matter how conservative and pro–balanced budget a congressional member might be, that member has a constituency that benefits from federal programs. Budget issues, especially when they involve real trade-offs between programs and revenues, force members to choose what to do regarding programs that benefit their constituents. To the extent that they fight to preserve benefits, and win, they may be seen as either moving policy to the left or as making it hard to achieve balanced budgets.

Our point is that decisions on the budget (and thus on most legislation) are even more complex than we have been able to describe thus far. Since we cannot deal with the hundreds of local issues that affect expenditure levels, we choose to give one example as an illustration of the process. Our example is the 1995 reconciliation budget's agricultural appropriations for dairy farmers. Agricultural politics is a good choice because much has been written on the subject. Grant

McConnell (1953, 1966) and Theodore Lowi (1969) feature agricultural politics in their theories of interest group liberalism. Roughly, there exists in agricultural politics an iron triangle of interests that exchange goods, services, votes, and campaign contributions, which in combination formulate policy. Farmers want programs that benefit them—price supports, parity payments, favorable tax legislation, and so on—and in order to get these programs, they and their organizations (interest groups) support candidates who favor them. In turn, those elected representatives serve on committees (Agriculture and Appropriations) that prepare policies beneficial to their constituents. These benefits programs are administered by bureaucratic agencies (mainly in the Department of Agriculture) that make the payments—that deliver the services to the constituents. The bureaucrats benefit because, by administering the programs that the farm interests desire, they develop a clientele that supports their agency. In short, politicians exchange favorable policies for financial and electoral support; farmers and farm interests exchange votes for programs; and the agencies formulate and administer programs that farmers and representatives want, thus ensuring their careers and their agencies' continued existence.

Recent work, especially Mark Hansen's *Gaining Access* (1991), has modified this picture somewhat by showing that elected representatives want information about how different policies will affect them politically, and that over time the interest groups with the best information win out. Nevertheless, the general picture is that since the passage of the 1933 Agricultural Adjustment Act, the federal government has been subsidizing various crops and products. Nowhere have these subsidies been more noticeable than in the area of dairy products and especially milk. John Connelly, a former Secretary of the Treasury and Republican presidential hopeful, was brought to trial over his alleged link to increases in the subsidy for milk prices. Present policy bases price supports for milk on regions. Since 1937 the country has been divided into geographical regions and each region has milk marketing orders that determine how much the milk processors, like those who make cheese, dried milk, and ice cream, must pay farmers for raw milk. The regional price is based on a set of complicated factors such as how far a particular farmer lives from the nation's center of efficient milk production—Eau Claire, Wisconsin.

The intention of the legislation in 1937 was to take into account the costs of the factors of production, which vary by climate, soil fertility, and other conditions. For purely economic reasons the upper Midwest, particularly Wisconsin, is where milk can be produced most efficiently. More recently, however, sophisticated methods of refrigeration and fast transportation have made it economically efficient for the upper Midwest to produce a greater percentage of the nation's milk. Freeing the market from milk subsidies would save taxpayers money (in reduced subsidies) and lower the price to consumers; it would also, however, in all probability greatly reduce the number of dairy farmers, particularly in the eastern United States where milk can only be produced inefficiently.

The original House version of the 1995 reconciliation budget reduced aid to farmers who raise wheat, corn, rice, cotton, peanuts, and almost every other crop. This legislation dropped milk marketing orders entirely. Dropping the subsidy to milk producers was supported by dairy farmers in the Midwest and opposed by dairy farmers in the East. Enter Representative Gerald Solomon (R., N.Y.), the Chair of the Rules Committee. Representative Solomon represents the twenty-fourth district in New York, which is essentially the upper Hudson Valley including Saratoga Springs. The district is safely Republican, and Solomon averaged over 70 percent of the vote across his nine consecutive elections to the House. Representative Solomon's district is the twentieth largest milk-producing district in the country and although he serves on the Rules Committee and not the Agriculture Committee, he has consistently voted for agriculture bills containing subsidies for his milk producers. Given his position as Rules Chair, Solomon led the way, along with Representative Drier (R., Calif.), in configuring the special rules under which the Contract with America was voted through the House. In short, Representative Solomon has been a key player in the Republican leadership.

But how should Representative Solomon behave in regard to the cuts in milk subsidies? Should he go with the Speaker and do his share to cut the deficit or should he fight to retain the milk subsidies for his constituents? If he wins concessions for his constituents, then he keeps expenditures higher than they would be if he were to go with the cuts. Obviously, Solomon chose to fight the subsidy reduction. On December 6 the *New York Times* reported that Representative Solomon had told the House leadership—while the bill was in a House-Senate conference committee—that unless they restored the milk subsidies he would lead the entire New York Republican delegation in a vote against the entire reconciliation budget. Solomon said, "Never in my life have I ever joined a rump group, but I did it because it's a matter of life or death." The Republican leadership could not afford to lose the New York delegation votes, so they stripped the bill of the antimilk subsidy provisions, thus ensuring the continuance of regional subsidies. In short, this action pushed expenditures to the left by keeping the milk subsidies, and moved the deficit higher.

In some sense budget decisions represent a hodgepodge of little arrangements like the milk subsidy settlement. Of course, not all members chair the Rules Committee and some members, particularly the class of 1994 Republicans, have given ground on issues important to their constituents. Nevertheless, the Solomon story is not unrepresentative, as congressional members worry much less about benefits that do not affect their own constituents; and to the extent that members succeed in serving their constituents the budget is harder to balance. Programs like Social Security that have significant numbers of beneficiaries in every district are particularly hard to change. Even programs like inefficient milk subsidies are, as we have seen, hard to cut.

Representative Solomon's case shows the continued power of individuals in the 104th Congress. Despite talk of strong Republican activities, individual Repub-

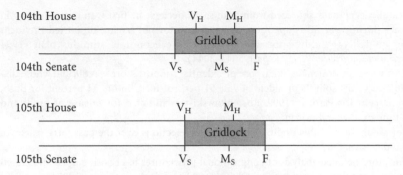

FIGURE 6.4   The 1996 Elections

licans and groups of Republicans—such as the freshman class—often act on their own against the wishes of their leadership. Again the story comes down to the individual preferences and positions of members of Congress. Although the 1994 elections led to a major shift to the right in the House, the combined opposition of the moderate Senate and the presidential veto made it impossible for those conservative representatives to have their way on most issues. When the most conservative members of the Republican Party realized that they needed to moderate their positions to achieve policy successes, they were forced to choose between accepting only minor policy changes or waiting for the 1996 election in the hopes that a Republican presidential victory would ease the constraint on policy movement to the right.

However, the 1996 elections left the gridlock region largely unchanged, as Figure 6.4 illustrates. Clinton's victory, along with a shift to the left in the House and a slight shift to the right in the Senate, means that policy changes will still be constrained by the presidential veto. Now it will be as difficult to override the veto in the House as it has been in the Senate. Gridlock continues.

NOTES

1. The policy enacted by the majority party in a parliamentary system is not expected to be at that party's median. If the median party position is eighty for the majority party and forty for the minority party, with fifty-one majority members and fifty minority members, and the fifty-first majority member has a preference of fifty, then that member could combine with the minority party to achieve a policy result of fifty. Thus it is clear that the "party position" may not be the place where policy ends up. Again it is the individual pivotal voters who can hold out and defect in order to achieve their ideal policy outcomes.

2. This advertisement understandably drew a great deal of coverage and commentary. All the same, it was not entirely novel for an incumbent to be running against his own party's leadership. Cain, Ferejohn, and Fiorina (1987, 198) note the example of Democrat Jim Jones who circulated a pamphlet on his differences with Speaker Tip O'Neill in 1984.

3. Mann was actually squeezed from both sides, because he first won only narrowly in a primary during which his opponent attacked him for not having supported President Clinton on federal funding for abortions and the economic stimulus plan (1994 *Congressional Quarterly Weekly Report*, 3043–3044).

4. This was Dan Rostenkowski, whose presidential support score was 80, and whose district (Illinois's 5th) split its presidential vote 51 percent for Clinton, 33 percent for Bush, and 16 percent for Perot in 1992. Rostenkowski was indicted for misuse of funds and served time in a federal prison.

5. For an analysis of this finding with regard to elections over the past forty years, see Brady and Cogan 1997.

6. For more detailed analysis of congressional procedures in choosing open and closed rules, as well as other procedures, see Oleszek 1989 and Bach and Smith 1988.

7. The standard unified budget has been used to assess the deficit by both parties for over a quarter of a century. In this standard budget, Social Security and other trust funds are included on the revenue side. Budgets not including Social Security and other trust funds show even higher deficits.

8. The actual numbers totaled sixty-six, one shy of the necessary two-thirds. In the final vote, however, Bob Dole voted against the amendment in a tactic that would allow him to raise the amendment again if an additional vote could be found.

9. For a history and political assessment of campaign financing and attempts at reform, see Sorauf 1992.

10. This was noted by a variety of surveys, which were beautifully compiled on the Internet's World Wide Web by Politics Now at http://www.politicsnow.com/resource/polltrak.

11. The survey asked Americans if they approved or disapproved of the job that Newt Gingrich was doing as Speaker of the House.

7

Conclusion

The freshman Republicans in the 104th Congress, like their counterparts in the 103rd Congress, came to Washington to "change" policy. Yet in both cases their hopes exceeded their achievements. Many of the Democratic freshmen elected to the 103rd House suffered the fate of Marjorie Margolies-Mezvinsky (Penn.) and were not reelected to the 104th House. Eleven members of the freshman Republican class of 1994 met the same end and were not reelected. As they returned to the towns, cities, and prairies of home, they faced an electorate that wanted to know what they had achieved. Why had they not achieved more or why had they achieved as much as they did? Both the Democrats in 1992 and the Republicans in 1994 had reason to believe when they first came to Washington that their victories were part of a larger whole, wherein their elections and votes would count for change. The Democrats in the 103rd were part of the first unified government in twelve years, led by a dynamic young President. The Republicans in the 104th Congress were members of the first Republican-controlled Congress in forty years. No wonder they felt that "change" was in the air.

Implicit in these members' notions of being a part of change was that their individual victories were part of a bigger, significant electoral shift, the first group to a unified government and the second to a Republican revolution. The premise is that elections matter and that certain elections move the elected representatives relatively uniformly toward policy changes. The literature on electoral politics backs up this notion. From V. O. Key's theories on "ballots not bullets" and critical elections to Popkin's theory (1991) of rational ignorance, the scholarly consensus is that some elections matter more than others. Certain elections, some argue, shift the majority party, which in turn changes policy; whereas others argue that elections don't predict policy shifts accurately but that electoral results can nevertheless account for policy (Mayhew 1974a). In short, elections create majorities that derive their power from the fact that the governed have consented to be governed and have put their imprimatur on these members via the electoral process. The policy process in its most basic sense prescribes that the majority of those elected by the people are free to legislate at least until the next election. The American system of representation thus relies on the people's consent to be governed by a majority of those elected, and leads freshman members in Congresses like the 103rd and 104th to believe that rapid change is forthcoming. Both the freshman Democrats and Republicans in the 103rd House expected battles over important reforms. Minority leader Robert Michel (R., Ill.) said that forty of the forty-seven new Republicans were hard-liners, creating a GOP conference that was "the most conservative and antagonistic to the other side" that he had seen in his 40 years (1993 *Congressional Quarterly Weekly Report,* 810). The Democratic freshmen were just as optimistic going in, and many of those defeated for reelection to the 104th Congress attributed their defeat to the failure of the 103rd Congress to enact new legislation.

The revolving gridlock theory is about elections and policy outcomes. Members of Congress develop preferences over policies that reflect, among other things, the views of their districts and their desire to be reelected. These preferences translate into policy outcomes through the majority and supermajority institutions surrounding the policymaking process. The harsh reality that new members discover is that developing supermajority coalitions around complex issues is difficult. Policy gridlock is the result of not being able to build such coalitions without violating the trust of the folks back home.

Soon after the 1993 legislative session began, Speaker Tom Foley (D., Wash.) commented, "The euphoria of the inauguration has been tempered by the reality of the problems" (*National Journal,* March 13, 1993, 606). As the session moved along and gridlock set in, members' views grew darker. On the now-famous budget vote, Democrats from moderate districts were caught between party and constituency. Said one senior House Democrat:

> The day before the vote a few [Democrats] said they intended to vote no but if their votes were crucial they would vote for the budget. When it was tied a lot of us were arguing with Ray [Thornton, Ark.], Pat [Williams, Mont.], and Marjorie [Margolies-Mezvinsky], trying to get them to vote for it. Then Ray said he couldn't do it and walked away. So Pat and Marjorie voted for it. . . . Sure we were wondering why Ray [from a safe district] made Marjorie take the hit. He saw his state as conservative, and he didn't want to vote for a tax increase. Sure we were yelling, and we were pissed at him. But there was little we could do. (Matsui 1995, 28)

Congresswoman Margolies-Mezvinsky lost her seat in 1994.

Health care never came to the floor, as moderate and conservative Democrats were not supportive. First-year representative Blanche Lambert (D., Ark.) said: "The nation is too diverse and the legislation was too much too soon." Pat Williams said: "I think the preparation of the President's legislation was poorly handled, as was the selling of it" (Matsui 1995, 30–31). Other Democrats felt essentially the same and health care died.

Political reform did not fare well in the 103rd House. PAC reforms went nowhere. One senior Democrat said: "If you eliminate PACs it will be to the disadvantage of Democrats because they take more from them." As the session wore down with little achieved, members began to take on the party leadership. Anna

Eshoo (D., Calif.) lamented: "My experience was for the most part . . . well you had better sit down and listen to us because we are in charge. . . . [Reform] was not welcomed." After the election of 1994 a senior Democratic leader said: "We should have given them something. They [the freshmen] needed something to take back to their districts, and we denied it all to them" (Matsui 1995, 39, 40, 41).

The Republican majority in the 104th Congress barely avoided defeat. In the end they campaigned on welfare reform, budget cuts, and reform in the House, as well as term limits, balanced budgets, and other reforms. But in both cases, the freshman members' notions of change were dramatically modified by election time. The reality of changing policy had replaced the euphoria of the election.

There is nothing new about the fact that congressional freshmen are excited about changing things. John Kingdon (1973) and others have found this phenomenon to be long standing. The phenomenon is not limited to members of Congress; newly elected Presidents often overestimate their power and potential to bring about change. John Kennedy, in a famous interview at the end of his first two years, said that what surprised him most was "how hard it was to get things done around here." Lyndon Johnson went from being the greatest legislator in 1965 and 1966 to resigning from the presidency in 1968. Presidential honeymoons with the public, the Congress, and the bureaucracy are short lived. The enthusiasm to bring about change in policy and process exceeds the ability to actually effect change; this holds true for Presidents as well as members of Congress.

What happens between the November election with its euphoria and anticipation, and the reality of the first two years in office?

The newly elected Congress and President arrive in Washington, ready and willing to enact the people's wishes; yet, except under very rare circumstances, this does not occur. In this book we offered a partial explanation of why change is usually not forthcoming. First, members of Congress and the President are dealing with complex issues about which there is little consensus, especially when it comes to change. Everyone agrees the that United States cannot continue its entitlement programs at present levels without (1) increasing taxes, (2) decreasing benefits, or (3) increasing the deficit and thus the burden on future generations. But the issue is more complex than a simple multiple-choice test. Some favor increasing taxes; others favor decreasing expenditures; many favor a mixed strategy; but what generally happens is an increase in the national debt. Complex problems generate complex solutions, and both are grounded in the complex and varied preferences underlying policy choices. Thus building policy majorities is hard.

The second reason for gridlock is that supermajority institutions, particularly the President's veto and Rule XXII in the Senate authorizing the filibuster, exacerbate the problems of building a consensus for change. They enable actors far from the median to affect policy outcomes beyond their single vote. The sixtieth (filibuster pivot) or sixty-seventh (veto pivot) Senator can move policy their way or keep the status quo even though a majority favors change.

In addition, not only is there a lack of consensus in the Congress, there is a lack of consensus among the public about what should be done.[1] "The budget should be balanced while taxes are cut and expenses increased" is a classic example of the American public's contradictory views on policy. It is hard to determine whether voters are inherently unrealistic or whether they have been induced to be unrealistic. Consider the budget problem. The public (a majority of respondents in various surveys) believes that we can reduce taxes, increase expenditures (in different areas, depending on the respondent's particulars), and have a balanced budget all at the same time.[2] One view drawn from such results is that the public is uninformed, irrational, and/or unrealistic. A counter to this would be: What should we expect from a public that has for decades been told that solving the budget problem will be painless? From Jimmy Carter's energy crises as "the moral equivalent of war" to Walter Mondale's pledge to raise taxes, to George Bush breaking his opposing pledge of "no new taxes," politicians who admitted that pain was involved in problem solving have not fared well at the polls. Politicians from LBJ (with his Great Society) to Ronald Reagan (with his Morning in America) who focused on the positive have done much better at the polls. In short, politicians often tell the public that problems can be solved without pain. Whether right or wrong, the 1996 campaign for the presidency took Social Security and Medicare off the table as policy areas vulnerable to change. Both parties' candidates spent considerable time assuring citizens that they were better able to protect these entitlements than their opponents. President Clinton had a real advantage over Dole on this issue, forcing Dole to claim time and again that Medicare would be safe under him. After twenty years of being told that budget problems can be solved without cutting middle-class entitlements or raising middle-class taxes, the public may well have begun to believe it.

Yet making public policy differs from talking about it in an election. President Clinton and the Democratic platform may boast about how they will protect Medicare from the Republican Congress, but after his reelection President Clinton had to propose cuts in Medicare's projected growth in order to avoid major fiscal problems. In the policy world, Presidents must propose the specifics of how they are going to reduce the deficit, enhance health care coverage, deal with Saddam Hussein and other foreign entanglements, and improve educational opportunities for American children. Such proposals entail trade-offs that have real consequences for citizens and thus for their elected representatives. These hard choices make it difficult for the Congress and the President to actually shift policy. In short, the status quo is hard to change for a variety of legitimate reasons.

The major causes of gridlock are the lack of a public consensus, and the power of the supermajority institutions that make shifting policy even harder. Members of the President's party cannot always be relied upon to vote for his legislation—especially legislation that shifts policy out of the gridlock region. In fact, some recent work suggests that, in House elections, the members who lose are those who have been pulled by their President to the left or right of their district's preferences (Brady, Cogan, and Rivers 1995; Brady and Cogan 1998). Thus rational members must vote their district, not the President or the party leadership. The ability of members to vote against their President and be reelected weakens parties, reducing party unity and making it more difficult to arrive at a coordinated goal. Under a strong party system, the goals problem could be solved (in principle) by a strong leader asserting the party's agenda. Once leaders establish goals, they use their powers (incentives and punishments) to get members to vote for the policy shifts. In the American system, even under the supposedly more partisan regime of today, the coordination of goals is difficult. The President has no real sanctions; he cannot deny members renomination, strip them of committee slots, or otherwise punish them. Thus the President and his congressional party must coordinate or bargain over policy goals; and, even if a consensus is reached, not all members will subscribe. Add the need to secure supermajorities, and the difficulty of finding consensus is even more acute because members of the other party must now be included. The further the policy proposal moves toward the other party, the more discontented the heart of the President's party becomes. With regard to the 103rd and 104th Congresses, we showed how difficult such consensus is to achieve.

Although we have reached a conclusion—the continuation of gridlock—similar to that reached by others, we believe that the revolving gridlock theory provides an explanation of policymaking strikingly different from those found elsewhere. For example, everyone has now reached the conclusion that health care reform in 1994 was plagued by the disease of gridlock. Hacker (1997) focuses on the Clinton plan as trying to appear moderate to moderates and liberal to liberals. Skocpol (1996) argues that Clinton lost labor support due to his position on NAFTA. Broder and Johnson (1996) believe that no policy change was possible. Although they capture the details of the health care reform attempts, they show how the big picture can be missed by politicians, scholars, and journalists alike. Our argument is that a shift to the left, such as Clinton's reform proposal, must appeal to those at the median and to the right of the median (here the filibuster pivot). The exclusion of and inability to address the concerns of these pivotal members—conservative Democrats such as Mike Andrews (Tex.) and liberal-to-moderate Republicans—meant one of two things. Either the proposals were focused on the wrong members, or the status quo policy was already inside the gridlock region. In order to understand policy outcomes, we must pay greater attention to those pivotal members necessary in forming the requisite majorities and supermajorities. This is an important lesson not only for those of us observing the process, but also for those attempting to bring about policy change. Where this lesson has not been learned, gridlock becomes even more likely.

What resolves gridlock? In our view, elections that give direction to the President and the Congress are the major vehicles for breaking gridlock. Scholars have referred to such elections as critical or realigning (Brady 1988; Burnham 1965, 1970; Glad 1966; Key 1955). Even though the realignment literature has fallen out of favor, it seems clear that without something like a realignment or a critical election that gives control to one party (or like-minded politicians regardless of party) with a majority sufficient to break gridlock, the status quo will prevail. Particularly with regard to budget-related policy, the complexity of the issues along with the threat of a presidential veto means that little can be accomplished without some preference alignment between Congress and the President. Yet even unified government does not ensure that preferences will be aligned.

The 1996 elections had the potential to break gridlock (as do all elections). Instead, the electorate returned Bill Clinton to the presidency with about 50 percent of the vote, and returned a diminished Republican majority to the House, while it increased the Republican majority in the Senate. The continuation of a government with divided party control and diverse preferences until at least 1998 (and more likely 2000) means that policy will remain left of where the median House and Senate Republican members prefer it and right of where President Clinton would prefer it. In terms of the budget, presidential proposals based on campaign rhetoric of banning Medicare and Medicaid cuts and passing tax cuts favored mostly by Democrats will not fly. Likewise, Republican proposals that are perceived as too conservative will be vetoed by the President. The compromises necessary to move toward a balanced budget by 2002 will be difficult to come by, and will probably rely on rosy economic figures, technicalities such as using geometric means to calculate indexation of federal programs, and extensions of changes made in 1990 and 1993 (with regard to Medicare and other programs). In sum, the 1996 elections ensured that policy will be to the right of the congressional Democrats, and the presidential veto ensures that policy will be to the left of the core of the congressional Republican party. When the resultant policy is called gridlock, it may, and in fact will, be attributed to divided government. However, as we have shown, it is the result of preferences, supermajority institutions, and a lack of electoral consensus.

Until we have an election that definitively shifts and aligns the preferences of Congress and the President, change will be hard to come by. Even if such an election occurred and were to shift policy, the majority party would have to gain reelection in order to firmly establish the new policy order. In 1981 Ronald Reagan came very close to achieving this.[3] The 1980 elections shifted preferences and policy rightward, but the recession of 1982 and the loss of twenty-six House seats kept the Republicans from becoming the majority party. Neither the 1992 nor the 1994 elections came as close as the Reagan revolution did to achieving policy realignment.

Given the mixed results of the 1996 election, the public will continue to perceive the President and the Congress as muddling through at best—struggling to find consensus and appearing to be out of touch with regard to where Americans expect them to be. Public dissatisfaction with Congress, as Hibbing and Theiss-Morse (1995) have shown, in part results because the public does not like the give-and-take of politics—the debate and subsequent compromise. In part, as pointed out earlier, the public perceives that policy solutions are easier to achieve than in fact they are. In one sense, supermajority institutions have added to the dissatisfaction, making politics more cumbersome and perhaps more heated. Jones (1994) reminds us of the complexity of policymaking given the separation of powers, yet he does not call for a simplification of the system. On the other hand, Binder and Smith (1996) argue that the gridlock resulting from the filibuster gives reason enough to abandon this supermajority institution. We do not take such a normative stand here. We believe, rather, that an inability to override vetoes or end filibusters is a further testimony to the lack of policy consensus in the United States.

This is not to say that we are not troubled by policy gridlock. If the median member of Congress is representative of the median in the country as a whole, then it follows that policy change preferred by a majority in Congress is preferred by a majority of U.S. citizens.[4] The revolving gridlock theory predicts that often the majority view is tempered by the need to secure supermajorities, and by the complexity of the issues. Where the will of the majority is continually thwarted by diverse preferences and supermajority institutions, the public may turn to elections to align politicians' preferences. But when politicians are already representing diverse district preferences, gridlock continues. Gridlock thus represents a lack of policy consensus regarding the difficult decisions we ask our representatives to make. Whether caused by complex issues or supermajority institutions, the political wrangling and subsequent inability to break gridlock leaves the public feeling dissatisfied.

The predicament of contemporary politics in America could be relieved by lowering public expectations about what the government is able to achieve, given the diversity of views held by Americans and the complexity of the problems with which the country is faced. Some commentators point to political reform—campaign finance reform, balanced budgets, and electoral reforms—as ways to improve the overall situation.[5] In general, we do not believe that political reforms will solve these more fundamental problems. Democratic countries from Japan and Korea in the Far East to Europe and Canada all face the same problems—corporate downsizing, high wages in the face of competition from the third world, exorbitant entitlements, electorates unhappy with high tax rates, aging populations, and questions about foreign policy in the post–Cold War world. Forms of government in these countries range from strong parliamentary systems to decentralized American-style governments. None has the answer, and in fact one could argue that America has moved further toward solving these common problems than have other countries, perhaps due to the policy gridlock of the past, which resisted public preferences for policies that were unsustainable in the long run: dramatic increases in entitlements, changes in the tax codes, and increased government regulation.

We do not mean to claim that all political reforms are therefore hopeless; rather, our point is that such reforms as those mentioned above are not likely to resolve the dilemmas and policy problems faced by modern nations. No political reform will provide a consensus on the proper mix of taxes and entitlement spending. If political reform then is not the answer, what is? Our view is that the answer is patience, time, and struggle. In a democracy like the United States, policy is worked out through elections, debate about policy changes, further elections, and finally the passage of policy changes. When Bill Clinton and the Democrats pushed too hard to the left in 1993 and Newt Gingrich led Republicans down the primrose path when he shut the government down over Christmas, the American electorate brought them back to reality. The Republicans of the 105th Congress and President Clinton will make progress toward a balanced budget as they did in the 104th. In the process they will displease the public—the debate will get heated and the result will probably anger both sides. Nevertheless, until the debate over the direction of the country is resolved by the public voting into office a President and a Congress with a common vision, Americans shall continue to muddle through.

NOTES

1. This lack of consensus may lead voters to place checks on politicians whom they believe would move policy too far in one direction or the other (Alesina and Rosenthal 1989, 1995), often leading to divided government (Fiorina 1991a, 1996).

2. Mark Hansen (1996) argues that these responses come from surveys offering the public a "free lunch." Anyone offered a tax cut, lower deficit, or more spending without other consequences would rightly take it. He reports results from surveys that explore the trade-offs more fully, with many interesting findings.

3. Martin Anderson (1990) gives an interesting close-up view of the Reagan revolution and its resultant policy legacy.

4. While we both feel that Congress generally reflects public preferences, we are divided in opinion over just how representative it is. For example, some segments of the population may be less well-represented than others, the public may vote for politicians to "balance out" other politicians already in office, and the weighting of district and state preferences may skew representation. As such, it may not be the case that the congressional median and population median are identical. Nevertheless, we both feel that changes in the public view lead, through elections, to changes in membership and preferences in Congress. We are deeply concerned that political institutions (whether electoral, within Congress, or elsewhere) might not allow the will of the people to be carried out.

5. See Sundquist 1993, 1995.

Appendix:
Distribution of Real ADA Scores

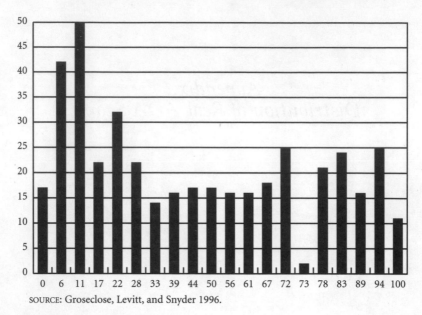

SOURCE: Groseclose, Levitt, and Snyder 1996.

FIGURE A.1   1980 "Real" ADA Scores

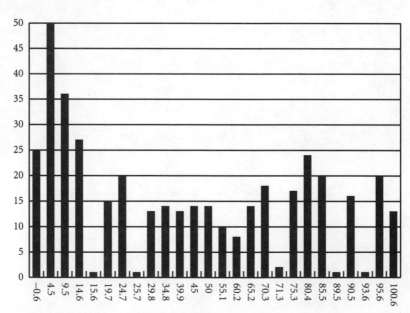

SOURCE: Groseclose, Levitt, and Snyder 1996.

FIGURE A.2   1982 "Real" ADA Scores

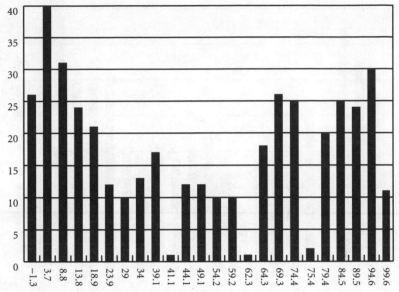

SOURCE: Groseclose, Levitt, and Snyder 1996.

FIGURE A.3   1984 "Real" ADA Scores

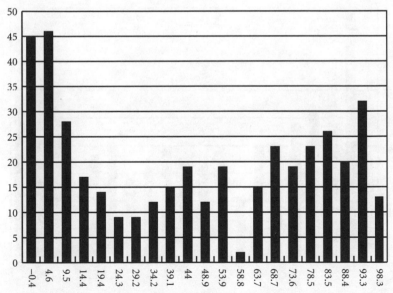

SOURCE: Groseclose, Levitt, and Snyder 1996.

FIGURE A.4   1986 "Real" ADA Scores

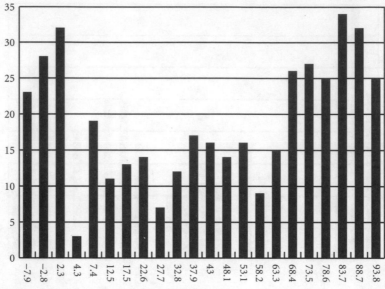

SOURCE: Groseclose, Levitt, and Snyder 1996.

FIGURE A.5   1988 "Real" ADA Scores

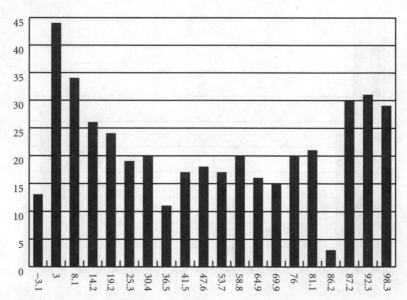

SOURCE: Groseclose, Levitt, and Snyder 1996.

FIGURE A.6   1990 "Real" ADA Scores

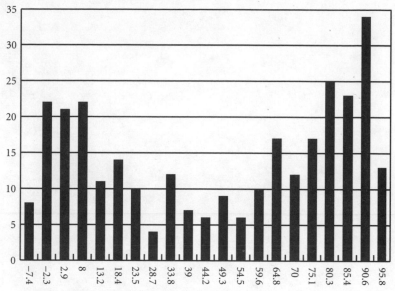

FIGURE A.7   1992 "Real" ADA Scores

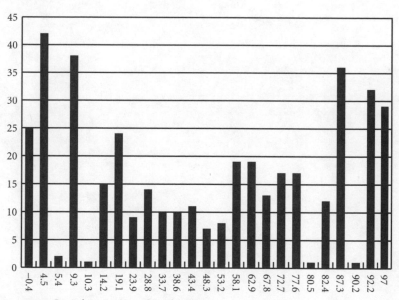

FIGURE A.8   1993 "Real" ADA Scores

Bibliography

Aberbach, Joel. 1991. The President and the Executive Branch. In *The Bush Presidency: First Appraisals*, edited by Colin Campbell and Bert Rockman. Chatham, N.J.: Chatham House Publishers.

Aldrich, John H. 1995. *Why Parties? The Origin and Transformation of Party Politics in America*. Chicago: University of Chicago Press.

Alesina, Alberto, and Geoffrey Carliner, eds. 1991. *Politics and Economics in the Eighties*. Chicago: University of Chicago Press.

Alesina, Alberto, and Howard Rosenthal. 1989. Partisan Cycles in Congressional Elections and the Macroeconomy. *American Political Science Review* 83(2):373–398.

———. 1995. *Partisan Politics, Divided Government, and the Economy*. Cambridge: Cambridge University Press.

Alford, John, and David Brady. 1993. Personal and Partisan Advantage in U.S. Congressional Elections, 1846–1990. In *Congress Reconsidered*. 5th ed., edited by Lawrence Dodd and Bruce I. Oppenheimer. Washington, D.C.: Congressional Quarterly Press.

Alt, James, and Robert Lowrey. 1994. Divided Government, Fiscal Institutions, and Budget Deficits: Evidence from the States. *American Political Science Review* 88:811–828.

Alt, James, and Kenneth Shepsle, eds. 1990. *Perspectives on Positive Political Economy*. Cambridge: Cambridge University Press.

American Political Science Association. 1950. *Toward a More Responsible Two-Party System*. Washington, D.C.: American Political Science Association.

Anderson, Martin. 1990. *Revolution: The Reagan Legacy*. Stanford: Hoover Institution Press.

Ansolabehere, Steven, David Brady, and Morris Fiorina. 1992. The Vanishing Marginals and Electoral Responsiveness. *British Journal of Political Science* 22:21–38.

Arnold, R. Douglas. 1990. *The Logic of Congressional Action*. New Haven: Yale University Press.

Arrow, Kenneth Joseph. 1951. *Social Choice and Individual Values*. New York: John Wiley.

Bach, Stanley, and Steven Smith. 1988. *Managing Uncertainty in the House of Representatives: Adaptation and Innovation in Special Rules*. Washington, D.C.: Brookings Institution.

Baron, David, and John Ferejohn. 1989. Bargaining in Legislatures. *American Political Science Review* 83(4):1181–1206.

Beam, David R., Timothy Conlan, and Margaret Wrightson. 1990. Solving the Riddle of Tax Reform: Party Competition and the Politics of Ideas. *Political Science Quarterly* 105(2):193–217.

Binder, Sarah A., and Steven S. Smith. 1996. *Politics or Principle? Filibustering in the United States Senate*. Washington, D.C.: Brookings Institution.

Birnbaum, Jeffrey H., and Alan S. Murray. 1987. *Showdown At Gucci Gulch*. New York: Random House.

Black, Duncan. 1958. *The Theory of Committees and Elections*. Cambridge: Cambridge University Press.

Black, Duncan, and R. A. Newing. 1951. *Committee Decisions with Complementary Valuation*. London: Hodge.

Brady, David W. 1988. *Critical Elections and Congressional Policy Making*. Stanford: Stanford University Press.

Brady, David W., and Kara M. Buckley. 1995. Health Care Reform in the 103rd Congress: A Predictable Failure. *The Journal of Health Politics, Policy, and Law* 2:447–457.

Brady, David W., and John F. Cogan. 1998. *Getting It Wrong: Liberal Democrats and Conservative Republicans in Elections, 1954–96*. Stanford: Stanford University Press.

Brady, David W., John F. Cogan, and Douglas Rivers. 1995. *How the Republicans Captured the House*. Stanford: Hoover Institution Press.

Brady, David W., and David Epstein. 1997. Intraparty Preferences, Heterogeneity, and the Origins of the Modern Congress: Progressive Reformers in the House and Senate, 1890–1920. *Journal of Law, Economics, and Organization* 13:26–49.

Broder, David, and Haynes Johnson. 1996. *The System: The American Way of Politics at the Breaking Point*. Boston: Little, Brown.

Brody, Richard A. 1991. *Assessing the President*. Stanford: Stanford University Press.

Burnham, Walter Dean. 1965. The Changing Shape of the American Political Universe. *American Political Science Review* 59(1):7–29.

———. 1970. *Critical Elections and the Mainsprings of American Politics*. New York: W. W. Norton.

———. 1995. Realignment Lives: The 1994 Earthquake and Its Implications. In *The Clinton Presidency: First Appraisals*, edited by Colin Campbell and Bert Rockman. Chatham, N.J.: Chatham House Publishers.

Burns, James MacGregor. 1963. *The Deadlock of Democracy*. Englewood Cliffs, N.J.: Prentice-Hall.

Cain, Bruce, John Ferejohn, and Morris Fiorina. 1987. *The Personal Vote: Constituency Service and Electoral Independence*. Cambridge: Harvard University Press.

Campbell, Colin. 1991. The White House and Cabinet Under the "Let's Deal" Presidency. In *The Bush Presidency: First Appraisals*, edited by Colin Campbell and Bert Rockman. Chatham, N.J.: Chatham House Publishers.

Campbell, Colin, and Bert Rockman, eds. 1991. *The Bush Presidency: First Appraisals*. Chatham, N.J.: Chatham House Publishers.

———. 1996. *The Clinton Presidency: First Appraisals*. Chatham, N.J.: Chatham House Publishers.

Carmines, Edward G., and James A. Stimson. 1989. *Issue Evolution: Race and the Transformation of American Politics*. Princeton: Princeton University Press.

Chubb, John E., and Paul Peterson, eds. 1985. *The New Directions in American Politics*. Washington, D.C.: Brookings Institution.

———. 1989. *Can the Government Govern?* Washington, D.C.: Brookings Institution.

Cogan, John F. 1997. *The Federal Budget: A Consistent Historical Data Base*. Manuscript, Hoover Institution.

Cogan, John F., Timothy Muris, and Allen Schick. 1994. *The Budget Puzzle: Understanding Federal Spending*. Stanford: Stanford University Press.

Cohen, R. 1993. Leadership Test. *National Journal* (March 13):606.

Collender, Stanley. 1991. The Guide to the Federal Budget. Washington, D.C.: Urban Institute Press.

Collier, Kenneth, and Terry Sullivan. 1995. New Evidence Undercutting the Linkage of Approval with Presidential Support and Influence. *Journal of Politics* 57(1):197–209.

Cooper, Joseph, and Gary Young. 1997. Partisanship, Bipartisanship and Crosspartisanship Since the New Deal. In *Congress Reconsidered*. 6th ed., edited by Lawrence C. Dodd and Bruce I. Oppenheimer. Washington, D.C.: Congressional Quarterly Press.

Cox, Gary W., and Samuel Kernell, eds. 1991. *The Politics of Divided Government*. Boulder: Westview Press.

Cox, Gary W., and Mathew D. McCubbins. 1993. *Legislative Leviathan: Party Government in the House*. Berkeley: University of California Press.

Cronin, Thomas. 1977. *The Presidency Reappraised*. 2nd ed. New York: Praeger.

———. 1982. *Rethinking the Presidency*. Boston: Little, Brown.

Cutler, Lloyd. 1987. The Cost of Divided Government. *New York Times,* November 22.

———. 1988. Some Reflections About Divided Government. *Presidential Studies Quarterly* 17:490.

———. 1989. Now Is the Time for All Good Men. *William and Mary Law Review* 30:387–402.

Davidson, Roger. 1985. Senate Leaders: Janitors for an Untidy Chamber? In *Congress Reconsidered*. 3rd ed., edited by Lawrence C. Dodd and Bruce I. Oppenheimer. Washington, D.C.: Congressional Quarterly Press.

Davidson, Roger, ed. 1992. *The Post-Reform Congress*. New York: St. Martin's Press.

Dodd, Lawrence C., and Bruce I. Oppenheimer, eds. 1985. *Congress Reconsidered*. 3rd ed. Washington, D.C.: Congressional Quarterly Press.

———. 1993. *Congress Reconsidered*. 5th ed. Washington, D.C.: Congressional Quarterly Press.

Downs, Anthony. 1957. *An Economic Theory of Democracy*. New York: Harper and Row.

Edwards, George. 1989. *At the Margins*. New Haven: Yale University Press.

———. 1991. George Bush and the Public Presidency: The Politics of Inclusion. In *The Bush Presidency: First Appraisals*, edited by Colin Campbell and Bert Rockman. Chatham, N.J.: Chatham House Publishers.

Edwards, George, John Kessel, and Bert Rockman, eds. 1993. *Researching the Presidency: Vital Questions, New Approaches*. Pittsburgh: University of Pittsburgh Press.

Epstein, David, and Sharyn O'Halloran. 1996. Divided Government and the Design of Administrative Procedures: A Formal Model and Empirical Test. *Journal of Politics* 58(2):373–397.

Erikson, Robert S. 1976. Is There Such a Thing as a Safe Seat? *Polity* 8:623–632.

———. 1988. The Puzzle of Midterm Loss. *Journal of Politics* 50(4):1011–1029.

———. 1989. Why the Democrats Lose Presidential Elections: Toward a Theory of Optimal Loss. *Political Science and Politics* 22(1):30–35.

———. 1990. Roll Calls, Reputation, and Representation in the U.S. Senate. *Legislative Studies Quarterly* 15:630.

Feldstein, Martin, ed. 1994. *American Economic Policy in the 1980s*. Chicago: University of Chicago Press.

Fenno, Richard F., Jr. 1973. *Congressmen in Committees*. Boston: Little, Brown.

——. 1975. If, as Ralph Nader Says, Congress Is "The Broken Branch," How Come We Love Our Congressmen So Much? In *Congress in Change: Evolution and Reform*, edited by Norman J. Ornstein. New York: Praeger.

——. 1978. *Homestyle: House Members in Their Districts*. Boston: Little, Brown.

Ferejohn, John. 1991. Changes in Welfare Policy in the 1980s. In *Politics and Economics in the Eighties*, edited by Alberto Alesina and Geoffrey Carliner. Chicago: University of Chicago Press.

Ferejohn, John, and Randall Calvert. 1984. Presidential Coattails in Historical Perspective. *American Journal of Political Science* 28(1):127–146.

Fiorina, Morris. 1991a. Divided Government in the States. In *The Politics of Divided Government*, edited by Gary W. Cox and Samuel Kernell. Boulder: Westview Press.

——. 1991b. Elections and the Economy in the 1980s: Short- and Long-Term Effects. In *Politics and Economics in the Eighties*, edited by Alberto Alesina and Geoffrey Carliner. Chicago: University of Chicago Press.

——. 1996. *Divided Government*. 2nd ed. Boston: Allyn and Bacon.

Fiorina, Morris, and Timothy Prinz. 1992. Legislative Incumbency and Insulation. In *Encyclopedia of the American Legislative System*, edited by Joel Silbey. New York: Charles Scribner's Sons.

Fullerton, Don. 1993. *Who Bears the Lifetime Tax Burden?* Washington, D.C.: Brookings Institution.

——. 1994. Tax Policy. In *American Economic Policy in the 1980s*, edited by Martin Feldstein. Chicago: University of Chicago Press.

Gilligan, Thomas W., and Keith Krehbiel. 1987. Collective Decision-Making and Standing Committees: An Informational Rationale for Restrictive Amendment Procedures. *Journal of Law, Economics, and Organization* 3:287–335.

——. 1990. Organization of Informative Committees by a Rational Legislature. *American Journal of Political Science* 34(2):531–564.

Gilmour, John B. 1995. *Strategic Disagreement: Stalemate in American Politics*. Pittsburgh: University of Pittsburgh Press.

Ginsburg, Benjamin, and Martin Shefter. 1990. *Politics by Other Means*. New York: Basic Books.

Glad, Paul. 1966. *The Trumpet Soundeth: William Jennings Bryan and His Democracy, 1896–1912*. Lincoln: University of Nebraska Press.

Greenstein, Fred I. 1982. *The Hidden-Hand Presidency: Eisenhower as Leader*. New York: Basic Books.

Groseclose, Timothy. 1995. An Examination of the Market for Favors and Votes in Congress. *Economic Inquiry* 30:320–340.

Groseclose, Timothy, and James M. Snyder. 1996. Buying Supermajorities. *American Political Science Review* 90(2):303–315.

Groseclose, Timothy, Steve Levitt, and James M. Snyder. 1996. An Inflation Index for ADA Scores. Manuscript, Massachusetts Institute of Technology.

Hacker, Jacob S. 1997. *The Road to Nowhere: The Genesis of President Clinton's Plan for Health Security*. Princeton: Princeton University Press.

Hall, Richard L. 1996. *Participation in Congress*. New Haven: Yale University Press.

Hansen, John Mark. 1991. *Gaining Access: Congress and the Farm Lobby, 1919–1981*. Chicago: University of Chicago Press.

————. 1996. Public Preferences over Public Finance: Individual and Aggregate Properties of Public Opinion on Spending, Taxes, and Deficits. Paper presented at annual meeting, American Political Science Association, San Francisco.

Heclo, Hugh. 1977. *A Government of Strangers*. Washington, D.C.: Brookings Institution.

Hetherington, Marc J. 1996. The Media's Role in Forming Voters' National Economic Evaluations in 1992. *American Journal of Political Science* 40(2):372–395.

Hibbing, John R. 1991. *Congressional Careers*. Chapel Hill: University of North Carolina Press.

Hibbing, John R., and Elizabeth Theiss-Morse. 1995. *Congress As Public Enemy*. Cambridge: Cambridge University Press.

Jacobson, Gary C. 1981. Incumbents' Advantages in the 1978 United States Congressional Elections. *Legislative Studies Quarterly* 6(2):183–200.

————. 1983. *Strategy and Choice in Congressional Elections*. 2nd ed. New Haven: Yale University Press.

————. 1989. Strategic Politicians and the Dynamics of United States House Elections, 1946–86. *American Political Science Review* 83(3):773–793.

————. 1990. *The Electoral Origins of Divided Government*. Boulder: Westview Press.

————. 1991. The Persistence of Democratic House Majorities. In *The Politics of Divided Government*, edited by Gary W. Cox and Samuel Kernell. Boulder: Westview Press.

————. 1993. Deficit-Cutting Politics and Congressional Elections. *Political Science Quarterly* 108(3):375–402.

Jacobson, Gary C., and Samuel Kernell. 1982. Strategy and Choice in the 1982 Congressional Elections. *Political Science and Politics* 15(3):423–430.

Jones, Charles. 1991. Meeting Low Expectations: Strategy and Prospects of the Bush Presidency. In *The Bush Presidency: First Appraisals*, edited by Colin Campbell and Bert Rockman. Chatham, N.J.: Chatham House Publishers.

————. 1994. *The Presidency in a Separated System*. Washington, D.C.: Brookings Institution.

Kernell, Samuel. 1993. *Going Public*. 2nd ed. Washington, D.C.: Congressional Quarterly Press.

Kettl, Donald F. 1992. *Deficit Politics: Public Budgeting in Its Institutional and Historical Context*. New York: Macmillan.

Key, V. O. 1955. Theory of Critical Elections. *Journal of Politics* 17(1):3–18.

————. 1961. *Public Opinion and American Democracy*. New York: Alfred A. Knopf.

————. 1964. *Politics, Parties, & Pressure Groups*. 5th ed. New York: Crowell.

————. 1966. *The Responsible Electorate*. Cambridge: Harvard University Press, Belknap Press.

Kiewiet, D. Roderick, and Mathew D. McCubbins. 1988. Presidential Influence on Congressional Appropriations Decisions. *American Journal of Political Science* 32:713–736.

————. 1991. *The Logic of Delegation: Congressional Parties and the Appropriations Process*. Chicago: University of Chicago Press.

King, Anthony, ed. 1990. *The New American Political System*. 2nd ed. Washington, D.C.: AEI Press.

King, Anthony, and Giles Alston. 1991. Good Government and the Politics of High Exposure. In *The Bush Presidency: First Appraisals*, edited by Colin Campbell and Bert Rockman. Chatham, N.J.: Chatham House Publishers.

King, Gary, and Andrew Gelman. 1991. Systemic Consequences of Incumbency Advantage in U.S. House Elections. *American Journal of Political Science* 35:110–138.

Kingdon, John W. 1973. *Congressmen's Voting Decisions.* New York: Harper and Row.

Krehbiel, Keith. 1988. Spatial Models of Legislative Choice. *Legislative Studies Quarterly* 13(3):259–319.

———. 1991. *Information and Legislative Organization.* Ann Arbor: University of Michigan Press.

———. 1993. Where's the Party? *British Journal of Political Science* 23:235–266.

———. 1995. Cosponsors and Wafflers from A to Z. *American Journal of Political Science* 39(4):906–923.

———. 1996. Institutional and Partisan Sources of Gridlock: A Theory of Divided and Unified Government. *Journal of Theoretical Politics* 8(1):7–40.

———. 1997. Pivotal Politics: A Theory of U.S. Lawmaking. Stanford University Graduate School of Business. Typescript.

Krehbiel, Keith, and Douglas Rivers. 1988. The Analysis of Committee Power: An Application to Senate Voting on the Minimum Wage. *American Journal of Political Science* 32(4):1151–1174.

Light, Paul. 1983. *The President's Agenda.* Baltimore: Johns Hopkins University Press.

Lowi, Theodore. 1969. *The End of Liberalism: Ideology, Policy, and the Crisis of Public Authority.* New York: W. W. Norton.

Manley, John. 1970. *The Politics of Finance: The House Committee on Ways and Means.* Boston: Little, Brown.

Matsui, Brian. 1995. The Politics of Reelection Versus Change. Senior honors thesis, Stanford University.

Mayhew, David R. 1974a. *Congress: The Electoral Connection.* New Haven: Yale University Press.

———. 1974b. Congressional Elections: The Case of the Vanishing Marginals. *Polity* 6:295–317.

———. 1991. *Divided We Govern.* New Haven: Yale University Press.

———. 1997a. Clinton, the 103rd Congress, and Unified Party Control: What Are the Lessons? Working paper, Yale University.

———. 1997b. Important Laws, 1995–96. Working paper, Yale University.

McConnell, Grant. 1953. *The Decline of Agrarian Democracy.* Berkeley: University of California Press.

———. 1966. *Private Power and American Democracy.* New York: Alfred A. Knopf.

McCubbins, Mathew D. 1991. Party Governance and U.S. Budget Deficits: Divided Government and Fiscal Stalemate. In *Politics and Economics in the Eighties,* edited by Alberto Alesina and Geoffrey Carliner. Chicago: University of Chicago Press.

McKelvey, Richard. 1976. Intransitivities in Multidimensional Voting Models and Some Implications for Agenda Control. *Journal of Economic Theory* 12:472–482.

McKenzie, Calvin, and Saranna Thornton. 1996. *Bucking the Deficit: Economic Policymaking in America.* Boulder: Westview Press.

Merrill, Peter R., Stanley E. Collender, and Eric W. Cook. 1990. Tax Legislation and the Budget in the 1980s. In *National Tax Association—Proceedings of the Eighty-Second Annual Conference, 1989, Atlanta, Georgia.* Columbus, Ohio: National Tax Association.

Mezey, Michael. 1991. *Legislatures in the Policy Process.* Cambridge: Cambridge University Press.

Moe, Terry. 1985. The Politicized Presidency. In *The New Directions in American Politics*, edited by John E. Chubb and Paul Peterson. Washington, D.C.: Brookings Institution.

———. 1993. Presidents, Institutions, and Theory. In *Researching the Presidency: Vital Questions, New Approaches*, edited by George Edwards, John Kessel, and Bert Rockman. Pittsburgh: University of Pittsburgh Press.

Neustadt, Richard Elliott. 1960. *Presidential Power.* New York: John Wiley.

Oleszek, Walter. 1989. *Congressional Procedures and the Policy Process.* 3rd ed. Washington, D.C.: Congressional Quarterly Press.

Palazzolo, Daniel. 1992. *The Speaker and the Budget.* Pittsburgh: University of Pittsburgh Press.

Petrocik, John R. 1991. Divided Government: Is It All in the Campaigns? In *The Politics of Divided Government*, edited by Gary W. Cox and Samuel Kernell. Boulder: Westview Press.

Plott, Charles. 1967. A Notion of Equilibrium and Its Possibility Under Majority Rule. *American Economic Review* 57:787–806.

Poole, Keith, and Howard Rosenthal. 1991a. Patterns of Congressional Voting. *American Journal of Political Science* 35: 228–278.

———. 1991b. The Spatial Mapping of Minimum Wage Legislation. In *Politics and Economics in the Eighties*, edited by Alberto Alesina and Geoffrey Carliner. Chicago: University of Chicago Press.

———. 1997. *Congress: A Political-Economic History of Roll Call Voting.* Oxford: Oxford University Press.

Popkin, Samuel. 1991. *The Reasoning Vote: Communication and Persuasion in Presidential Campaigns.* Chicago: University of Chicago Press.

Quirk, Paul. 1991. Domestic Policy: Divided Government and Cooperative Presidential Leadership. In *The Bush Presidency: First Appraisals*, edited by Colin Campbell and Bert Rockman. Chatham, N.J.: Chatham House Publishers.

Rivers, Douglas, and Nancy Rose. 1985. Passing the President's Program: Public Opinion and Presidential Influence in Congress. *American Journal of Political Science* 29(2):183–196.

Rockman, Bert. 1991. The Leadership Style of George Bush. In *The Bush Presidency: First Appraisals*, edited by Colin Campbell and Bert Rockman. Chatham, N.J.: Chatham House Publishers.

Rohde, David W. 1991. *Parties and Leaders in the Postreform House.* Chicago: University of Chicago Press.

Romer, Thomas, and Howard Rosenthal. 1978. Political Resource Allocation, Controlled Agendas, and the Status Quo. *Public Choice* 33:27–43.

Romer, Thomas, and Barry Weingast. 1991. Political Foundations of the Thrift Debacle. In *Politics and Economics in the Eighties*, edited by Alberto Alesina and Geoffrey Carliner. Chicago: University of Chicago Press.

Rosenstone, Steven J. 1983. *Forecasting Presidential Elections.* New Haven: Yale University Press.

Rosenstone, Steven J., and John Mark Hansen. 1993. *Mobilization, Participation, and Democracy in America.* New York: Macmillan.

Schattschneider, E. E. 1942. *Party Government.* New York: Holt, Rinehart and Winston.

Schick, Allen. 1981. *Reconciliation and the Congressional Budget Process.* Washington, D.C.: AEI Press.

————. 1995. *The Federal Budget.* Washington, D.C.: Brookings Institution.

Shepsle, Kenneth. 1979. Institutional Arrangements and Equilibrium in Multidimensional Voting Models. *American Journal of Political Science* 23:27–60.

Shuman, Howard E. 1984. *Politics and the Budget.* Englewood Cliffs, N.J.: Prentice-Hall.

Silbey, Joel, ed. 1992. *Encyclopedia of the American Legislative System.* New York: Charles Scribner's Sons.

Sinclair, Barbara. 1989. *The Transformation of the U.S. Senate.* Baltimore: Johns Hopkins University Press.

————. 1991. Governing Unheroically (and Sometimes Unappetizingly): Bush and the 101st Congress. In *The Bush Presidency: First Appraisals,* edited by Colin Campbell and Bert Rockman. Chatham, N.J.: Chatham House Publishers.

Skocpol, Theda. 1996. *Boomerang: Clinton's Health Security Effort and the Turn Against Government in U.S. Politics.* New York: W. W. Norton.

Skowronek, Stephen. 1993. *The Politics Presidents Make.* Cambridge: Harvard University Press, Belknap Press.

Snyder, James M. 1991. On Buying Legislatures. *Economics and Politics* 3:93–109.

Sorauf, Frank. 1992. *Inside Campaign Finance.* New Haven: Yale University Press.

Steuerle, C. Eugene. 1992. *The Tax Decade.* Washington, D.C.: Urban Institute Press.

Stewart, Charles H., III. 1991. The Politics of Tax Reform in the 1980s. In *Politics and Economics in the Eighties,* edited by Alberto Alesina and Geoffrey Carliner. Chicago: University of Chicago Press.

Sundquist, James L. 1981. *The Decline and Resurgence of Congress.* Washington, D.C.: Brookings Institution.

————. 1988. Needed: A Political Theory for the New Era of Coalition Government in the United States. *Political Science Quarterly* 103(4):613–635.

————. 1993. *Beyond Gridlock?* Washington, D.C.: Brookings Institution.

————. 1995. *Back to Gridlock?* Washington, D.C.: Brookings Institution.

Thurber, James A., ed. 1991. *Divided Democracy: Cooperation and Conflict Between the President and Congress.* Washington: Congressional Quarterly Press.

Truman, David. 1959. *The Congressional Party.* New York: John Wiley.

Volden, Craig. 1997. Sophisticated Voting in Supermajoritarian Settings. *Journal of Politics.* Forthcoming.

Weaver, R. Kent. 1986. The Politics of Blame Avoidance. *Journal of Public Policy* 6:371–398.

————. 1988. *Automatic Government.* Washington, D.C.: Brookings Institution.

Wildavsky, Aaron B. 1988. *The New Politics of the Budgetary Process.* Glenview, Ill.: Scott, Foresman.

Index